# The U.S.-Mexican War

## *A Binational Reader*

# The U.S.-Mexican War

## *A Binational Reader*

Edited, with an Introduction, by
CHRISTOPHER CONWAY

Translations by
GUSTAVO PELLÓN

Hackett Publishing Company, Inc.
Indianapolis/Cambridge

Copyright © 2010 by Hackett Publishing Company, Inc.

All rights reserved
Printed in the United States of America

14 13 12 11 10   1 2 3 4 5 6 7

For further information, please address
Hackett Publishing Company, Inc.
P.O. Box 44937
Indianapolis, Indiana 46244-0937

www.hackettpublishing.com

Cover design by Abigail Coyle
Interior design by Mary Vasquez
Composition by William Hartman
Printed at Sheridan Books, Inc.

**Library of Congress Cataloging-in-Publication Data**

The U.S.-Mexican War : a binational reader / edited, with an introduction, by Christopher Conway ; translations by Gustavo Pellón.

p. cm.

Includes bibliographical references.

ISBN 978-1-60384-220-4 (paper : alk. paper) —

ISBN 978-1-60384-221-1 (cloth : alk. paper)

1. Mexican War, 1846–1848—Sources. 2. Mexican War, 1846–1848—Personal narratives, Mexican. 3. Mexican War, 1846–1848—Personal narratives, American. I. Conway, Christopher B., 1969– II. Title: US-Mexican War.

E404.U17 2010

973.6'209—dc22

2009043100

The paper used in this publication meets the minimum requirements of American National Standard for Information Sciences—Permanence of Paper for Printed Library Materials, ANSI Z39.48–1984.

# Contents

# Acknowledgments

The generosity of others has played a central role in making this book possible. At the University of Texas at Arlington, I am grateful for the generous financial support of the Office of the Provost, the College of Liberal Arts, the Center for Greater Southwestern Studies and the History of Cartography, and the Center for Mexican American Studies. I thank professors Jesse Aleman, Dana Dunn, Richard Francaviglia, John Garrigus, Susan González Baker, Sam Haynes, Antoinette Sol, Roberto Treviño, Kimberly Van Noort, Beth Wright, and Christian Zlolniski. I am particularly indebted to Professor A. Ray Elliott, the chair of the Department of Modern Languages, whose friendship and support was instrumental in enabling me to work on this and other projects while carrying out my other professional responsibilities. Becky Rosenboom and Melissa Miner have been invaluable in helping me arrange travel and other logistical support for my research.

I am humbled by the generosity, knowledge, and professionalism of all of the librarians and archivists at the Special Collections department of the University of Texas at Arlington, which houses one of the finest collections of materials relating to the U.S.-Mexican War in the nation. Without their assistance and guidance, many of the archival treasures featured in this book would not have been found. I thank Anne E. Hodges, the director of Special Collections, and particularly Maritza Arrigunaga, Ben Huseman, and Lea Worcester for making my visits to their collection so rewarding. I want to express my gratitude to Mr. Jenkins Garrett for seeding the U.S.-Mexican War collection at the University of Texas at Arlington by donating his outstanding private collection to the library. It is thanks to the zeal, expertise, and generosity of private collectors like Mr. Garrett that knowledge about the past is preserved, enriched, and disseminated. I also thank the always welcoming and friendly staff at the Rare Books and Manuscripts department of the Benson Collection at the University of Texas, Austin. My outstanding research assistant Melody Woods is also deserving of special mention. Melody took many hours to proof my footnotes and carefully summarized and excerpted the dime novel *Captain Ray: The Young Leader of the Forlorn Hope,* which appears in Part VI of this book. I also thank Armando Villareal y Talamantes for providing assistance at the early stages of this project.

I owe a special debt of gratitude to Professor Desirée Henderson, who taught me about the U.S.-Mexican War, inter-American studies, and nineteenth-century U.S. culture and politics before I began working on this project. Her thoughtful counsel and insight is everywhere in evidence in different parts of this book. I thank Rick Todhunter at Hackett Publishing for providing much needed encouragement at different stages of this difficult project and for his friendship. I am also deeply grateful for the privilege of working with one of the best translators in the business, the distinguished literary and cultural critic Gustavo Pellón of the University of Virginia. I thank Gustavo for his enlightening insights into this project and for vibrantly rendering the Spanish language selections into English. I also thank my father, John Phillip Conway, for always lending a friendly ear to this and other projects.

Several undergraduate students at the University of Texas at Arlington taught me about the U.S.-Mexican War by doing archival projects and mapping out the possibilities for a book like this one: Benjamín Arreguín, Oscar Carrillo, Dejanira Castillejos, Gabriela González-Briones, Jesús González Hernández, Andrew Gooding, Jorge Guerrero, Andrea Hoang, Javier Loyo, and Joseph B. Rodríguez. In gratitude for their intelligence, creativity, and hard work as junior scholars, I dedicate this book to them and to the staff of Special Collections at the University of Texas at Arlington for making books like this one possible.

# Introduction

To appreciate the foundational importance of the U.S.-Mexican War of 1846–1848, all we need to do is look at a map of the United States. Before the war, the lands comprising present-day California, Nevada, Arizona, Utah, and New Mexico as well as parts of Colorado, Kansas, and Wyoming all belonged to Mexico. The defeat of Mexico in the war enabled the United States to gain control of this extensive territory and its inhabitants and fulfill the ideology of Manifest Destiny, which argued that the entirety of the North American continent belonged by divine right to white American settlers. The collision of cultures that occurred between the new settlers and Mexican and indigenous people in these lands laid the multicultural foundations of the modern American West. Equally important is the fact that the acquisition of so much Mexican land intensified debates over American slavery and how far it should be allowed to extend. President Ulysses S. Grant, who had fought in the Mexican War, believed that the U.S. Civil War was caused by the unjust war with Mexico. "Nations," he wrote, "like individuals, are punished for their transgressions. We got our punishment in the most sanguinary and expensive war of modern times."[1]

The effects of the war on Mexico were equally significant. Since its independence in 1821, Mexico had struggled to organize itself politically as centralists and federalists clashed with one another over who should control the state. Military coup followed military coup, and the presidency seesawed between different political interests, even as the U.S. Army invaded Mexico. At the center of it all was Antonio López de Santa Anna, a military leader who had made a name for himself during the Mexican War of Independence and who masterfully played all factions against one another in order to hold on to power. Mexico's loss to the United States marked the beginning of the end of his influence over Mexican politics. It also led to the reorganization of the federalists, who united and overthrew Santa Anna once and for all in 1855. Led by Benito Juárez, who became Mexico's first Indian president, the new liberals effectively promoted secularism and a modern, nationalist Mexican culture.

### Shifting Borders

The annexation of Texas by the United States in 1845 and a dispute over the border of Texas with Mexico precipitated the U.S.-Mexican War of 1846–1848. In a broader sense, however, the conflict can be traced to centuries of shifting borders on the North American continent. In the seventeenth and eighteenth

---

1. Ulysses S. Grant, *Memoirs and Selected Letters: Personal Memoirs of U.S. Grant, Selected Letters 1839–1865* (New York: Library of America, 1990), 42.

centuries, the great colonial powers of Great Britain, Spain, and France struggled to define, expand, and defend their claims to large expanses of the continent. At the dawn of the nineteenth century, the emergent and expansive republic of the United States became an actor in the drama of competing borders in the New World, negotiating and fighting to remove European claims to a vast continent that it increasingly saw as its birthright. The changing geopolitics of the New World is thus central to an understanding of the belligerence over borders that contributed to the outbreak of war in 1846.

By the middle of the eighteenth century, the Spanish Viceroyalty of New Spain extended from central Mexico far into North America, where it was bordered by the large French claim of Louisiana that extended from the Appalachians to the Rockies. The British claim was east of the Appalachians from Florida in the south to Nova Scotia in the north. The borders between these claims were flashpoints for violence and territorial competition. On French Louisiana's western border, the Spanish tried to colonize and militarize Texas between 1716 and 1719 in order to protect it from French incursions. In the east, tensions between French and English colonists and several Indian nations allied with the French led to the start of the French and Indian War in 1754. Most importantly, the conflict over territory on the North American continent grew into the Seven Years' War (1756–1763), which drew several European powers into a world war that was fought in Europe, the Caribbean, India, and Africa. The defeat of France and its allies reorganized land claims in North America. France lost its possessions east of the Mississippi to Great Britain and ceded Louisiana to Spain, and Spain lost Florida to Great Britain. Eager to avoid further conflict with the Indian nations who had allied themselves with the French during the French and Indian War, Britain restricted its settlements east of the Appalachian Mountains with the Proclamation of 1763.

From the eighteenth century onward, the borders of North America continued to shift. After the diplomatic consummation of American independence in 1783, Spain recovered Florida from Great Britain. The region became a thorn in the side of the new republic for decades to come because it was a haven for runaway slaves and Indian raiders as well as a suspected staging ground for British conspiracies against the United States. When Spain ceded Louisiana back to France in 1800, U.S. access to the vital port of New Orleans, which had been assured by a treaty with Spain, was endangered. Napoleon Bonaparte's imperial designs on the New World also troubled President Thomas Jefferson, who purchased Louisiana from France for $15 million in 1803. With the exception of Florida, the northern frontier of New Spain, and the largely unexplored Pacific Northwest, the United States now controlled a vast swath of the North American continent. Yet, the question of whether Texas was a part of the Louisiana Purchase or not was a source of disagreement between Spain and the United States until the Adams-Onís Treaty of 1819, which ceded Florida to the United States and drew the western boundary of Louisiana along the Sabine River in Texas northward to the forty-second parallel. Spain, which had eyed the meteoric demographic growth and expansionism of the new American Republic since its independence, now sought to bar the unchecked entry of U.S. settlers into Texas. When Mexican insurgents and U.S. expeditioners used the territory of Louisiana as a base for raids on royalists during the Mexican War of Independence (1810–1821), Spanish authorities understood as they had never before the dangers of sharing a border with their neighbor to the north, and this fear was inherited by the leaders of the Mexican Republic.

Many in the United States believed that John Quincy Adams, who had negotiated the treaty of 1819 with Spanish foreign minister Luis de Onís, had unjustly excluded Texas from the Louisiana Purchase. As president, Adams himself attempted to buy Texas from Mexico in 1827, as did his successor Andrew Jackson, but U.S. emissaries to Mexico proved to be controversial men who only succeeded in increasing Mexican resentment toward the United States. Even more tempting than Texas was California, which had become an important whaling hub and a thriving center for trade in cowhide, tallow, and sea otter pelts. Popular books, such as Henry Dana's *Two Years before the Mast* (1840) and Lansford Hastings' *Emigrant's Guide to Oregon and California* (1845), disseminated news of the natural wealth of California and the great opportunities it promised to enterprising North American settlers. To the north, fertile Oregon had attracted thousands of U.S. settlers as well, but the area was jointly claimed by Great Britain and the United States. American fears of a British alliance with Mexico and of British designs on Oregon and Texas colored President James K. Polk's assertive nationalist foreign policy as he began his presidential term in 1845. The war with Mexico that began on his watch would end the shifting of borders in North America and make the United States the unrivaled master of the continent.

## The Settlement and Independence of Texas

The story of Mexican Texas, which became home to a burgeoning colony of U.S. settlers in 1821, is essential for an understanding of the U.S.-Mexican War. The Anglo-American colonization of Texas began with one man, Moses Austin, a merchant from Connecticut who received dispensation from the Spanish Crown in 1798 to settle and mine for lead in the northern frontier of the Viceroyalty of New Spain in present-day Missouri. In 1820, Austin traveled to San Antonio de Béjar in Texas to ask license from Governor Antonio María Martínez for starting a colony of three hundred U.S. settlers in Texas. The concession was given, but Moses Austin died before he could carry out his plans, which fell into the hands of his son, Stephen F. Austin, who founded his colony on the Brazos River in the Gulf Coast region of Texas in December 1821, in an area known today as Fort Bend.

The end of Spanish rule in Mexico, however, dictated that Austin travel to Mexico City in 1822 to renegotiate his colonization plans. The reauthorization of land grants to U.S. settlers was decreed by the Mexican Imperial Colonization Law of 1823, which offered individual farmers 177 acres, ranchers 4,428 acres, and settlers who farmed and ranched 4,605 acres. The settlers were exempted from taxation for the first six years of their land tenancy and were required to pay reduced taxes for the second six years, after which they would be subject to normal taxation under Mexican law. All foreign settlers were required to profess the Catholic faith and to cultivate or utilize their lands for grazing within two years or else risk losing their property. The law also prohibited the sale and purchase of slaves and provided for the liberty of the children of slaves at the age of fourteen. The eagerness of Mexico to populate its undeveloped northeastern frontier was evident in the treatment and definition of land agents, or *empresarios,* in the Imperial Law and subsequent legislation about the colonization of Texas. The *empresarios* who brought hundreds of families into Mexico for the purpose of settlement were rewarded for their services with large tracts of property.

Mexico's policies on the incorporation of U.S. settlers within its borders were ambivalent. On the one hand, the enthusiastic interest of U.S. settlers promised to raise revenue, promote agricultural development, and encourage the founding of new towns in a part of the Mexican territory that was underpopulated and underdeveloped. By attracting Anglo-American colonists and trying to acculturate them into Mexican culture and society, the Mexican authorities hoped to create a border region that would serve as a buffer against U.S. encroachment into Texas. This paradoxical strategy was not new; Spanish authorities had done the same in the late eighteenth century when men like Moses Austin were allowed land grants in the territory that later became part of the Louisiana Purchase. The Colonization Law of 1825, for example, stated that applications to settle within twenty leagues of the border with the United States were subject to stricter scrutiny than other applications and stipulated that preferential treatment would be given to prospective settlers who were Mexican soldiers and citizens and to foreigners who married Mexican women.

Despite such cautionary measures, the rapid influx of Anglo-American settlers into Texas and the great distances that separated central Mexico from its northern frontier made effective political control over the territory difficult, if not impossible. Many settlers did not convert to Catholicism, learn Spanish, or follow Mexican law, and the continuous flood of Anglo-Americans into Texas rendered Mexicans a minority within their own country. In 1828, President Guadalupe Victoria sent Manuel Mier y Terán to gather information about where the border between Texas and the United States should be drawn and to form impressions about life in Texas. Mier y Terán observed that the Texans outnumbered the Mexicans ten to one and that the Mexicans of Texas were too poor and uneducated to counter the influence of the new settlers. Mier y Terán warned his president to take timely measures because "Texas could throw the whole nation into revolution."[2]

As a result of Mier y Terán's report, the Mexican government passed the Law of April 6, 1830, which forbade U.S. immigration into Texas, introduced

2. Alleine Howren, "Causes and Origins of the Decree of April 6, 1830," *The Southwestern Historical Quarterly* 16, no. 4 (1912/1913): 395.

a stronger military presence in the region, halted the importation of slaves, and encouraged Mexican and European settlement in Texas. In 1832 and 1833, the Texas colonists organized two conventions and petitioned Mexican authorities to lift some of the restrictions of the Law of April 6, 1830, and to confer upon them more regional autonomy by approving their separation from the state of Coahuila. When Stephen F. Austin traveled to Mexico City to argue for these reforms, he found the government too distracted by internal discord and an outbreak of cholera to act on his petitions. After the disillusioned Austin wrote a fateful letter advising Texans to move forward with their plans, the authorities intercepted it and arrested him for sedition, holding him in prison until December 1834. Moreover, tensions between Texas and Mexico City worsened when Santa Anna, who had identified himself with federalism, renounced this ideology in favor of centralism and began waging war against his enemies.

A few words on federalists and centralists are in order, as these competing political visions in Mexico shaped the events that subsequently led to the war with the United States. The centralists espoused executive power and the influence of the church and the military, whereas the federalists sought to expand regional autonomy and limit presidential and church powers. As far as the centralists were concerned, federalism threatened to engulf Mexico into chaos, anarchy, and mob rule. In contrast, the federalists believed that centralism was a return to the tyrannical structures of power of the colonial era and a violation of the true tenets of republicanism. In the words of the editors of federalist newspaper *La Voz del Pueblo,* federation symbolized patriotism and freedom and represented the interests of the middle and working classes, whereas centralism was the emblem of opulence, privilege, egotism, and slavery. In 1833, Texas had sought to separate from the Mexican state of Coahuila under the auspices of Mexican federalism but soon found itself at odds with the newly centralist and belligerent administration of Santa Anna.

Although many Texans clamored for independence, political consensus was not achieved until March 2, 1836, four days before a massive force led by Santa Anna stormed the Alamo and massacred the small force of Texans defending the old mission. Another tragic defeat occurred when more than 350 Texas insurgents led by James Fannin were captured and executed at Goliad on March 27, 1836. A few weeks later, the Texas army led by Sam Houston caught the Mexicans off guard at the Battle of San Jacinto and captured Santa Anna. At Velasco, Santa Anna signed two treaties: one public and one private. The first stipulated the cessation of hostilities, the return of prisoners, and the withdrawal of Mexican forces across the Rio Grande, whereas the private treaty stated that Santa Anna would use his influence to gain recognition of Texan independence from the Mexican government. Texas was now an independent republic, although its existence as such would be short-lived.

Despite pro-annexationist sentiment in Texas, President Andrew Jackson did not want to alienate antislavery interests that saw annexation as a threat to the balance of power between free and slaveholding states in the Union. Jackson was also reticent to spark an international incident with Mexico, which had not ratified the Treaties of Velasco or recognized the independence of Texas. For this reason, between 1836 and 1845, Texas made its way alone, struggling to achieve recognition from other nations, waging war on the Cherokee and the Comanche, and trying to protect itself against Mexican raids. Mexico did not forget the humiliation of losing Texas and harbored hopes of recovering it, but the state's coffers were too low to fund another war and its politicians too divided to effectively organize a campaign. It was not until the U.S. Congress passed a resolution annexing Texas to the United States in 1844 that President Santa Anna began to prepare for war. In the United States, the election of the expansionist Democrat James K. Polk to the presidency that year also set the stage for confrontation. Polk would not waver in his determination to aggressively confront Mexico and Great Britain about U.S. claims to Texas and Oregon.

## The Annexation of Texas and the Slavery Question

In a newspaper article first published in 1829 and widely circulated as a part of David Woodman Jr.'s *Guide to Texas Emigrants* (1835), an anonymous commentator praised the prospect of the United States annexing Texas and dividing it into four separate states of the Union. The soil of the region was so fertile that it would break dependence on British sugar and French wine, spread U.S. tobacco across Europe, and produce some of the finest cotton in the Americas. Texas also promised to supply the United States with an overabundance of cedar and oak wood, fruit, and vegetables. In sum, Texas would "make this nation, what all nations desire to be, independent of the world for the necessaries, the comforts, and with very few exceptions, the luxuries of life."[3] By the 1830s and 1840s, the ideology of Manifest Destiny had also taken hold in the United States as a rationale for annexation. In the words of John O'Sullivan, who coined the phrase Manifest Destiny, it was the right of the United States to "overspread and to possess the whole of the continent which Providence has given us for the development of the great experiment of Liberty and federated self-government entrusted to us."[4] Moreover, the rise of anti-Catholic sentiment fed the belief that it was the responsibility of the United States to protect its freedom-loving political brethren in Texas from the threat of a "barbaric" and Catholic Mexico. But the question of slavery made annexing Texas the most internally divisive foreign policy issue of the time.

Political life in the United States on the eve of the U.S.-Mexican War was defined by the Second Party System. The Democrats, associated with the popular Andrew Jackson, sought to limit government and promoted westward expansion.

3. David Woodman Jr., *Guide to Texas Emigrants* (Boston: printed by M. Hawes, 1835), 125–27.

4. Robert J. Miller, *Native America, Discovered and Conquered: Thomas Jefferson, Lewis & Clark, and Manifest Destiny* (Santa Barbara: Greenwood Publishing Company, 2006), 119.

They drew much of their strength from populist appeals to Westerners and the working class. The Whigs favored the expansion of government and struck a more cautious note on the subject of westward expansion. The Democrats spearheaded calls for annexation, but the Whigs were opposed because they feared that the incorporation of Texas into the Union would result in the creation of new slave states. In the Missouri Compromise of 1820, the U.S. Congress had avoided a sectional crisis by admitting Missouri as a slave state and Maine as a free state, thus maintaining the equilibrium between slave- and nonslaveholding states (twelve each). The compromise also stipulated that slavery would not be permitted in any future states above Missouri's southern boundary, at 36°30′. Texas was well south of this boundary, meaning that it would enter as a slave state if annexation succeeded. The prospect of the extension of slavery fueled the passionate resistance of an emergent and increasingly well-organized antislavery movement.

President John Tyler, who had gained the highest office after the sudden death of President William Henry Harrison in 1842, was at first cautious on the annexation question. However, worries over Britain's close relationship with Texas and its diplomatic ventures in Mexico on behalf of the recognition of Texan independence changed his mind. If Britain brokered a peace between Texas and Mexico, and gained enough influence to abolish slavery in Texas, slavery in the United States would be threatened. When Tyler's treaty of annexation failed to get the two-thirds majority required to pass the Senate in June 1844, he resubmitted it as a joint resolution (requiring only a simple majority of both houses) and got it approved in February 1845. Four months later, on July 4, Texas ratified the agreement and entered the Union in December.

Shortly after the passage of annexation, Democrat James K. Polk took the office of president. In his public statements and approach to foreign policy questions, Polk made it clear that he would militarily defend Texas against reprisals from Mexico and that the United States should not share Oregon with the British. Great Britain's territorial ambitions on the North American continent were a source of great anxiety during this time. Tensions over a disputed boundary between Maine and New Brunswick had threatened to spark a wider war between the powers. In October 1842, Commodore Thomas Cateby Jones of the U.S. Pacific Squadron claimed California for the United States on erroneous military intelligence that suggested that Mexico was ceding California to Great Britain. One day after raising the American flag over Monterey, an embarrassed Jones lowered it and apologized to Mexican Governor Manuel Micheltorena. It was in this atmosphere of distrust, fueled by Britain's diplomatic overtures toward Texas and suspicions of its designs on California, that Polk asserted himself incontrovertibly. "No future European colony or dominion," he wrote in his first annual message to Congress in December 1845, "shall with our consent be planted or established on any part of the North American continent."[5] In April

5. U.S. Congress. House, *Abridgement of the Debates of Congress, from 1789 to 1856: Dec. 4, 1843–June 18, 1846* (New York: D. Appleton and Company, 1868), 854.

1846, when Congress repealed the agreement by which the United States and Great Britain shared Oregon, the British reopened negotiations that resulted in the United States acquiring all of Oregon to the forty-ninth parallel. Although such an arrangement fell short of the popular expansionist motto of "54°40′ or fight!", it averted conflict with a formidable foe and made the United States a transcontinental power for the first time in its history.

As a result of congressional approval for the annexation of Texas, Mexico broke off diplomatic relations with the United States and readied itself to defend its borders. At the heart of the ever-increasing acrimony between the two nations was the southern border of Texas. The United States claimed that the border should be drawn at the Rio Grande, whereas Mexico put it more than one hundred miles north at the Nueces River. (See Map 1.) Polk ordered General Zachary Taylor to lead his 3,500-strong Army of Observation to the Rio Grande to prevent Mexico from threatening Texas. In March 1846, Taylor and his men arrived at the north bank of the Rio Grande, right across from the town of Matamoros. Mexican general Pedro de Ampudia wrote to Taylor from Matamoros and demanded that U.S. forces withdraw to the Nueces River. "If you insist on remaining upon the soil of the Department of Tamaulipas," wrote Ampudia, "it will clearly result that arms and arms alone must decide the question; and in that case I advise you that we accept the war which, with so much injustice on your part, you provoke on us."[6]

## Mexico Divided

On the eve of war with the United States, the political elites of Mexico did not unite in the face of a common enemy. Since the end of the Mexican War of Independence in 1821, they had struggled unsuccessfully to establish a stable system of government. The centralists were beholden to the church and to the military and distrusted constitutional arrangements that limited presidential power. In contrast, the federalists were heirs of the Enlightenment who sought to promote a more decentralized and secular national politics. In this regard, and following more contemporary parlance, centralists may be considered conservatives and federalists, liberals. Yet, within the ranks of the federalists, there were factions as well. The *moderados* favored a more conciliatory approach toward the problem of state-church relations and sought to curtail the role of the urban poor in politics. The radicals, or *puros,* were less compromising in their quest to limit church influence and sought to mobilize the urban masses to their cause.

The symbolic linchpin of the federalist agenda was the Constitution of 1824, a charter that provided Texas and other regions of Mexico with a template for

---

6. United States. President (1845–1849: Polk), *Messages of the President of the United States, with the Correspondence, therewith communicated, between the Secretary of War and other Officers of the Government, on the Subject of The Mexican War* (Washington, DC: Wendell and Van Benthuysen, 1848), 140.

state rights in the 1830s. Federalism, however, suffered a significant setback in 1835 with the passing of the Seven Laws, which reorganized Mexico into tightly controlled departments (as opposed to states) and extended the presidential term of office from four to eight years. When the congress sought to reform this charter in 1842, President Santa Anna and his supporters disbanded that body and instituted the *Bases Orgánicas* in 1843. The new, more conservative constitution expanded presidential powers, defended church and military interests, and strengthened financial restrictions on who could vote and serve in the senate. The *Bases Orgánicas* remained in effect until after the start of the war with the United States, when the Constitution of 1824 was reinstituted in August 1846.

The question of military power also divided the governing elites of Mexico in the 1840s: federalists supported the creation and maintenance of civilian militias, whereas centralists were inherently distrustful of how such militias concentrated power in the hands of the masses. The status of the army also proved to be a flashpoint. When President Joaquín de Herrera, a *moderado,* sought to modernize that institution and curtail its power, he stirred up the centralists, who had always championed military privilege as a part of its programs, but he also provoked the *puros,* who decided to capitalize on military discontent to try to topple him in 1845. Worst of all was the fact that the Mexican military provided centralists, *puros,* and *moderados* with the means to forcibly impose their political programs on the country. The military was not an independent institution dedicated to national defense but a political player in its own right.

When news of the impending annexation of Texas arrived in Mexico in 1844, Mexicans were divided about what course to pursue. In 1836, after the defeat of Santa Anna in Texas, Mexico had refused to recognize Texan independence and raided the republic twice, in the spring and fall of 1842. Yet, Mexico was too unstable to fund a real war of reconquest. In 1841, the federalists overthrew President Anastasio Bustamante but were then removed from power by Santa Anna. Despite the humiliation of losing Texas in 1836, Santa Anna had rehabilitated himself politically and militarily by leading Mexican forces against the French at Veracruz in 1839 (where he lost his left leg in battle). Santa Anna's commitment to funding and raising an army to reconquer Texas in 1844 alienated powerful interests and led to his overthrow by the *moderado* José Joaquín de Herrera, who in turn was overthrown by the centralist Manuel Paredes y Arrillaga in 1845. President Herrera's pragmatism about the consequences of rushing into a war with the United States had paradoxically alienated him from both *puros* and centralists, who demanded a more assertive leader.

In late 1845, as Taylor and his Army of Observation were encamped on the Nueces, Commissioner John Slidell arrived in Mexico City with instructions from President Polk to negotiate the border dispute between Texas and Mexico. If Mexico accepted the U.S. claim to the corridor between the Nueces and the Rio Grande, Polk instructed, Slidell was to offer to buy both California and New Mexico for $30 million and cancel Mexican debts to the United States (which totaled nearly $2 million). Herrera and his centralist successor, Paredes, refused to receive Slidell over diplomatic technicalities, leading to the envoy's empty-handed departure in February 1846. Two months later, while U.S. and Mexican forces faced off on the border with no hope in sight of a diplomatic resolution, Paredes ordered the Mexican army to protect its homeland in the event of U.S. aggression: "I have commanded the general in chief of the division of our northern border to attack the army that is attacking us, to answer the enemy who makes war on us with war, and I invoke the God of Battles to preserve the valor of our soldiers, our unquestionable right to our territory, and the decorum of our arms that are going to be employed only in the defense of justice."[7]

In the months leading up to the war, Paredes had become the target of impassioned condemnations when it became clear that his administration was entertaining a return to a monarchical system of government. The Mexican polity may have been deeply divided, but *puros* and *moderados,* and even many centralists, could find patriotic common ground in rejecting such a retrograde proposal. Paredes was overthrown a few months after the start of the war in August 1846 and replaced by Santa Anna, who had been living in exile in Cuba. A true master of political intrigue, Santa Anna had succeeded in persuading his *puro* foes that he would ally himself with their cause if he returned to Mexico. He also convinced President Polk to allow him past the U.S. naval embargo of Mexico so that he could help resolve the conflict peaceably and accommodate the territorial demands of the United States. Instead, upon his return to Mexico, Santa Anna turned his attention to resisting the U.S. invasion.

## The Course of the War, 1846–1848

On April 24, 1846, a Mexican force led by General Mariano Arista ambushed a party of sixty-three U.S. Dragoons on patrol near Taylor's Fort Texas in the disputed area between the Nueces and the Rio Grande. Sixteen U.S. soldiers were killed or wounded and the rest were captured. Two weeks later, Arista put the fort under siege while Taylor was away on a resupply mission. On May 8 and 9, respectively, in the fields of Palo Alto and the adjoining Resaca de la Palma, 2,300 U.S. soldiers under Taylor's command battled over five thousand Mexican soldiers and defeated them. On the same day that U.S. forces were fighting at Resaca de la Palma on May 9, President Polk received news of the April skirmish and called on the U.S. Congress to declare war on Mexico. In his recounting of the events of April 24, Polk famously declared that Mexico had invaded the United States and "shed the blood of our fellow citizens on our own soil." On May 11, the U.S. Congress declared war on Mexico. On July 2, months after the commencement of hostilities between the two nations, the Mexican congress formally declared war on the United States.

Although the United States' armed forces suffered significant casualties during the war, they defeated Mexican resistance in all of the major battles of the conflict. The specific details of troop movements and military strategy need

7. "Manifesto of April 23, 1846," in Part II of this book.

not occupy us in this introduction. More information on specific engagements may be found in this edition's chronology, maps, selected documents, and headnotes. What follows is an abbreviated overview of the campaigns that resulted in the defeat of Mexico. (See Map 2.) The U.S. attack on Mexico consisted of four major campaigns targeting different geographical regions. General Zachary Taylor's campaign in northern Mexico began with the outbreak of hostilities on the Rio Grande and continued in the northeastern interior of Mexico at the battles of Monterrey in September 1846 and Buena Vista in February 1847. General Winfield Scott's central Mexican campaign began with a massive U.S. amphibious assault on the city of Veracruz on the Gulf Coast of Mexico in March 1847 and continued westward through the Mexican interior, clashing with Mexican forces at Cerro Gordo in April, Contreras and Churubusco in August, and Molino del Rey and Mexico City in September. The third major campaign involved Colonel Stephen W. Kearny's Army of the West, which departed from Kansas on an expedition to secure New Mexico shortly after the outbreak of the war. The Army of the West occupied Santa Fe in August 1846 without encountering resistance. Kearny ordered one regiment of volunteers under the command of Colonel Alexander Doniphan to move south into the northern Mexican state of Chihuahua, where they defeated Mexican forces at Brazitos in December 1846 and Sacramento in February 1847. Meanwhile, several U.S. commanders took part in the campaign for California, beginning in June 1846 and ending in January 1847: Commodores John Sloat and Robert Stockton of the U.S. Pacific Squadron, a combined force of riflemen and Anglo-American California settlers led by the famed adventurer and explorer Lieutenant John Charles Frémont, and a small detachment of the Army of the West led by Kearny.

The U.S. military that participated in the war was composed of two branches: soldiers and sailors who belonged to the standing army of the country (the regulars) and volunteers who were recruited through a state-run militia system. Volunteer units elected their own officers and had a strong sense of regional identity and distinct uniforms. Conflicts between regional volunteer units were not uncommon, and discipline problems led to harsh punishments and many desertions. Although the Mexican military did contain some highly trained troops, the bulk was composed of forcibly conscripted soldiers who felt little or no loyalty to the concept of *Patria Grande* (the large homeland or the nation). Frequent political conflict in Mexico had sown disillusionment and oriented the military toward political intrigue and localized civil wars rather than national defense. In addition, the U.S. Army was equipped with more effective, modern weapons, such as an early version of the Colt revolver, the .54 caliber Mississippi rifle, and artillery that was lighter and more mobile than Mexican cannons. Mexican small arms consisted largely of older pistols and muskets, many of which malfunctioned on a regular basis. In addition to such firearms, soldiers on both sides were armed with sabers, daggers, and, in the case of the Mexican cavalry, long lances. Once the war had begun, atrocities were committed on both sides. U.S. soldiers reported seeing Mexicans murdering wounded American soldiers on the battlefield and stealing their clothes and personal possessions, while angry U.S. soldiers went on a killing spree against civilians in Huamantla in October 1847.

In the major battles of the northern and central Mexican campaigns, the combatants on both sides typically numbered in the thousands, with Mexican forces overwhelmingly outnumbering their U.S. counterparts. For example, five thousand U.S. soldiers defeated fifteen thousand Mexican soldiers at the Battle of Buena Vista, numbers that were proportionally repeated at a subsequent battle at Molino del Rey. Casualties in the major battles were in the hundreds, with heavier Mexican losses estimated in the thousands in the battles of Cerro Gordo, Churubusco, and Mexico City. That said, the war exacted a very heavy human price from U.S. forces, especially in a period in which modern standards of medical sanitation were not practiced, resulting in large numbers of mortal infections after limb amputations and rudimentary surgeries to remove shrapnel. Diseases such as cholera, dysentery, and yellow fever also took a heavy toll on U.S. forces.

While U.S. and Mexican soldiers were dying on the battlefield, the war was having a political impact on both countries. Opposition to the war in the United States was pronounced among Whig politicians and foes of slavery who considered the war a pretext for acquiring more land in the name of slavery. In August 1846, Congressman David Wilmot, a Democrat from Pennsylvania, appended a proviso to a war appropriations bill prohibiting slavery in any lands acquired from Mexico. The Wilmot Proviso failed to pass the Senate but it was repeatedly reintroduced during the war. Another critic of the war was a Whig congressman from Illinois named Abraham Lincoln, who challenged Polk's justification for the war on more than one occasion by introducing "Spot Resolutions," which demanded more information on the question of whether or not American blood had been shed on American soil at the start of the war in April 1846. Another source of controversy was the question of whether or not a victorious United States should annex all of Mexico's territory, but fears over the human and financial cost of an uncompromising war of territorial conquest, as well as the signing of the Treaty of Guadalupe Hidalgo in 1848, blocked such designs.

In Mexico, political division continued to cripple the war effort. While Santa Anna was away from Mexico City leading the Mexican army in January and February 1847, his vice president, the *puro* firebrand Valentín Gómez Farías, tried to raise war funds by expropriating church capital and land, outraging supporters of church interest. The deep animosity of *moderados* and centralists toward Farías, as well as controversy surrounding the vice president's motives in trying to manipulate civilian militias loyal to his political enemies, sparked a month-long series of violent disturbances in Mexico City known as the Polkos Revolt. At first Santa Anna was outraged over the outbreak of violence, but upon his return to Mexico City in March 1847, he adroitly removed Farías from office and replaced him with General Pedro María Anaya. Santa Anna was a realist: to effectively lead in the defense of Mexico, he needed Mexico City to be quiet.

Meanwhile, General Winfield Scott's forces struck inland from Veracruz and defeated Mexican forces at Cerro Gordo (April 18), Contreras and Churubusco (August 19–20), and Molino del Rey (September 8). On August 22, as the U.S.

Army stood within striking distance of Mexico City, Scott and Santa Anna signed an armistice during which Mexican peace commissioners and Polk's envoy Nicholas P. Trist discussed terms for resolving the conflict. After the breakdown of talks on September 6, Scott's forces battled their way to the gates of Mexico City and accepted the unconditional surrender of the Mexican capital on September 14. The Mexican congress fled northward to unoccupied Querétaro while Santa Anna resigned his office and left Mexico. Trist continued negotiations with Santa Anna's successors until their representatives signed the Treaty of Guadalupe Hidalgo (named after a village south of Mexico City) on February 2, 1848. The treaty ceded all of Alta California and New Mexico to the United States and recognized the Rio Grande as the border of Texas. In exchange for this cession, consisting of more than five hundred thousand square miles of land, the United States agreed to pay Mexico $15 million and cancel Mexican debts. The treaty was ratified by the U.S. Congress in March and by the Mexican congress in May. The ratification of the treaty in the Mexican congress of Querétaro was not easy. Many argued passionately against the treaty and called for the continuation of hostilities, among them Benito Juárez, a delegate from Oaxaca who ten years later became one of Mexico's most influential presidents. The *moderado* advocates for peace prevailed, however, fearing that Mexico was too weak to continue to resist the United States in a protracted war.

## Legacies of the Treaty of Guadalupe Hidalgo

One of the most important legacies of the U.S.-Mexican War was its contribution to the sectional crisis in the United States that led to the Civil War. Since the Missouri Compromise boundary line did not extend across the continent to the Pacific Ocean, the acquisition of California and New Mexico by the United States in 1848 intensified debate over whether or not slavery should be permitted in these lands. The Compromise of 1850 admitted California as a free state and New Mexico as a territory where slavery could be instituted at a later date. The passage of the Kansas-Nebraska Act of 1854 repealed the Missouri Compromise and instituted the concept of popular sovereignty by which territorial legislatures could decide for themselves whether or not to institute slavery. The struggle to protect the institution of slavery in an ever-expanding nation, a concern that had marked all debates about the annexation of Texas and the meaning of Mexico's defeat in the U.S.-Mexican War, was showing strain. What followed is well known to students of American history: the birth of the Republican Party (1855), Bleeding Kansas (1855), the Dred Scott Decision (1856), John Brown's Raid (1859), the election of Abraham Lincoln to the presidency (1860), and the formation of the Confederated States of America and the start of the Civil War (1861). In this manner, the issue of slavery in Texas and the vast new lands acquired from Mexico in 1848 played a role in the chain of events that led to the Civil War.

In Mexico, Santa Anna returned from exile and took the reins of power again in 1853 and sold a large tract of land south of the Gila River on the Mexico-New Mexico border to the United States for $10 million (the Gadsden Purchase; see

Map 3). In 1855, a younger and more united generation of liberals that included Benito Juárez overthrew Santa Anna and took power. The new liberals, heirs of the federalist cause, defeated the conservatives in a civil war and fought a successful guerilla war against French invaders between 1861 and 1867. Unlike their *puro* and *moderado* predecessors, who conspired against each other in the years leading up to and during the war with the United States, Juárez and his followers were able to maintain enough unity to defeat a foreign invader and begin the process of building more stable republican institutions. The triumph of Juárez transformed liberalism from a partisan ideology into, in the words of Charles Hale, "a unifying political myth" central to the very foundation of the modern Mexican state.[8] As a result, Mexico saw a flowering of cultural nation building in the last quarter of the nineteenth century that had not been possible at midcentury when political instability, military coups, and foreign intervention were the order of the day.

The incorporation of the Mexican territories out of which the modern U.S. states of California, Nevada, Arizona, Utah, and New Mexico and much of Colorado emerged is very significant. After the war, a land rush fueled by the promise of vast expanses of land and California gold overwhelmed the Mexican and native peoples of the west and southwest, dispossessing them of their lands and relegating them to a marginal status. Although the Treaty of Guadalupe Hidalgo provided protection for property held by Mexicans and their descendants, many Mexican land grants were challenged and defeated in court in the second half of the nineteenth century owing to faulty or missing documentation as well as political and legal corruption. The Mexican inhabitants of the U.S. Southwest also became the targets of racism, violence, and arbitrary persecution, as in the case of California's original Anti-Vagrancy Law of 1855, which called Mexicans "Greasers" and justified their arrest on the vaguest and most insubstantial charges. Other flashpoints of racial conflict after the war included civil disturbances in Los Angeles, California, over the murder of Antonio Ruiz (1856) and several conflicts in Texas, such as the San Antonio Cart War (1857), a revolt by Juan Cortina in Brownsville (1859), and the El Paso Salt War (1877). Finally, tribes such as the Navajo, which had roamed almost freely on the Spanish frontier, became exiled peoples when they were forcibly removed from their ancestral lands to reservations. In 1883, a young Mission Indian boy from California wrote to President Chester A. Arthur and complained that white people wanted to take his village's land. "We think it is ours, for God gave it to us first. . . ." Ramon Cavavi wrote, "We are so poor that we have not enough good food for the sick, and sometimes I am afraid that we are all going to die."[9]

---

8. Charles Hale, *The Transformation of Liberalism in Late Nineteenth-Century Mexico* (Princeton: Princeton University Press, 1989), 3.

9. Helen Hunt Jackson and Abbot Kinney, *Report on the Condition and Needs of the Mission Indians of California* (Washington, DC: Washington Government Printing Office, 1883), 17.

In some ways, the U.S.-Mexican War is so important to so many subsequent historical contexts, actors, and events that it is almost impossible to take a full measure of its impact on both countries. The war set modern borders and deepened the ethnic diversity of the United States in ways that continue to be relevant to culture and politics. Mexico's defeat and the painful and contradictory realities of the U.S.-Mexico border have kept the war and its legacies very much alive in the minds of Mexicans and Mexican Americans. In short, the present-day and future inhabitants of Mexico and the United States are sons and daughters of the Treaty of Guadalupe Hidalgo.

## About This Edition

Although many English-language anthologies of primary documents relating to the U.S.-Mexican War have been published, this is the first one to give full voice to the Mexican side of the conflict. Yet, while striving to present "both sides" of the conflict, this book does not set a monolithic U.S. perspective against a Mexican one but rather presents a mosaic of voices that often dissent with each other from within their respective national designations. Whether they are on the Mexican or U.S. side, the voices of men and women and of whites and people of color dialogue and challenge each other in the pages that follow. Often, I have staged stark contrasts by juxtaposing U.S. views with Mexican ones, especially in Part III, which deals with the actual military conflict on the ground. In order to create such contrasts and, most importantly, give voice to the Mexican side, I have recovered lesser-known and previously untranslated voices that will hopefully stimulate students, lay readers, and scholars.

Since this book grew out of a desire to bring to the fore Mexican voices that have gone largely unheard in the United States, I have elected to use the phrase "The U.S.-Mexican War" to refer to the conflict rather than "The Mexican War" or the less favored "The Mexican-American War." The parallel construction in the title "U.S.-Mexican War," popularized by the 1998 Public Broadcasting Service television documentary on the war, reflects my attempt to set U.S. and Mexican texts in true, binational dialogue. "The Mexican War" could not highlight my purpose as well, while "The Mexican-American War" has fallen in estimation because of the contemporaneous usage of "Mexican American" to refer to an ethnic group.

To enable the broadest selection of voices, most documents in this reader are presented in selected form, but each one seeks to capture the essence of a problem or theme in a way that is both accessible and conceptually rewarding. I have also tried to highlight documents and authors that older, more conventional accounts may have overlooked because they were considered of marginal importance. For example, lists of items for the emigrant to take to settle in Texas or popular songs are not the stuff of traditional political or military histories, but they can undoubtedly be the most illuminating and humanizing of cultural artifacts. Each document and selection is annotated to facilitate accessibility and immediacy for the reader, who should not have to consult encyclopedias and dictionaries to understand archaic or culturally specific words and expressions. Headnotes perform a similar role by briefly framing each document featured in the collection.

The great Peruvian writer, historian, and humorist Ricardo Palma once referred to the writer and editor of historical anecdotes as a tailor who works with scraps of cloth. This is, undoubtedly, the best description of this book, with its multitude of voices, perspectives, and vistas. Hopefully its patterns and piecework will serve as an invitation to readers to take needle and thread and seek out the many other pieces of the story that did not fit here.

Christopher Conway
The University of Texas at Arlington

# Chronology of Texas and the U.S.-Mexican War, 1821–1848

| | |
|---|---|
| 1821–1825 | Moses and Stephen Austin commence the colonization of Texas. Mexican colonization laws in 1823, 1824, and 1825 regulate the colonization of Mexico. |
| 1826 | A revolt by Texas colonists against Mexican authorities is defeated in Nacogdoches (December 21, the Fredonia Rebellion). |
| 1830 | Inspired by troublesome reports of the weakness of Mexican political administration in Texas and the large number of U.S. settlers there, Mexico prohibits the introduction of further colonists into Texas, militarizes the area, and forces restrictions on the existing colonists (Law of April 6, 1830). |
| 1835–1836 | A convention of Texas notables at Washington-on-the-Brazos declares independence from Mexico (March 2, 1836) while a small band of insurgents defends the Mission of the Alamo against an overwhelmingly superior Mexican force (February 23–March 6). Sam Houston defeats Santa Anna at the Battle of San Jacinto (April 21) and secures the independence of Texas. |
| 1844 | President John Tyler submits to the U.S. Senate a treaty calling for the annexation of Texas to the United States (April 22), but it is defeated (June 8). Democrat James Knox Polk elected president (December 4). |
| 1845 | The U.S. Congress approves a joint resolution annexing Texas to the United States (March 1). Inauguration of President Polk (March 2). Mexico breaks off relations with the United States (March 28). Polk's envoy John Slidell arrives in Mexico City with instructions to buy California and New Mexico and to resolve a dispute about the boundary separating Texas from Mexico (December 6). President Herrera's administration refuses to recognize Slidell's diplomatic credentials (December 16). General Mariano Paredes y Arrillaga overthrows Herrera (December 31). |
| 1846 | President Polk orders General Zachary Taylor to the disputed boundary of Texas, between the Nueces and Rio Grande (January 13). After failing to make headway with the Paredes administration, Slidell leaves Mexico (March). The Mexican |

army skirmishes with sixty-three U.S. Dragoons outside of Matamoros, killing eleven and capturing the rest (April 24). War commences with the Battles of Palo Alto and Resaca de Palma (May 8–9). Polk delivers his war message to the Congress (May 11), which in turn declares war on Mexico (May 13). In California, U.S. settlers in Sonoma revolt against Mexican authorities and receive the assistance of Captain John Charles Frémont (June 10–July 5). Commodore John D. Sloat of the U.S. Pacific Squadron claims California for the United States (July 7). The Mexican congress formally declares war on the United States (July 2). Congressman David Wilmot of Pennsylvania introduces the Wilmot Proviso as an amendment to a war-funding bill (August 8). The proviso prohibits the introduction of slavery in any lands conquered from Mexico, but it is not approved by Congress. Stephen Kearny of the Army of the West claims New Mexico for the United States (August 15). Santa Anna returns to Mexico from exile after convincing the U.S. to allow him through the naval blockade of his country in exchange for help ending the war and securing U.S. demands (August 16). General Taylor takes the city of Monterrey (September 25). The Doniphan expedition departs from Santa Fe (late October) and defeats the Mexicans at the Battle of El Brazito (December 25). Santa Anna becomes president of Mexico (December 6) after the overthrow of Paredes (August 6) and the interim presidency of Mariano Salas.

1847 Taylor wins the Battle of Buena Vista (February 22–23). General Winfield Scott's expeditionary force captures Veracruz after a destructive siege (March 27). Scott's army is victorious at the Battles of Cerro Gordo (April 18), Contreras and Churubusco (August 19–20), Molino del Rey (September 8), and Mexico City (September 14). Peace commissioner Nicholas Trist arrives in Mexico on confidential orders to negotiate peace and Mexican concessions to the United States (May 6). Santa Anna resigns the presidency (September 16) and is replaced by interim president Pedro María Anaya (November 11). The Mexican government establishes itself in the city of Querétaro, north of Mexico City.

1848 Manuel de la Peña y Peña becomes president of Mexico (January 8). The Treaty of Guadalupe Hidalgo is signed in the village of the same name (February 2) and is ratified in the United States (March 10) and in Mexico (May 25). U.S. troops depart from Mexico City (June 12).

Map 1. Texas 1846–1850

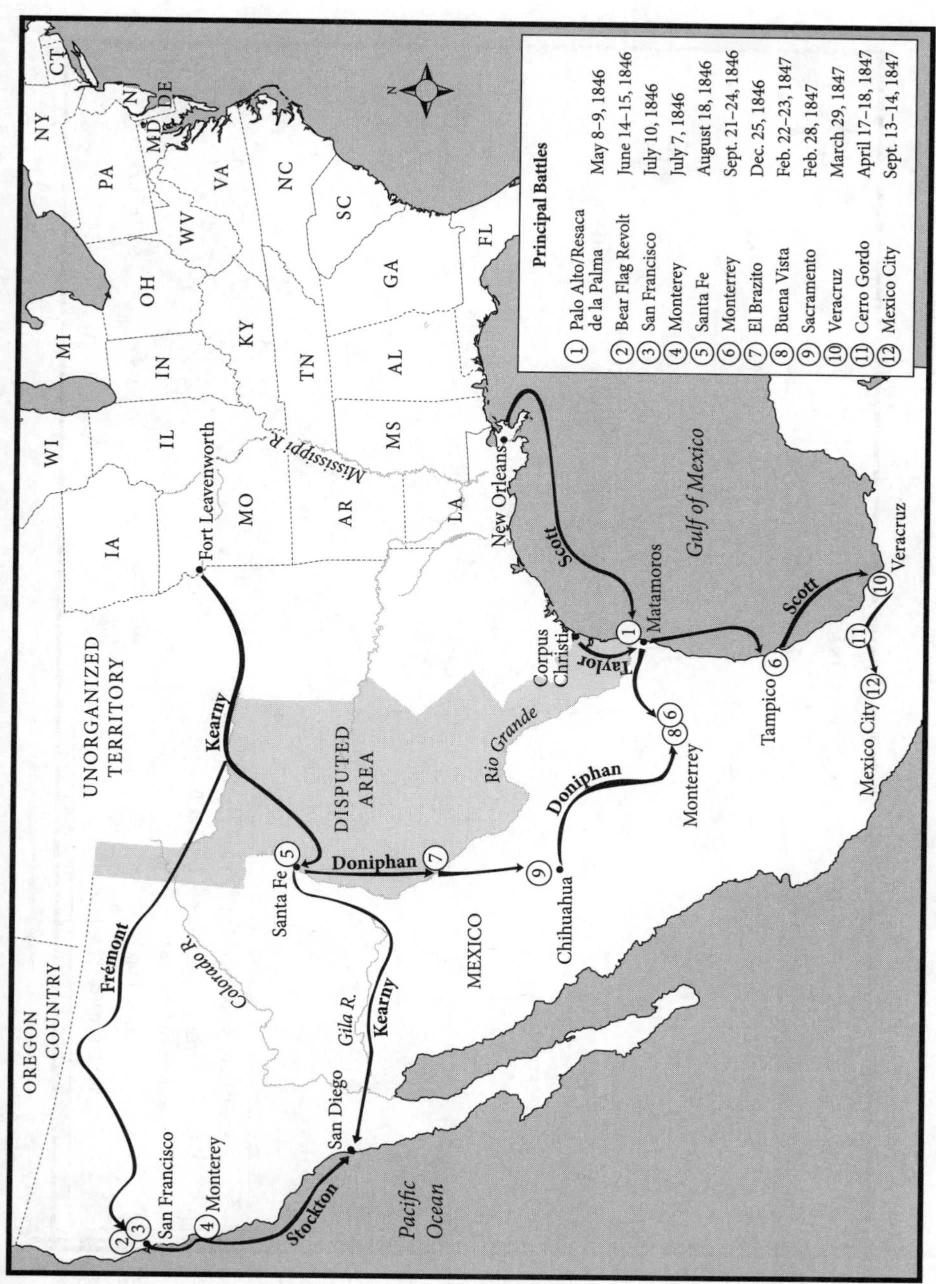

Map 2. The Principal Battles and Campaigns of the U.S.-Mexican War

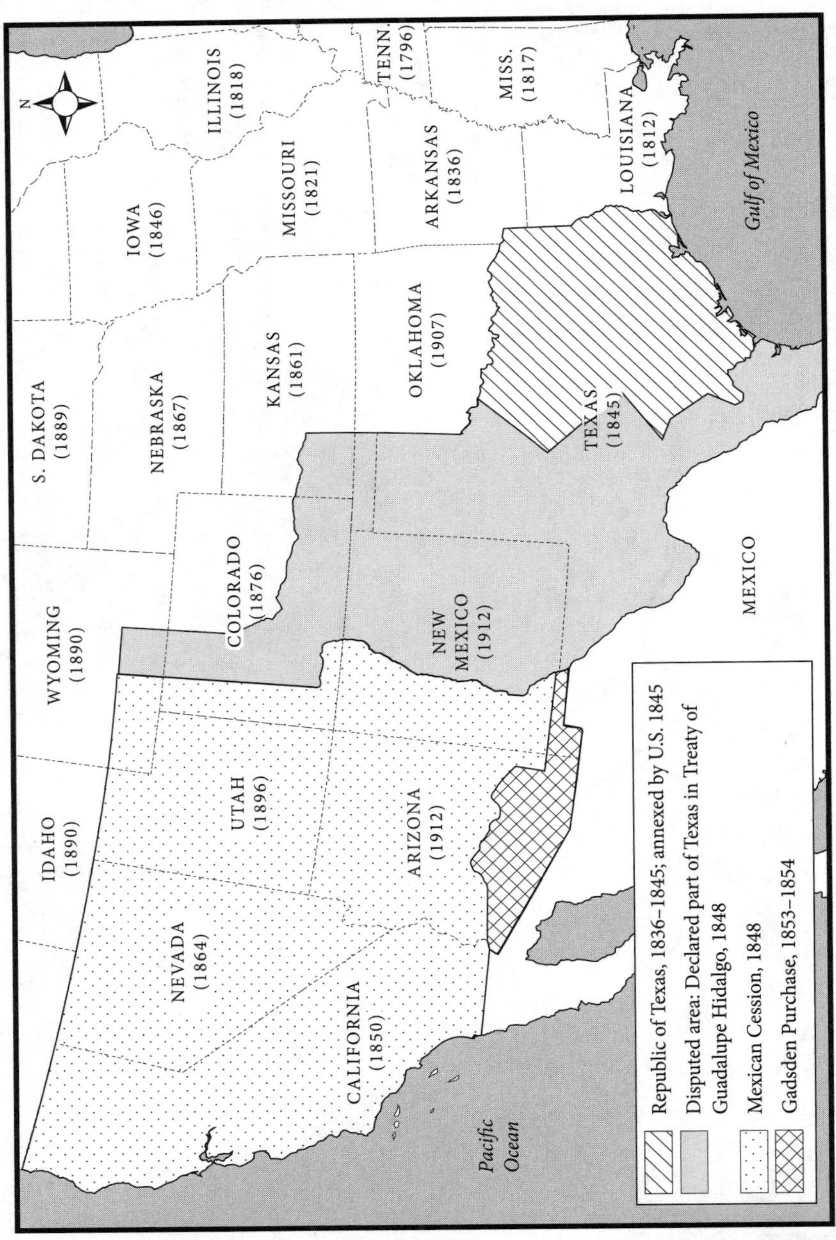


Map 3. The Treaty of Guadalupe Hidalgo (1848) and the Gadsden Purchase (1853–1854)

# I

# The Settlement and Independence of Texas

## The Imperial Colonization Law (1823)[1]

*The colonization of Texas by Anglo-American settlers began with the efforts of Moses Austin (1761–1821), who secured permission from the Spanish authorities in 1821 to start a colony of three hundred settlers in Texas. Upon his death, his son Stephen F. Austin (1793–1836) took up the venture and organized the first Texas colony on the banks of the Brazos River. In 1823, Austin successfully renegotiated the colonization grant with Emperor Agustín de Iturbide (1783–1824) of the newly independent Mexican empire. Iturbide's Imperial Colonization Law (1823) established the basic principles of Mexican policy toward the colonization of Texas: generous land grants, the requirement that colonists convert to Catholicism and obey Mexican law, and the* empresario *system, in which a colonizing agent (*empresario*) was rewarded with land for introducing colonists into Texas. In 1824, the Mexican congress stipulated that state legislatures would be charged with enacting specific colonization laws. The Imperial Colonization Law of 1823, which we present in its entirety below in Stephen F. Austin's own English translation, was followed by the State Colonization Law of 1825.*

Augustin, by Divine Providence, and by the Congress of the Nation, 1st Constitutional Emperor of Mexico, and Grand Master of the Imperial Order of Guadalupe; To all who shall see these presents, Know Ye,—That the *Junta Nacional Instituyente* of the Mexican Empire, has decreed, and we sanction the following:—

The *Junta Nacional Instituyente* of the Mexican Empire, being convinced by the urgent recommendations of the government, of the necessity and importance of giving to the empire a general law of colonization, have thought proper to decree as follows.

1. Stephen Fuller Austin, *Translation of the Laws, Orders, and Contracts on Colonization, from January, 1821, Up to This Time* (San Felipe de Austin, TX: Godwin B. Cotten, 1829), 41–48.

Art. 1. The government of the Mexican nation will protect the liberty, property, and civil rights of all foreigners, who profess the Roman Catholic apostolic religion, the established religion of the empire.

Art. 2. To facilitate their establishment, the executive will distribute lands to them, under the conditions and terms herein expressed.

Art. 3. The *empresarios,* by whom is understood those who introduce at least two hundred families, shall previously contract with the executive, and inform it what branch of industry they propose to follow, the property or resources they intend to introduce for that purpose; and any other particulars they may deem necessary, in order that with this necessary information, the executive may designate the province to which they must direct themselves; the lands which they can occupy with the right of property, and the other circumstances which may be considered necessary.[2]

Art. 4. Families who emigrate, not included in a contract, shall immediately present themselves to the *Ayuntamiento*[3] of the place where they wish to settle, in order that this body, in conformity with the instructions of the executive, may designate the lands corresponding to them, agreeably to the industry which they may establish.

Art. 5. The measurement of land shall be the following—establishing the *vara,* at three geometrical feet, a straight line of five thousand *varas* shall be a league; a square, each of whose sides, shall be one league, shall be called a *Sitio;*[4] and this shall be the unity of counting one, two, or more *Sitios;* five *Sitios* shall compose one Hacienda.

Art. 6. In the distribution made by government, of lands to the colonists, for the formation of villages, towns, cities, and provinces, a distinction shall be made between grazing lands, destined for the raising of stock, and lands suitable for farming, or planting, on account of the facility of irrigation.

Art. 7. One *labor* shall be composed of one million square *varas,* that is to say, one thousand *varas* on each side, which measurement shall be the unity for counting one, two or more *labors.*[5] These *labors* can be divided into halves and quarters, but not less.

---

2. The *empresarios* were colonization and immigration agents who operated under the authority of Mexican law to constitute and oversee colonies in Texas. *Empresarios* were compensated for their services with land.

3. An *ayuntamiento* is a town council, presided over by an *alcalde* and other municipal officers.

4. A *sitio* is equivalent to 4,428 acres.

5. A *labor* is equivalent to 177 acres.

Art. 8. To the colonists whose occupation is farming, there cannot be given less than one *labor,* and those whose occupation is stock raising there cannot be given less than one *Sitio.*

Art. 9. The government of itself, or by means or the authorities authorized for that purpose, can augment said portions of land as may be deemed proper, agreeably to the conditions and circumstances of the colonists.

Art. 10. Establishments made under the former government which are now pending, shall be regulated by this law in all matters that may occur, but those that are finished shall remain in that state.

Art. 11. As one of the principal objects of laws in free governments, ought to be to approximate, so far as is possible, to an equal distribution of property, the government taking into consideration the provisions of this law, will adopt measures for dividing out the lands, which, may have accumulated in large portions, in the hands of individuals or corporations, and which are not cultivated, indemnifying the proprietors, for the just price of such lands to be fixed by appraisers.

Art. 12. The union of many families at one place, shall be called a village, town, or city, agreeably to the number of its inhabitants, its extension locality, and other circumstances which may characterize it, in conformity with the law on that subject. The same regulations for its internal government and police shall be observed as in the others of the same class in the empire.

Art. 13. Care shall be taken in the formation of said new towns, that, so far as the situation of the ground will permit, the streets shall be laid off straight, running north and south, east and west.[6]

Art. 14. Provinces shall be formed whose *superficie*[7] shall be six thousand square leagues.

Art. 15. As soon as a sufficient number of families may be united to form one or more towns, their local government shall be regulated, and the constitutional *Ayuntamiento*s and other local establishments formed in conformity with the laws.

Art. 16. The government shall take care, in accord with the respective ecclesiastical authority, that these new towns are provided with a sufficient number of spiritual pastors, and in like manner, it will propose to congress a plan for their decent support.

---

6. This grid or checkerboard pattern was the model for urban planning in the Spanish New World since the sixteenth century.

7. *Superficie* is a surface or area of space.

Art. 17. In the distribution of lands for settlement among the different provinces, the government shall take care, that the colonists shall be located in those, which it may consider the most important to settle. As a general rule, the colonists who arrive first, shall have the preference in the selection of land.

Art. 18. Natives of the country shall have a preference in the distribution of land; and particularly the military of the army of the three guarantees, in conformity with the decree of the 27th. of March, 1821; and also those who served in the first epoch of the insurrection.

Art. 19. To each Empresario, who introduces and establishes families in any of the provinces designated for colonization, there shall be granted at the rate of three haciendas and two labors, for each two hundred families so introduced by him, but he will lose the right of property, over said lands, should they not have populated and cultivated them in twelve years from the date of the concession. The premium cannot exceed nine haciendas, and six labors, whatever may be the number of families he introduces.

Art. 20. At the end of twenty years the proprietors of the lands, acquired in virtue of the foregoing article, must alienate two thirds part of said lands, either by sale, donation, or in any other manner he pleases. The law authorizes him to hold in full property and dominion one third part.

Art. 21. The two foregoing articles are to be understood as governing the contracts made within six months, as after that time, counting from the day of the promulgation of this law, the executive can diminish the premium as it may deem proper, giving an account thereof to congress, with such information as may be deemed necessary.

Art. 22. The date of the concession for lands constitutes an inviolable law, for the right of property and legal ownership; should any one through error or by subsequent concession occupy land belonging to another, he shall have no right to it, further than a preference in case of sale, at the current price.

Art. 23. If after two years from the date of the concession, the colonist should not have cultivated his land, the right of property shall be considered as renounced; in which case, the respective *Ayuntamiento* can grant it to another.

Art. 24. During the first six years from the date of the concession, the colonists shall not pay tithes, duties on their produce, nor any contribution under whatever name it may be called.

Art. 25. The next six years from the same date, they shall pay half tithes and the half of the contributions whether direct or indirect, that are paid by the other citizens of the empire. After this time, they shall in all things relating to taxes and contributions, be placed on the same footing with the other citizens.

Art. 26. All instruments of husbandry, machinery, and other utensils, that are introduced by the colonists for their use, at the time of their coming to the empire, shall be free, as also the merchandise introduced by each family, to the amount of two thousand dollars.

Art. 27. All foreigners, who come to establish themselves in the empire, shall be considered as naturalized, should they exercise any useful profession or industry by which, at the end of three years, they have a capital to support themselves with decency, and are married. Those who with the foregoing qualifications marry Mexicans will acquire particular merit for obtaining letters of citizenship.

Art, 28. Congress will grant letters of citizenship to those who solicit them in conformity with the constitution of the empire.

Art. 29. Every individual shall be free to leave the empire, and can alienate the lands over which he may have acquired the right of property, agreeably to the tenor of this law, and he can likewise take away from the country all his property, by paying the duties established by law.

Art. 30. After the publication of this law, there can be no sale or purchase of slaves which may be introduced into the empire. The children of slaves born in the empire shall be free at fourteen years of age.[8]

Art. 31. All foreigners who may have established themselves in any of the provinces of the empire, under permission of the former government, will remain on the lands which they may have occupied, being governed by the tenor of this law, in the distribution of said lands.

Art. 32. The executive, as it may conceive necessary, will sell or lease the lands, which on account of their local situation, may be the most important, being governed with respect to all others, by the provisions of this law.

---

8. The 1827 state constitution of Coahuila outlawed slavery, but the Texas colonists found a way around the law by freeing slaves and making them sign contracts for indentured service. When Presidente Guadalupe Victoria decreed an end to slavery in Mexico in 1829, Texas was allowed to keep its slaves.

This law shall be presented to His Imperial Majesty, for his sanction, publication, and fulfillment.—Mexico, 3rd January, 1823—3rd of the independence of the empire.—

Juan Francisco, Bishop of Durango, President.—Antonio de Mier, Member and Secretary.—Juan Batista Arispe, Member and Secretary

Therefore, we order all tribunals, Judges, Chiefs, Governors, and all other authorities, as well civil, as military, and ecclesiastical, of whatever class or dignity they may be, to comply with this decree, and cause it to be complied with, in all its parts, and you will cause it to be printed, published, and circulated. —Given in Mexico, 4th January, 1823. —Signed by The Emperor.

## The Village of San Felipe de Austin (1831)[9]

*The following anonymous description of the town of Austin is one of the earliest published descriptions of life in Stephen F. Austin's colony in Mexican Texas before the Texas Revolution.*

At length we arrived at San Felipe; and learnt that one reason why we had seen the lights so far, was the elevation of the ground on which the town is situated. We found there were two public houses in the place, and stopped at Whitehouse's, where we lodged. In the morning we had an opportunity to look around us.

San Felipe de Austin, (St. Philip,) stands on the west bank of the Brazos, at the head of boat navigation, and on ground about 40 feet above the surface of the water when at its usual level. From the nature of the country where the river rises, and the height of the banks, the floods rise here at particular seasons thirty feet. The shores are broken sand banks, quite steep, and destitute of soil and trees on the immediate margin of the stream, as well as greatly deficient in beauty. The village, as was naturally to be expected, presented nothing fine or particularly interesting. It contains about fifty houses, all built of logs, except one, which is framed, and very comfortable. About a mile distant is the residence of Mr. Williams, the secretary of Col. Austin, from whom are obtained the land titles conveyed to settlers. Several wagons and other carriages which I observed in the street gave an air of business and thrift which I had not before seen in Texas.

At the inn I found twenty or thirty men who had come from different quarters in pursuit of places to settle. These persons, commonly called land-hunters, were almost all from the United States, and generally from the Southwestern States.

---

9. Anonymous, *A Visit to Texas: The Journal of a Traveller through Those Parts Most Interesting to American Settlers with Descriptions of Scenery, Habits, &c &c* (New York: Goodrich & Wiley, 1834), 213–15.

I saw one, however, who had come from Ohio, and was inquiring for a tract on which he might undertake with advantage the raising of sheep. Among these strangers I found a number of very intelligent men but I learn that a portion of them had fled from justice, or as they chose to call it, from the law, in their own country. It is a well known fact, that a considerable proportion of our countrymen who are found in Texas, are of this character. . . . So accustomed are the inhabitants to the appearance of fugitives from justice, that they are particularly careful to make inquiries of the characters of new-comers, and generally obtain early and circumstantial information concerning strangers. Indeed it is very common to hear the inquiry made: "what did he do that made him leave home?" or "what have you come to Texas for?" intimating almost an assurance of one's being a criminal. Notwithstanding this state of things, however, the good of the public and of each individual is so evidently dependant on the public morals, that all appear ready to discountenance and punish crimes. . . .

. . .

There is now at San Felipe an *ayuntamiento*, or council, an *alcalde*, or chief civil officer, and several persons of some education who perform the part of advocates, much on the principles of the laws of the United States. Men accused of high crimes are however made over to the Mexican authorities, at the seat of government of the state of Coahuila and Texas. Two men were now at San Felipe under a charge of murder, under keeping and restraint, but were allowed to move about the village.

A few native Mexicans are settled in this part of the province, and I witnessed one afternoon a Spanish fandango danced in the open air by a party of these people, evidently of a low class. There was nothing worthy of particular remark in the style of the performance; and the music, which was that of a violin, was poor indeed. A billiard table is publicly kept in the place, and found players even among such a limited population.

. . .

There were several small stores in San Felipe, their stocks of goods being brought from New Orleans through Brazoria, chiefly by land. Most of the inhabitants of the town have lands in the vicinity: the terms offered by the Mexican Government through the *empresarios,* here as well as elsewhere in the province, being extremely tempting, to those who can submit to the laws of the country. Here were many persons who had come into possession, with good titles, of beautiful estates, merely for occupying them, and paying the expenses of surveying, recording &c., altogether not exceeding one hundred and fifty dollars. Single men are thus found, in the enjoyment of their quarter leagues: more beautiful and fertile, as well as more extensive than some old family possessions of Europe, which have been the objects of envy from age to age; and by merely becoming a married man, each is entitled to an addition of three times as much more, instead of becoming by that measure, as in many other parts of the world, almost of necessity a beggar.

## Articles to Be Taken by the Emigrant (1835)[10]

*David Woodman Jr.'s* Guide to Texas Emigrants *(1835) was an early and influential handbook for prospective Texas colonists. Woodman's book was composed of letters by Texas residents and visitors who described its terrain, peoples, and living conditions. The guide also featured newspaper articles on whether the United States should annex Texas or not. In a similar vein,* The Emigrant's Guide to Oregon and California *(1845) by Lansford Hastings assiduously promoted U.S. expansion into California and Oregon. The following selection from Woodman's guide provides some insight into the kinds of supplies colonists needed to establish themselves successfully in Texas. Most of the medicines listed below, such as magnesia, castor oil, and Epsom salts, were laxatives.*

Emigrants going to the grants, had better be provided with sufficient bread stuffs and groceries to last them for six or seven months.

The settler would do well to turn his little stock of money into Spanish dollars and doubloons. Although United States' bills are generally above par, yet there would be a difficulty in getting them changed, provided the settler were going inland. All Spanish silver money passes, and nothing will be lost in making use of it.

He should be provided with a passport.

A family should take the following medicines with them:

| | |
|---|---|
| 1/2 lb. calcined Magnesia and bottle, | $1.50 |
| 2 oz. Rhubarb powder, | 0.38 |
| 3 lbs. best Epsom Salts, 1s. 6d., | 0.56 |
| 2 oz. Essence of Peppermint[11] and vial, | 0.25 |
| 2 oz. of Laudanum[12] and vial, | 0.25 |
| 6 doz. Calomel and Jalap, | 0.75 |
| 1 doz. Emetics,[13] | 0.50 |
| 2 pint bottles Castor Oil, | 1.00 |
| 6 oz. Soap liniment[14] and vial, | 0.50 |
| 3 oz. Hartshorn[15] and vial, | 0.31 |

10. David Woodman Jr., *Guide to Texas Emigrants* (Boston: M. Hawes, 1835), 187–88.

11. Peppermint was used to treat stomach discomfort.

12. A narcotic created by mixing opium in alcohol. Laudanum was used to treat a variety of maladies.

13. Emetics are substances used to induce vomiting.

14. An ointment made out of a variety of ingredients, including soap and camphor, and used topically to treat soreness.

15. Another topical ointment.

| | |
|---|---|
| 2 oz. Spirits of Camphor[16] and vial, | 0.25 |
| Box, | 0.18 |
| | $ 6.93 |

Emigrants should be well provided with necessary farming utensils, a wagon, comfortable clothing, principally of cotton stuff, a good rifle, and a strong dog. Seeds of useful plants and different grains must not be forgotten. It would be best to carry tents or sail-cloth, for covering, until the house is built.

The settler who does not want to spend his money in luxuries, would find the following table of necessaries sufficient to last a family of five persons during a voyage from New York to Texas, (say, twenty-five days), viz: ten lbs. of sugar. One and a half lb. of coffee (ground, if possible.) One lb. of tea. Two lbs. of soap. One pint salt. One oz. pepper. One quart vinegar, and a jar. Four lbs. cheese. One and a half lbs. rice. One cwt.[17] biscuit. Two gallons flour. Thirty-seven lbs. beef, ham or bacon, or a proportion of each. One cwt. of potatoes. Half lb. of currants or raisins. Two doz. eggs. Six lbs. butter. Half gallon molasses. Two lbs. split peas. One dozen lemons, a pleasant drink, and allays sea-sickness. Half bushel apples. A loaf or two of bread cut into slices and toasted slowly. A small jar of pickles.

Some utensils should also be taken. The following would serve: two pots for boiling, (a large and a small one), one hook pot; one tin chamber and cover; one tin water-can; tinder-box and matches; three lbs. of candles; one tin hand basin; two tin pint cups; two square, deep tin baking pans; one wooden bowl to mix paste, &c.; three tin plates; knives, forks and spoons; and a small washtub.

The light travelling wagons of our own country are hardly strong enough for Texas. A party of emigrants who had to go inland, should have a strong large wagon, and buy a couple of oxen at the place of landing, and travel by the side of their baggage. These will be invaluable to the settler when he commences working his lands.

The farming utensils which are used in America and England, will be required in Texas. Wagon and yoke harness for horses, spades, ploughs, hoes, shovels and axes. Box of carpenter's tools. Ropes, &c., will be found useful. Also, such articles of bedding as the family possesses.

## Mexican Views of Texas

*Although Texas held agricultural and commercial promise for Mexico, it was also a place of troubling cultural collisions between Protestant Anglo-Americans settlers and Catholic Mexicans. What had once been a frontier was now a site*

16. A strong stimulant resulting from the mixture of camphor with alcohol and used both topically and internally for a variety of maladies, including the common cold.

17. Cwt. is a unit of measurement signifying 100 lbs., also known as "hundredweight."

*where Mexican sovereignty might be undermined by immigration. The following selections illustrate the perspectives of three notable Mexicans of the 1830s on the Texas question. The first is by Lieutenant José María Sánchez (1801?–1834), who accompanied Manuel de Mier y Terán on a fact-finding tour of Texas in 1828. The second is by Lorenzo de Zavala (1788–1836), a federalist and one of the early Mexican republic's most accomplished and cosmopolitan political figures. Persecuted on more than one occasion by centralist political enemies, including Antonio López de Santa Anna, Zavala traveled to Texas, where he signed its declaration of independence and became its first vice president, in 1836. The third selection is by Juan Nepomuceno Almonte (1803–1869), who was charged by Santa Anna to study the Texas question in 1835. After fighting against the Texas insurgents at the Alamo and San Jacinto, he served as ambassador to the United States on the eve of the U.S.-Mexican War and as secretary of war under President Mariano Paredes y Arrillaga in 1846.*

## Artillery Lieutenant José María Sánchez (1828)[18]

North Americans have taken possession of almost all of the eastern part of Texas, in most cases without the knowledge of the authorities, since they emigrate incessantly without anyone to hinder them, taking possession of whatever place suits them, without asking, needing only to dismount and build their dwellings. Thus, the majority of the inhabitants of the department are North Americans, the Mexican population being reduced to only Béjar,[19] Nacogdoches, and Bahía del Espíritu Santo, miserable towns that between them have no more than three thousand inhabitants, and the new village of Guadalupe Victoria, which barely has little more than seventy inhabitants. The government of the state, residing in Saltillo, which should watch over the conservation of its most important and precious department, by taking measures to prevent its being stolen by foreign hands, knows the least, not only about what is going on but even about the land itself. This assertion is confirmed by the report that the state government itself gave to the boundaries commission, about the land in Texas that it had granted to the *empresarios* of the colonies. By comparing this report to the map, we find that grants have been made of previously granted lands. . . . Frequent and forceful representations have been made to the supreme government of the federation asserting that this important department is in imminent danger of falling prey to greedy North Americans, but it has never taken what might be called safety measures, either because it has always been busy with the fatal convulsions that

18. José María Sánchez, *Viaje a Texas* (Mexico City: Talleres Gráficos de la Nación, 1926), 51–53. Translated by Gustavo Pellón.

19. San Antonio de Béjar.

have destroyed the republic[20] or because covert agents have deceived government officials into believing that there are no risks but merely the exaggerations of cowardly spirits. Thus they lull to sleep the vigilance of the government authorities, and meanwhile northern enemies never miss a chance to advance, even if just one step, to achieve the ends of their traitorous project, which is well known. . . .[21]

## Lorenzo de Zavala (1834)[22]

In my *Historical Essay* concerning Mexico's revolutions, I have made known my opinions regarding that beautiful and rich tract of land known previously as the province of Texas and today as an integral part of the State of Coahuila and Texas. Once the door was open to its colonization, as was fitting under a system of free government, it was predictable that within a few years a new generation would appear to populate part of the Mexican Republic and consequently that this new population would be totally heterogeneous with respect to the other provinces or states of the country. Fifteen or twenty thousand foreigners distributed throughout the vast territory of Mexico, Oaxaca, Veracruz, etc., disseminated among the old inhabitants, cannot bring about any sudden change in their customs and habits. Rather they are likely to adopt the inclinations, manners, language, religion, politics, and even the vices of the multitudes that surround them. An Englishman will become a Mexican in Mexico City, and a Mexican will become an Englishman in London. The same will not occur in the case of the colonies. These places that were totally deserted forests and woods, uninhabited twelve years ago, now turned suddenly into villages and towns by Germans,[23] Irish, and North Americans, will necessarily make up an entirely diverse nation, and it would be absurd to expect them to renounce their religion, their customs, and their most deeply held convictions. What will the results be?

I have already announced it many times. They will not be able to subject themselves to the military regime and the ecclesiastical government that unfortunately have persisted in Mexican territory despite the republico-democratic constitutions. They will invoke the institutions that should be governing the country, and they will want them to be not a lie, an illusion, but a reality. Whenever a military chief tries to intervene in civil transactions, they will resist and they will triumph. They will form popular assemblies to deal with public affairs, as is the practice in the United States and in England. They will erect chapels to different

---

20. Here Sánchez refers to Mexican civil wars.

21. Mexicans believed that the United States wanted to annex Texas to its territory.

22. Lorenzo de Zavala, *Viaje a los Estados Unidos del Norte de América* (Paris: Imprenta de Decourchant, 1834), 140–42, 366–68. Translated by Gustavo Pellón.

23. German immigrants to Mexican Texas in the 1830s and 1840s settled primarily in south central Texas in an area known as the "German Belt."

cults so as to adore the Creator according to their beliefs. Religious practices are a social necessity, one of the greatest consolations to the evils of humanity. Will the government of Mexico send to Texas a legion of soldiers to enforce the third article of the Mexican constitution that prohibits the practice of any religion other than Catholicism? Within a few years, this happy conquest of civilization will continue its course through other states toward the Southwest, and the states of Tamaulipas, Nuevo León, San Luis, Chihuahua, Durango, Jalisco, and Zacatecas will be the freest in the Mexican confederation, while those of Mexico, Puebla, Veracruz, Oaxaca, Michoacán, and Chiapas will have to endure for some time the military and ecclesiastical influence. . . .

Consequently the influence of the United States on Mexico, in time, will be through the force of opinion, through teaching, all the stronger because it will be a purely moral force founded on their doctrines and lessons. But there is more. Ten thousand citizens of the United States settle annually in the territory of the Mexican Republic, especially in the states of Chihuahua, Coahuila, and Texas, Tamaulipas, Nuevo León, San Luis Potosí, Durango, Zacatecas, Sonora, Sinaloa, and the territories of New Mexico and the Californias. Together with their industriousness, these settlers and merchants bring their habits of liberty, thrift, work, their austere and religious customs, their individual independence, and their republicanism. What changes will these enterprising guests not make on the moral and material existence of the ancient inhabitants? Cartagena was a Carthaginian city, Cadiz a Phoenician city, Marseilles a Greek city for many centuries, because their settlers were from these countries. Within a few years, the Mexican Republic will come to be molded by a regime that combines the American system with Spanish customs and traditions. . . .

The end result, all the same, will be the triumph of liberty in those states, and over the Gothic rubble of untenable privileges will rise a new, glorious, and enlightened generation. By putting into motion all their abundant, rich resources, this generation will finally unite that indigenous class, degraded and vilified even today, to the civilized family, teaching it to think and to value its dignity, elevating its thoughts. What barrier can withstand this torrent, born twenty-four years ago in a small town of the Bajío, obscure in origin, without direction or bounds, devastating all in its path, but today a majestic river that receives pure and crystalline waters from other countries, and will fertilize the entire territory of Mexico? Useless will be the opposition of a vilified generation, heir to Castilian traditions and beliefs, which defends its antisocial doctrines despite a lack of results. The American system will obtain a complete though bloody victory.

## Juan Nepomuceno Almonte (1835)[24]

It is not difficult to foresee what will happen if you pay attention to the immense advances of industry there and if you consider its advantageous geographical location, its ports, the easy navigation of its rivers, the variety of its products, the fertility of its soil, climate, etc.; it must be admitted that Texas will very soon be the most flourishing region of the republic. It is not difficult to find the reason for this prosperity, if you consider that, with the exception of a few troublemakers, no one there thinks about anything but planting sugarcane, cotton, corn, wheat, tobacco, raising cattle, making roads, and making rivers navigable; and that the effects of our political commotions are not even felt, and sometimes they learn of them only by chance.

Situated as Texas is, 450 leagues from the capital of the federation, it is easy to understand how its population and industry will increase rapidly. Living beyond the reach of the civil wars that have unfortunately destroyed us, those inhabitants have been able and will be able without interruption to devote themselves to work and business, in this way endowing with value the country and lands with which the supreme government's munificence favored them. If the situation of Texas is so advantageous, what keeps Mexicans from having a share of so many benefits? Are they not the owners of these precious lands? Do they not know how to face the dangers with constancy and resolution? Therefore, let small companies be formed; let families of farmers be contracted; let each of these companies name the steward, agent, or director of the colony, and I guarantee that before one or two years, the concession of eleven *sitios*[25] that perhaps did not cost more than a sheet of stamped paper[26] will become a property worth more than 15,000 or 20,000 pesos. Whoever wants to confirm the truth of this may examine the haciendas of the settlers, and he shall see that what I say is not a dream. I have heard that an objection to the colonization of Texas by Mexicans is the distance between here and there, but those who argue that have undoubtedly not considered that to go to that territory it is not necessary to make the whole journey by land, since from here you can go to Veracruz in four days, and from there to Galveston or Brazoria in six or eight more days. It is therefore possible to assert that in less than twelve or fourteen days you can make the trip from here to Texas, and it is now clear that although the distance between here and there is considerable by land, by water it is too insignificant to present an obstacle to the realization of such a lucrative and honorable project. If, as I trust, I were to return to Texas as director of colonization, it would always give me the greatest pleasure to give to Mexican buyers of land and *empresarios* all the information I may have

---

24. Juan Almonte, *Noticia Estadística Sobre Tejas* (Mexico City: Ignacio Cumplido, 1835), 6–9. Translated by Gustavo Pellón.

25. See note 4.

26. Stamped paper (*papel sellado*) refers to embossed paper used for legal transactions.

to help them settle the land, and I am not afraid to assure, principally retired and invalid officers, that the best way to provide their families with a secure and comfortable living is to apply to the supreme government to receive land in lieu of their salaries and go to colonize Texas.[27] There, they will find peace and industry, and their old age will be restful, which will perhaps not be easy to obtain in the center of the republic.

## Mary Austin Holley on the People of Texas (1836)[28]

*Mary Phelps Austin Holley (1784–1846) was Stephen F. Austin's cousin and the author of* Texas: Observations Historical, Geographical and Descriptive *(1833) as well as the subsequent* Mrs. Holley's Texas *(1836). Holley was born in Connecticut and was the wife of the Reverend Horace Holley, a Unitarian minister who settled in Kentucky and served as president of Transylvania University. After her husband's death in 1828, Holley emigrated to Texas to live with her brother Henry Austin at the Bolivar plantation on the lower Brazos River, south of present-day Houston.*

The Mexicans are commonly very indolent, of loose morals, and, if not infidels of which there are many, involved in the grossest superstition. This view exhibits why it is by no means wonderful that this people have been the dupes and slaves of so many masters, or that the plans of intelligent and patriotic men, for the political regeneration of Mexico, have heretofore entirely failed. The moral education of this people must be improved, before their political condition can be ameliorated. There are many honorable and signal exceptions to this statement, it is true; but we believe the general character of the Mexicans in Texas and her vicinity has been pretty accurately drawn. Fortunately however, as we have seen, there are but few of the race within her confines.

The great majority of the population of Texas, and the most valuable portion of it, consists of emigrants from the United States. The active and enterprising New Englander—the bold and hardy western hunter—the high-spirited southern planter—meet here upon common ground, divested of all sectional influence, to lend their combined energies to the improvement of this infant but delightful and prosperous country. It has been said and published by certain individuals, for what cause we know not without it is in sheer enmity to this country, that Texas is the great penitentiary of America, where outlaws, murderers, thieves, and vagabonds resort, after having been compelled to flee from the judgments of

27. Based on the reports of Manuel Mier y Terán, the Mexican government sought to counteract U.S. influence in Texas by coaxing Mexican colonists to move there.

28. Mary Austin Holley, *Texas* (Lexington, KY: J. Clarke and Co., 1836), 128–34.

offended laws, or the scorn and detestation of society. This is a gross misrepresentation, and unworthy of any man who has the least regard for truth. . . . Never has any cis-Atlantic State[29] been peopled by a more honest, industrious, intelligent, and respectable emigration than Texas, and especially Austin's colony. Sturdy mechanics, substantial farmers, able professional men, and, not infrequently, wealthy planters, have sought and found a home in the Brazos valley; while the great body of settlers, though commonly poor, have been of the most respectable and enterprising character. The empresario, Gen. Austin, has never admitted into his colony any man known to be of disreputable standing, and has always, as far as practicable, made diligent enquiries in order to ascertain, if possible, the conduct and reputation of each applicant.

. . .

There are a considerable number of Negroes in Texas who, though slavery is prohibited, by an evasion of the law are "bound" for life, and are, *de facto,* the property of their masters. They are however, from the restraints of the law, invested with more liberty and less liable to abuse than the slaves of the Southern United States. The question of negro slavery in connection with the settlement of this country, is one of great importance, and perhaps may hereafter present a serious difficulty. The former constitution and laws totally prohibited this worst of evils.

. . .

The character of Leather-Stocking[30] is not uncommon in Texas. Many persons employ an individual of this class in the business of hunting, in all its branches; and thus are constantly supplied with provisions of every description, even to eggs, which are furnished by the immense number of wild fowl. These hunters are very profitable to their employers, and much cherished in the family, and often become spoiled by familiarity and indulgence. A roughness of manners, and a rudeness of speech are tolerated in them, which would not be brooked in other servants. They are a sort of privileged character. Indians and Mexicans are considered the best qualified for this important office. But it sometimes happens that a white man from the *States,* who has become somewhat decivilized, (to coin a word,) is substituted. The dress of these hunters is usually of deer-skin; hence the appropriate name of *Leather Stocking.* Their generic name, for they form a distinct class, is *Frontiers-men.*

---

29. On this side of the Atlantic.

30. A phrase referring to a frontiersman, first used as the nickname of Natty Bumppo, the protagonist of *The Pioneers* (1823), a novel belonging to a series of "Leatherstocking Tales" (1823–1845) by James Fenimore Cooper (1789–1851).

## The Texas Declaration of Independence (March 2, 1836)[31]

*A convention of Texas notables on the Washington-on-the-Brazos declared independence from Mexico on March 2, 1836, during the siege of the Alamo. The Texas declaration of independence was the culmination of a political process begun in 1832 and 1833, when Texas colonists began to formally organize themselves to request statehood from Mexico. The arrest of Stephen F. Austin in 1834, Santa Anna's rejection of federalism, and tensions between colonists and the Mexican military all contributed to the Texas Revolution. In November 1835, Texas delegates gathered in San Felipe de Austin, created a provisional government, and affirmed that they would declare independence if Mexico did not reinstate the federalist constitution of 1824. At a convention in March 1836, Texas declared independence from Mexico and drafted a constitution. The convention named Sam Houston (1793–1863) commander in chief of the Texas army and drafted a constitution. The convention also elected David G. Burnet (1788–1870) interim president and the Mexican-born Lorenzo de Zavala[32] vice president.*

### The Unanimous Declaration of Independence made by the Delegates of the People of Texas in General Convention at the town of Washington on the 2nd day of March 1836.

When a government has ceased to protect the lives, liberty, and property of the people, from whom its legitimate powers are derived, and for the advancement of whose happiness it was instituted, and so far from being a guarantee for the enjoyment of those inestimable and inalienable rights, becomes an instrument in the hands of evil rulers for their oppression.

When the Federal Republican Constitution of their country, which they have sworn to support, no longer has a substantial existence, and the whole nature of their government has been forcibly changed, without their consent, from a restricted federative republic, composed of sovereign states, to a consolidated central military despotism, in which every interest is disregarded but that of the army and the priesthood, both the eternal enemies of civil liberty, the ever ready minions of power, and the usual instruments of tyrants.

When, long after the spirit of the constitution has departed, moderation is at length so far lost by those in power, that even the semblance of freedom is removed, and the forms themselves of the constitution discontinued, and so far from their petitions and remonstrances being regarded, the agents who bear

---

31. H. P. N. Gammel, comp., "The Declaration of Independence Made by the Delegates of the People of Texas," in *The Laws of Texas, 1822–1897* (Austin, TX: Gammel Book Co., 1898), 1: 1063–66.

32. For more on Lorenzo de Zavala's life and views, see "Mexican Views of Texas."

them are thrown into dungeons, and mercenary armies sent forth to force a new government upon them at the point of the bayonet.

When, in consequence of such acts of malfeasance and abdication on the part of the government, anarchy prevails, and civil society is dissolved into its original elements. In such a crisis, the first law of nature, the right of self-preservation, the inherent and inalienable rights of the people to appeal to first principles, and take their political affairs into their own hands in extreme cases, enjoins it as a right towards themselves, and a sacred obligation to their posterity, to abolish such government, and create another in its stead, calculated to rescue them from impending dangers, and to secure their future welfare and happiness.

Nations, as well as individuals, are amenable for their acts to the public opinion of mankind. A statement of a part of our grievances is therefore submitted to an impartial world, in justification of the hazardous but unavoidable step now taken, of severing our political connection with the Mexican people, and assuming an independent attitude among the nations of the earth.

The Mexican government, by its colonization laws, invited and induced the Anglo-American population of Texas to colonize its wilderness under the pledged faith of a written constitution, that they should continue to enjoy that constitutional liberty and republican government to which they had been habituated in the land of their birth, the United States of America.

In this expectation they have been cruelly disappointed, inasmuch as the Mexican nation has acquiesced in the late changes made in the government by General Antonio López de Santa Anna,[33] who having overturned the constitution of his country, now offers us the cruel alternative, either to abandon our homes, acquired by so many privations, or submit to the most intolerable of all tyranny, the combined despotism of the sword and the priesthood.

It has sacrificed our welfare to the state of Coahuila, by which our interests have been continually depressed through a jealous and partial course of legislation, carried on at a far distant seat of government, by a hostile majority, in an unknown tongue, and this too, notwithstanding we have petitioned in the humblest terms for the establishment of a separate state government, and have, in accordance with the provisions of the national constitution, presented to the general Congress a republican constitution, which was, without just cause, contemptuously rejected.

It incarcerated in a dungeon, for a long time, one of our citizens,[34] for no other cause but a zealous endeavor to procure the acceptance of our constitution, and the establishment of a state government.

---

33. Although Antonio López de Santa Anna overthrew the centralist regime of Anastasio Bustamante in 1832, in 1835 he turned against the federalists and adopted a centralist regime that was hostile to the kind of regional autonomy requested by Texas on the eve of its independence.

34. This is an understatement because the citizen in question was the "Father of Texas," Stephen F. Austin himself. Austin was imprisoned for almost a year in 1834 because

It has failed and refused to secure, on a firm basis, the right of trial by jury, that palladium of civil liberty, and only safe guarantee for the life, liberty, and property of the citizen.

It has failed to establish any public system of education, although possessed of almost boundless resources, (the public domain,) and although it is an axiom in political science, that unless a people are educated and enlightened, it is idle to expect the continuance of civil liberty, or the capacity for self government.

It has suffered the military commandants, stationed among us, to exercise arbitrary acts of oppression and tyranny, thus trampling upon the most sacred rights of the citizens, and rendering the military superior to the civil power.

It has dissolved, by force of arms, the state Congress of Coahuila and Texas, and obliged our representatives to fly for their lives from the seat of government, thus depriving us of the fundamental political right of representation.

It has demanded the surrender of a number of our citizens, and ordered military detachments to seize and carry them into the Interior for trial, in contempt of the civil authorities, and in defiance of the laws and the constitution.

It has made piratical attacks upon our commerce, by commissioning foreign desperadoes, and authorizing them to seize our vessels, and convey the property of our citizens to far distant ports for confiscation.

It denies us the right of worshipping the Almighty according to the dictates of our own conscience, by the support of a national religion, calculated to promote the temporal interest of its human functionaries, rather than the glory of the true and living God.[35]

It has demanded us to deliver up our arms, which are essential to our defense, the rightful property of freemen, and formidable only to tyrannical governments.

It has invaded our country both by sea and by land, with intent to lay waste our territory, and drive us from our homes; and has now a large mercenary army advancing, to carry on against us a war of extermination.

It has, through its emissaries, incited the merciless savage, with the tomahawk and scalping knife, to massacre the inhabitants of our defenseless frontiers.

It hath been, during the whole time of our connection with it, the contemptible sport and victim of successive military revolutions, and hath continually exhibited every characteristic of a weak, corrupt, and tyrannical government.

These, and other grievances, were patiently borne by the people of Texas, until they reached that point at which forbearance ceases to be a virtue. We then took up arms in defence of the national constitution. We appealed to our Mexican brethren for assistance. Our appeal has been made in vain. Though months have elapsed, no sympathetic response has yet been heard from the Interior. We

---

authorities intercepted a letter in which he said that Texas should not wait for official consent to undertake its separation from the state of Coahuila.

35. Although enforcement was impossible, Mexican colonization laws required that foreigners who settled in Texas convert to Catholicism.

are, therefore, forced to the melancholy conclusion, that the Mexican people have acquiesced in the destruction of their liberty, and the substitution therefore of a military government; that they are unfit to be free, and incapable of self government.

The necessity of self-preservation, therefore, now decrees our eternal political separation.

We, therefore, the delegates with plenary powers of the people of Texas, in solemn convention assembled, appealing to a candid world for the necessities of our condition, do hereby resolve and declare, that our political connection with the Mexican nation has forever ended, and that the people of Texas do now constitute a free, Sovereign, and independent republic, and are fully invested with all the rights and attributes which properly belong to independent nations; and, conscious of the rectitude of our intentions, we fearlessly and confidently commit the issue to the decision of the Supreme arbiter of the destinies of nations.

## The Fall of the Alamo (March 6, 1836)

*After taking San Antonio in December 1835 during the Texas Revolution, Colonels William Travis (1809–1836) and Jim Bowie (1796–1836) stayed behind with a small force to defend the Mission of the Alamo against an overwhelmingly larger Mexican force under the command of President Santa Anna and General Vicente Filisola (1789–1850). On March 6, the Mexicans overwhelmed the mission and killed all of its defenders except one slave and some women and children. The Alamo became a rallying cry for Texan independence, as did the subsequent massacre of Goliad (March 27), when Santa Anna ordered the execution of hundreds of captured Texans. Below we present selected documents relating to the fall of the Alamo, including a selection from* Colonel Crockett's Exploits and Adventures in Texas *(1836), one of the first of many heroic and fictional recreations of the death of David Crockett (1786–1836), a much mythologized frontiersman and former congressman from Tennessee. The book was published a few months after the fall of the Alamo to capitalize on Crockett's fame and popular support for Texan independence in the United States.*

### Letter by William Travis (February 24, 1836)[36]

To the people of Texas and All Americans in the world—

---

36. Francis White Johnson, *A History of Texas and Texans*, ed. Eugene C. Barker with the assistance of Ernest William Winkler (Chicago: American Historical Society, 1914), 401.

Fellow citizens and compatriots:

I am besieged by a thousand or more of the Mexicans under Santa Anna. I have sustained a continual bombardment and cannonade for 24 hours and have not lost a man. The enemy has demanded a surrender at discretion,[37] otherwise the garrison are to be put to the sword, if the fort is taken. I have answered the demand with a cannon shot, and our flag still waves proudly from the walls. I shall never surrender or retreat. Then, I call on you in the name of liberty, of patriotism and everything dear to the American character to come to our aid with all dispatch. The enemy is receiving reinforcements daily and will no doubt increase to three or four thousand in four or five days. If this call is neglected, I am determined to sustain myself as long as possible and die like a soldier who never forgets what is due his own honor and that of his country, Victory or death.

William Barret Travis
Lt. Col. Comdt

## Antonio López de Santa Anna's Proclamation on the Fall of the Alamo (March 6, 1836)[38]

Army of Operations. Your Excellency[39]—Victory has accompanied the army; and at this moment, eight o'clock in the morning, it has just achieved the most complete and glorious one that will perpetuate its memory.

As I informed Your Excellency on the 27th of the previous month, when I announced the taking of this city, I was waiting for the first infantry brigade in order to take decisive action on the fortress of the Alamo, but since all the units that compose the brigade could not come, three battalions, by doubling their march, were able to reach us: Sappers, Aldama, and Toluca; from whose force, that of Matamoros, Jiménez, and San Luis Potosí, I was able to choose, excepting recruits, 1,400 infantrymen. Having divided them into four columns and a reserve, as indicated by yesterday's general order, a copy of which I enclose for Your Excellency, the attack was undertaken at five in the morning, encountering obstinate resistance, so that the fighting lasted more than an hour and a half, making it necessary to employ even the reserve.

The scene presented by this fight was extraordinary: the men fought hand to hand and vied with each other for heroic actions: twenty-one pieces of enemy artillery employed to great effect, the bright fire of musketry that seemed to

37. Surrendering unconditionally, without guarantees that life would be respected.

38. Vicente Filisola, *Memorias para la Historia de la Guerra de Tejas* (Mexico City: Ignacio Cumplido, 1849), 16. Translated by Gustavo Pellón.

39. Santa Anna addresses himself to General Don José María Tornel y Mendivil (1789–1853), secretary of war and navy.

illuminate the interior of the fort; and the moats and walls were not obstacles for the undaunted Mexicans: they did their duty bravely and deserve the recognition of the supreme government and the gratitude of their compatriots.

We were finally left in possession of the fort with its artillery, ammunition, etc., buried in their moats and trenches more than six hundred corpses,[40] all foreigners, and in the surrounding area a great number that we have not been able to examine yet, for as they tried to escape from the bayonets of the infantry, they fell under the sabers of the cavalry, which I had deployed at the appropriate spot. I can therefore guarantee that very few of them will have brought news of the event to their comrades.

Among the corpses mentioned were found those of the first and second commanders of the enemy: Bowie and Travis, self-styled colonels, that of the equally ranked Crockett and all the other commanders and officers who held commissions from the convention. On our side there are about seventy dead and three hundred wounded, including two commanders and twenty-three officers, whose loss is easier to bear because of the just cause we defend; for it is the duty of a Mexican soldier to die in the defense of the rights of his country, and they were all ready to make any sacrifice for such a dear objective, never to permit foreigners, wherever they may come from, to insult the fatherland and to dismember its territory.

In due course I will remit a detailed account of this important triumph, I close now with my congratulations to the nation and ask Your Excellency to please convey them to His Excellency the Interim President.

The bearer of this letter carries one of the flags of the enemy battalions taken today. It demonstrates well the true designs of the traitorous colonists and their collaborators who come from the ports of the United States of the North.

God and liberty. General Headquarters, Béjar, March 6, 1836.—Antonio López de Santa Anna.—To His Excellency the Secretary of War and Navy, General Don José María Tornel.

## General Vicente Filisola's Account (1849)[41]

That same afternoon, or shortly after night had fallen, it is said that Travis Barnet,[42] commander of the enemy garrison, proposed to the general in chief, through a woman, that he would surrender weapons and the fort, with everything

---

40. Santa Anna inflated these numbers. The likelier figure, as reported by other witnesses, is about two hundred dead. A likely estimate of Mexican casualties is five hundred with hundreds of wounded. See Todd Hansen, *The Alamo Reader: A Study in History* (Mechanicsburg, PA: Stackpole Books, 2003), 780–81.

41. Vicente Filisola, *Memorias para la Historia de la Guerra de Tejas* (Mexico City: Ignacio Cumplido, 1849), 13–15. Translated by Gustavo Pellón.

42. Filisola is referring to William Barret Travis.

in it, with the sole condition that his life and that of his comrades in arms be spared; but the reply had been that their surrender should be unconditional, without any guarantees, not even that of life itself, because traitors did not deserve them. Given this response, it is clear that they all were disposed to lose their lives only by selling them at the highest price, and consequently they kept a close watch so as not to be surprised at any hour of the day or night.

At four in the morning of the sixth, the Mexican troops were deployed according to the orders they had received in the instructions here included. The artillery, as can be deduced from the same instructions, remained out of action, because it had no orders, nor was it even possible, given the darkness and the disposition of the troops attacking the enclosure from all four sides, for the artillery to make fire, without blowing their own comrades to bits. Therefore, the enemy enjoyed the advantage of not suffering the ravages of our artillery for the duration of the attack. Their artillery was prepared and vigilant; so that when the fatal bugle sounded,[43] they had no doubt at all that they were in the extreme predicament of winning or dying; and if there was room for any doubt, it was soon dispelled by the assaulting columns' imprudent shouting and cheering for General Santa Anna. No sooner had they revealed their position than a storm of grapeshot and musket and rifle bullets fell on them, hurled by the besieged, who at the first blowing of the bugle, were standing at their posts, weapons in hand. . . .

Our losses were great and considerable: Colonel Don Francisco Duque was one of the first to be gravely wounded; and from the ground where he lay, trampled by his own subordinates, continued to urge them to attack. The primitive manner in which the attack was ordered, on the four sides of the enclosure, was eminently imprudent and unmilitary, since besides the fire from our enemies, our troops had to suffer that from our own soldiers, opposite them. Furthermore, since they attacked in close order formation, all the projectiles, whose trajectories descended a bit, pierced the backs of those who preceded them. Thus, the greater part of our dead and wounded were the result of this accident; as it is certain that no more than a quarter were due to enemy fire. . . .

In any case, the Mexicans were left in possession of the position, and its defenders are all dead; and it is regrettable that after the first moments of the heat of battle had passed, atrocities were authorized, unworthy of the valor and resolve with which that operation was executed, and which, of course, have left an indelible stain in history, although they were immediately condemned by those who were unfortunate enough to witness them; and afterward by the whole army, which was surely not motivated by such feelings, and received them with the horror and repugnance befitting Mexican valor and generosity, which is only compatible with noble and generous actions. We abstain from relating these deeds because of the displeasure it would give us to record events that, for the honor of

---

43. The *Degüello* was a trumpet call used in the Hispanic tradition to communicate that no living prisoners were to be taken. *Degüello* is derived from the Spanish *degollar*, meaning "to slit the throat."

the republic, we sincerely wish had never occurred. Likewise, we omit others that preceded them during that poor semblance of a siege or blockade that, although of a different kind and purely personal, are not less scandalous and cost several dead and wounded among the most zealous soldiers in the army.

In our opinion, the blood of our soldiers, like that shed by our enemies, was pointless, as its only object was an unthinking, puerile, and punishable vanity: to be able to say that Béjar had been reconquered by force of arms and that many men on both sides had perished in the assault. Because, as we have said, the defenders of the Alamo were ready to surrender, without any other condition but that their lives be spared. . . . How much more glorious it would have been for Mexico and its reputation if, instead of so much blood and so many dead, the lives of its gratuitous and ungrateful enemies, from the Alamo as well as from Refugio, Goliad, and Guadalupe Victoria, had been spared and sent to Mexico City, so that by laboring in public works they could have compensated in part for the expenses they made us incur!

## Selection from *Colonel Crockett's Exploits and Adventures in Texas* (1836)[44]

They were instantly surrounded, and ordered by General Castrillon to surrender, which they did, under a promise of his protection, finding that resistance any longer would be madness. Colonel Crockett was of the number. He stood alone in an angle of the fort, the barrel of his shattered rifle in his right hand, in his left his huge Bowie knife dripping blood. There was a frightful gash across his forehead, while around him there was a complete barrier of about twenty Mexicans, lying pell mell, dead, and dying. . . .

General Castrillon was brave and not cruel, and disposed to save the prisoners. He marched them up to that part of the fort where stood Santa Anna and his murderous crew. The steady fearless step and undaunted tread of Colonel Crockett, on this occasion, together with the bold demeanor of the hardy veteran, had a powerful effect on all present. Nothing daunted, he marched up boldly in front of Santa Anna, and looked him sternly in the face, while Castrillon addressed "His Excellency,"—"Sir, here are six prisoners I have taken alive; how shall I dispose of them?" Santa Anna looked at Castrillon fiercely, flew into a violent rage, and replied, "Have I not told you before how to dispose of them? Why do you bring them to me?" At the same time his brave officers plunged their swords into the

44. Davy Crockett, Charles T Beale, Richard Penn Smith, and Alex J Dumas, *Col. Crockett's Exploits and Adventures in Texas: Wherein Is Contained a Full Account of His Journey from Tennessee to the Red River and Nathchitoches, and thence across Texas to San Antonio; Including Many Hair-Breadth Escapes; Together with a Topographical, Historical, and Political View of Texas* (Philadelphia: T. K. and P. G. Collins, 1836), 203–6.

bosoms of their defenceless prisoners. Colonel Crockett, seeing the act of treachery, instantly sprang like a tiger at the ruffian chief, but before he could reach him a dozen swords were sheathed in his indomitable heart; and he fell and died without a groan, a frown on his brow, and a smile of scorn and defiance on his lips. Castrillon rushed from the scene, apparently horror-struck, sought his quarters, and did not leave them for several days, and hardly spoke to Santa Anna.[45]

The conduct of Colonel Bowie was characteristic to the last. When the fort was carried he was sick in bed. He had also one of the murderous butcher knives which bears his name. Lying in bed, he discharged his pistols and gun, and with each discharge brought down an enemy. So intimidated were the Mexicans by this act of desperate and cool bravery, that they dared not approach him, but shot him from the door; and as the cowards approached his bed, over the dead bodies of their companions, the dying Bowie, nerving himself for a last blow, plunged his knife into the heart of his nearest foe at the same instant that he expired.

The gallant Colonel Travis fought as if determined to verify his prediction, that he would make a victory more serious than a defeat to the enemy. He fell from the rampart, mortally wounded, into the fort; and his musket fell forward among the foe, who were scaling the wall. After a few minutes he recovered sufficiently to sit up when the Mexican officer who led that party attempted to cut his head off with a saber. The dying hero, with a death grasp, drew his sword and plunged it into the body of his antagonist, and both together sank into the arms of death. General Cos, who had commanded this fortress while in possession of the Mexicans, and from whom it was captured, on entering the fort after the battle, ordered the servant of Colonel Travis to point out the body of his master; he did so, when Cos drew his sword, waved it triumphantly over the corpse, and then mangled the face and limbs with the malignant feelings of a Comanche savage.[46]

## The Treaties of Velasco (May 14, 1836)

*After taking the Alamo (March 6, 1836), the massacre of Goliad (March 27), and burning the town of Harrisburg (April 18), Santa Anna lost the battle of San Jacinto (April 21) to Sam Houston. The Treaties of Velasco (May 14), one public*

---

45. The circumstances of David Crockett's death (whether he died in battle or was executed after the fall of the Alamo with a few other survivors) have been the subject of heated controversy among historians. For an overview of the debate, see Richard Flores, *Remembering the Alamo: Memory, Modernity, and the Master Symbol* (Austin: University of Texas Press, 2002), 135–39.

46. The representation of the deaths of Crockett, Bowie, and Travis in this narrative does not constitute a reliable historical account, but it ably illustrates the author's intent to cement their reputation as martyr-heroes in contrast to the "savage" Mexicans.

*and one secret, were signed in the town of Velasco on the Brazos River. Upon hearing the news of Santa Anna's defeat and capture, the interim president of Mexico, José Justo Corro (1794–1864), ordered the placement of black crape on the colors and standards of the troops of the Mexican army and the lowering of the Mexican flag to half-mast. The Mexican government did not ratify the agreements signed at Velasco, but Santa Anna's defeat and capture ended the war for Texan independence and augured the start of the Texas republic, which lasted until the United States annexed Texas in 1845.*

## Public Agreement[47]

Articles of an agreement entered into between His Excellency David G. Burnet, President of the Republic of Texas of the one part, and His Excellency General Antonio López de Santa Anna, President General in Chief of the other part:

**Article 1st.**

General Antonio López de Santa Anna agrees that he will not take up arms, nor will he exercise his influence to cause them to be taken up against the People of Texas, during the present war of independence.

**Article 2d.**

All hostilities between the Mexican and Texian[48] troops will cease immediately, both by land and water.

**Article 3d.**

The Mexican troops will evacuate the territory of Texas, passing to the other side of the Rio Grande del Norte.[49]

**Article 4th.**

The Mexican Army in its retreat shall not take the property of any person without his consent and just indemnification, using only such articles as may be

47. H. Niles, ed., *Niles Weekly Register. From March, 1836, to September, 1836—Vol. L. or Volume XIV.—Fourth Series* (Baltimore: printed by the editor, 1836), 336.

48. A term used to designate Texans during the revolution and the republican period.

49. This article was used by many in Texas and in the United States in the years leading up to the U.S.-Mexican War to argue that Santa Anna agreed that the Rio Grande, and not the Nueces River, was the boundary between Texas and Mexico.

necessary for its subsistence, in cases when the owner may not be present, and remitting to the commander of the army of Texas, or to the commissioners to be appointed for the adjustment of such matters, an account of the value of the property consumed, the place where taken, and the name of the owner if it can be ascertained.

**Article 5th.**

That all private property, including cattle, horses, negro slaves, or indentured persons of whatever denomination, that may have been captured by any portion of the Mexican Army, or may have taken refuge in the said army, since the commencement of the late invasion shall be restored to the commander of the Texian army, or to such other persons as may be appointed by the government of Texas to receive them.

**Article 6th.**

The troops of both armies will refrain from coming into contact with each other, and to this end the commander of the army of Texas will be careful not to approach within a shorter distance than five leagues.

**Article 7th.**

The Mexican Army shall not make any other delay on its march than that which is necessary to take up their hospitals, baggage &c. and cross the rivers; any delay not necessary to these purposes to be considered as an infraction of this agreement.

**Article 8th.**

By Express to be immediately dispatched, this agreement shall be sent to general Filisola and to general T. J. Rusk, Commander of the Texian army, in order that they may be apprised of its stipulation—and to this end they will exchange engagements to comply with the same.

**Article 9th.**

That all Texian prisoners now in possession of the Mexican Army or its authorities be forthwith released and furnished with free passports to return to their homes, in consideration of which a corresponding number of Mexican prisoners, rank and file, now in possession of the government of Texas, shall be immediately released. The remainder of the Mexican prisoners that continue in possession of the government of Texas to be treated with due humanity; any extraordinary comforts that may be furnished them, to be at the charge of the government of Mexico.

**Article 10th.**

General Antonio López de Santa Anna will be sent to Vera Cruz as soon as it shall be deemed proper.

The contracting parties sign this instrument for the above-mentioned purposes by duplicate at the Port of Velasco this 14th day of May 1836,

David G. Burnet, *president.*
JAS. Collingsworth, *secretary of state.*
Antonio López de Santa Anna.
B. Hardiman, *secretary of the treasury.*
P. W. Grayson, *attorney general.*

## Secret Treaty[50]

Antonio López de Santa Anna, General in Chief of the Army of Operations and President of the Republic of Mexico, before the Government established in Texas, solemnly pledges himself to fulfill the stipulations contained in the following Articles, so far as concerns himself:—

**Article 1.**

He will not take up arms, nor cause them to be taken up, against the People of Texas, during the present war for independence.

**Article 2.**

He will give his orders that, in the shortest time, the Mexican Troops may leave the Territory of Texas.

**Article 3.**

He will so prepare matters in the Cabinet of Mexico, that the Mission that may be sent thither by the Government of Texas may be well received, and that by means of negotiations all differences may be settled, and the independence that has been declared by the Convention may be acknowledged.

---

50. J. M. Morphis, *History of Texas: From Its Discovery and Settlement, with a Description of Its Principal Cities and Counties, and the Agricultural, Mineral, and Material Resources of the State* (New York: United States Publishing Co., 1875), 293–94.

**Article 4.**

A treaty of commerce, amity, and limits will be established between Mexico and Texas, the territory of the latter not to extend beyond the Río Bravo del Norte.

**Article 5.**

The present return of General Santa Anna to Vera Cruz being indispensable for the purpose of effecting his solemn engagements, the Government of Texas will provide for his immediate embarkation for said port.

**Article 6.**

This instrument, being obligatory on one part as well as on the other, will be signed in duplicate, remaining folded and sealed until the negotiation shall have been concluded, when it will be restored to his excellency General Santa Anna; no use of it to be made before that time, unless there should be an infraction by either of the contracting parties.

Port of Velasco, May the 14th, 1836

Antonio López de Santa Anna.
David G. Burnet.
James Collingsworth, *Secretary of State.*
Bailey Hardeman, *Secretary of the Treasury.*
P. H. Grayson, *Attorney General.*

## Manifesto of the Mexican Congress (1836)[51]

*News of the defeat of Santa Anna at San Jacinto was greeted with dismay by Mexican observers. Interim president José Justo Corro, secretary of war José María Tornel y Mendivil (1789–1853), and Mexican journalists called for a continuation of the war against the Texas insurgents. The following excerpt of a manifesto by the Mexican congress (July 29, 1836) captures the nationalist fervor that Mexican elites were trying to instill in the Mexican people in the face of Santa Anna's defeat in Texas. However, Mexico's troubled politics and finances did not allow for an effective campaign of reconquest.*

51. *Manifiesto del Congreso en el Presente Año* (Mexico City: Imprenta de J. M. F. de Lara, 1836), 3–4, 6–8. Translated by Gustavo Pellón.

Mexicans:

This name alone embraces everything that the congress of your representatives has to tell you today. In primitive times this name signified a great nation,[52] barbarous and superstitious as all have been in their infancy, whose fate was to be stalked from a distance of two thousand leagues by European ambition and greed, sought, found, and finally subdued, thus becoming foreign in its own soil that disappeared below its feet to be distributed among its new masters for whom, furthermore, it had to till it. Later it signified a rich colony, badly exploited by its owners; little known but all too envied by nations to which it did not belong, and peopled by a mixed race in which, the conquered and the conquerors were already blended and mixed. Then came the time of the nation's manhood. Nature made her irresistible voice heard, made clear the violence with which her designs had been eluded by trying to join extremes that she had separated by interposing the whole immense ocean; and it awakened in those who until then had been colonials the feeling of the dignity of man, the charm of liberty, and the yearning to be true masters of their home. They entered into the glorious fray, fought heroically, and in the end justice crowned their brow; they created for themselves a fatherland and became their own masters. Since then the name "Mexicans" has signified a sovereign, independent nation that determines its destiny and holds the distinguished rank among the nations of the globe that its natural circumstances and its efforts and sacrifices have won. . . .

Never, therefore, have we faced a more just and more truly national war, a war that affects our dignity and our honor, and jeopardizes our political existence. Unwary and in good faith we opened our arms and offered the warmth of our bosom to those whom helplessness, and perhaps their immorality and crimes, cast from other countries. With kindness we received them in the most fertile part of our territory; we granted them immunities and exemptions of every kind; we even tolerated their insult to humanity, by making it sweat, enslaved, for their profit; we allowed them total liberty in their municipal government, and required nothing of them except the unity of common government with their benefactors; but no sooner had they recovered life under our protection, than they sought to sink into our breast their venomous teeth to devour us. Not happy to be citizens, nor satisfied to share the dignity of being our compatriots, they want at all cost to be our masters, subject us to their whims, bind us to their irreligiousness, give us their laws.

And who have formed such a plan? Men without faith, without a country, with no more unity than that of ambition; born in different lands; at odds in terms of religion, education, customs; fugitives from the countries that gave them birth, because they do not fit in them; men unused to the hard work of war, who are bothered and oppressed by military splendor, and who perhaps tremble and

52. *Mexica* was the term that the Aztec inhabitants of Tenochtitlan and Tlatelolco used to refer to themselves. The name "Mexico" originates from this term.

turn their faces from the flash and detonation when they shoot a rifle: men, in short, incompatible with blind military discipline, inexperienced in the difficult science of government, men for whom all is contemptible except perversity and malice. . . .

The event that made those colonists arrogant is not one that ought to humiliate us; nor would it even merit being listed among the upsets so common in war, if it were not for an accidental circumstance. They did not triumph; chance suspended for a moment the rapid course of our victories. . . .

## General José María Tornel y Mendivil on the Texas Declaration of Independence (1837)[53]

*José María Tornel y Mendivil was a loyal supporter and confidant of Santa Anna. Tornel was a highly educated and articulate man of letters who distinguished himself in the Mexican War of Independence by serving as secretary to Santa Anna and Guadalupe Victoria. After a stint as ambassador to the United States (1829–1831), Tornel served as Santa Anna's secretary of war during the Texas revolution and as senior military officer of the Mexican army in 1847. He was also secretary of war under President Mariano Paredes y Arrillaga (1797–1849) between February and July 1846, during the start of the U.S.-Mexican War. Tornel was the author of an 1835 decree calling for any invading or subversive foreigner on Mexican soil to be treated and punished as a pirate, with no mercy.*

The day finally came when the colonists of Texas, seduced by the advantages that a thousand unforeseen circumstances afforded them, took flight and declared themselves independent *sans retour*[54] from the Mexican nation. The delegates assembled in Washington, district of Brazoria, and on March 2, 1836, issued their declaration of independence. This is nothing more than the expression of a fact and a desire that has been known for some time; but they attempt to support their right to do so through an astonishing collection of falsehoods. In it they assert that Texans were invited and admitted according to a certain pact, a written constitution, and that the latter being annulled, they are free of all their obligations. The nation, imprudently generous with the colonists, acceded to their pleas, admitting them into our association, because they desired and requested it. We have observed that when the first land grants were made to them, the government of the nation was a monarchy and that afterward several changes

53. José María Tornel y Mendivil, *Tejas y los Estados-Unidos de América en Sus Relaciones con la Republica Mexicana* (Mexico City: Ignacio Cumplido, 1837), 65–67. Translated by Gustavo Pellón.

54. *Sans retour* means "without return, definite."

have occurred that do not authorize them to withdraw their obedience, because no system of government was imposed as a condition. An insolent minority of the inhabitants of the republic cannot usurp its power to arrange its administration in the manner it sees fit. If that minority was not happy with the changes, it could abandon the country for which it had become a bothersome burden and a dangerous hindrance.

The rebels allege as the major motive for their complaint that they would not have been allowed to form an independent state and rule themselves according to the constitution that they had drafted *motu proprio*.[55] Assuming the permanence of the federal system, it would have been worth considering if Texas had the necessary rudiments and resources to acquire an independent existence; furthermore, they could not fail to consider the distrust that such a radical step would naturally inspire when the aim of all the petitions of the colonists was so well known. Since a change in the administration of the country was being effected, the colonists should have awaited the result of the fundamental changes that are planned, and we have seen that the congress raised Texas to the rank of department, separating it from Coahuila.

They accuse us of having neglected primary and elementary education in Texas; their bad faith is especially glaring in this charge. As is known, education, according to our laws, is the responsibility of the respective municipal governments, and those in Texas already enjoyed or usurped even those powers that do not pertain to this type of operation. Why did they not attend to what most interested them? Furthermore, in Texas, the municipalities imposed contributions and disposed of that revenue without the least intervention from Mexican officials; if they did not allocate it for the instruction of their children, it was their fault. Texans were represented in the state congress; that is where they should have sued for what they wanted as they did in the case of land, the first object of their desire, the principal motive of their insatiable greed.

The colonists complain most plaintively that their interests have always been sacrificed to those of Coahuila: this is a classic lie. The state authorities, if anything, went to the other extreme, without any reserve protecting Texans in their tireless petitions. In this same writ, we have seen the land grants that were made to them, and it is notable that among those favored there were not more than two or three Coahuiltexans whose lands had in great part been usurped. Sometimes they curse Coahuila for its supposed injustices, and others they curse the nation because they dream of abuses against Coahuila.

False are the acts of oppression and tyranny of which they accuse our military. Far from it, our soldiers have been exposed to the same contempt as all our public employees; they have been disarmed and cast from the positions they held in the performance of their duty. Any enforcement of the law has been called an assault; and the repression of crime has become an insult and an affront in the dictionary invented by the colonists, who continue to assert that their commerce

55. *Motu proprio* means "by his or her own will or accord."

has been exposed to unheard of restrictions and humiliations. For seven years all goods brought into Texas were exempted from duty, and afterward there has been nothing but smuggling along the border and all along the coast.

The prohibition against erecting churches and practicing ceremonies of any religion except the Catholic faith was a law of the land when the colonists arrived and they agreed to it without complaining. Why did they not stay in their country or erect churches in the desolate West? Nations adopt or refuse to adopt restrictions regarding religious beliefs as they see fit; and to expect to force us to accept religious toleration is to expect to exercise over us a right greater than the right of conquest, in which the religion, habits, and customs of the conquered country are always respected.

The rebels, finally, aspire to justify before God and men their criminal uprising on the grounds of the repressive measures that the most indulgent Mexican government has been forced to adopt. The use of force to contain the restless, punish the rebellious, and enforce obedience is a right inherent to the sovereignty of nations. What right but this is being invoked now in the United States by sending troops to the Floridas to punish the Seminole and Creek Indians?[56] What is just for one people is just for all: the attributes of sovereignty are equal for all. The civilized world has already pronounced judgment on the usurpation of the Texans and rejected the claims on which they seek to base their declaration of independence.

Convinced of the justice of the nation's cause, and not less of its power to triumph, the government diligently readied and deployed an army to march to repair the setbacks suffered by a handful of our troops and to give a severe lesson to those who had vilified the Mexican name. The circumstances in which the republic then found itself could not have been more difficult or complicated: the constitution of 1824 had been abolished and another had not been drafted. This produced an anxiety and uncertainty that intimidated even the most resolute spirits. The party inimical to changes in the fundamental law of the land was still powerful; its leaders still preserved the connections and prestige of the power they had held for long. Was it not reasonable to fear that by sending the best government troops far to Texas, the balance of power would tilt in favor of those contrary to the status quo? Thus thought many who fail to appraise the worth of Mexican honor, when the interests threatened are those of its glory. The government did not hesitate, it preferred to be left unarmed in the bosom of the nation, to the sad consolation of a safety purchased at the expense of our ignominy. I will always remember with tears in my eyes the memorable answer of President Barragán[57] to a man who advised him of the risks of our situation

56. This statement refers to General Andrew Jackson's 1818 campaign in Spanish Florida against the Seminole. Jackson's success in taking Florida helped John Quincy Adams negotiate its cession from Spain in 1819 through the Adams-Onís Treaty.

57. Miguel Barragán (1789–1836) was one of several men who held the office of president of Mexico while Santa Anna was away on campaign or resting in his hacienda.

and the danger that the party of Don Valentín Gómez Farías[58] would rise again if the interior of the republic was left unguarded and the best army corps sent to the rebellious colony. "Gómez Farías," he said, "is Mexican; and if he returns to power and locks me up in the Inquisition, the dishonor will be his; but if Texas is not recovered, the ignominy will be national." We must take pleasure in the nation's vindication of that noble, disinterested, and patriotic confidence: all votes were for Texas, and the government was left without worries about powerful upheavals in the interior. It is true that some Mexicans, though few, did not sacrifice their interests and resentments at the altar of the Fatherland.

But the vast majority sided with the government that with such good sense had considered as the basis for the conservation of peace what others considered the beginning of our ruin. Thus are the energies of a people deployed at great moments; and although they may fight against an inauspicious star, sooner or later their constancy conquers the rigors of destiny.

58. Valentín Gómez Farías (1781–1858) was the leader of the radical wing of the federalists, the *puros*.

# II

# The Annexation of Texas and the Road to War

## John Quincy Adams and Texas (1836)

*John Quincy Adams (1767–1848) was the sixth president of the United States (1825–1829) and subsequently a member of the U.S. Congress for the state of Massachusetts (1831–1848). Adams was a well-known critic of Texas annexation in Congress. In his address of May 25, 1836, Adams explores the geopolitics of slavery in relation to Texas and speaks out against the prospect of a war with Mexico.*

### Speech of the Hon. John Quincy Adams in the House of Representatives (May 25, 1836)[1]

The war now raging in Texas is a Mexican civil war, and a war for the re-establishment of slavery where it was abolished. It is not a servile war but a war between slavery and emancipation, and every possible effort has been made to drive us into the war, on the side of slavery.

It is indeed, a circumstance eminently fortunate for us, that this monster, Santa Anna, has been defeated and taken, though I cannot participate in that exquisite joy with which we have been told that every one having Anglo-Saxon[2] blood in his veins, must have been delighted on hearing that this ruffian has been shot, in cold blood, when a prisoner of war, by the Anglo-Saxon leader of the victorious Texian army.[3] Sir, I hope there is no member of this House, of other than Anglo-Saxon origin, who will deem it uncourteous, that I, being myself in part Anglo-Saxon, must, of course, hold that for the best blood that ever circulated in human veins. Oh! Yes, Sir; far be it from me to depreciate

---

1. John Adams, *Speech of the Hon. John Quincy Adams in the House of Representatives on the State of the Nation: Delivered May 25, 1836* (New York: H. R. Piercy, 1836), 8–15.

2. The Anglo-Saxons were the Germanic peoples who controlled England until the Norman invasion of 1066.

3. Santa Anna was not harmed by his Texas captors.

the glories of the Anglo-Saxon race; although there have been times when they bowed their necks and submitted to the law of conquest, beneath the ascendency of the Norman race. But, Sir, it has struck me as no inconsiderable evidence of the spirit which is spurring us into this war of aggression, of conquest, and of slave-making, that all the fires of ancient hereditary national hatred are to be kindled, to familiarize us with the ferocious spirit of rejoicing at the massacre of prisoners in cold blood! . . .

And this is the nation with which, at the instigation of your executive government, you are now rushing into war—into a war of conquest, commenced by aggression on your part, and for the re-establishment of slavery, where it has been abolished, throughout the Mexican Republic. For your war will be with Mexico—with a republic of twenty-four states, and a population of eight or nine millions of souls. It seems to be considered that this victory over twelve hundred men, with the capture of their commander, the President of the Mexican Republic, has already achieved the conquest of the whole republic. That it may have achieved the independence of Texas, is not impossible. But Texas is to the Mexican Republic not more, nor so much, as the state of Michigan is to yours; that state of Michigan, the people of which are in vain claiming of you the performance of that sacred promise you made them, of admitting her as a state in the Union[4]; that state of Michigan, which has greater grievances and heavier wrongs to allege against you, for a declaration of her independence, if she were disposed to declare it, than the people of Texas have for breaking off their union with the Republic of Mexico. Texas is an extreme boundary portion of the Republic of Mexico—a wilderness inhabited only by Indians, till after the revolution which separated Mexico from Spain—not sufficiently populous at the organization of the Mexican confederacy to form a state by itself, and therefore united with Coahuila, where the greatest part of the indigenous population reside. . . .

As to the annexation of Texas to your confederation, for what do you want it? Are you not large and unwieldy enough already? Do not two millions of square miles cover surface enough for the insatiate rapacity of your land-jobbers?[5] I hope there are none of them within the sound of my voice. Have you not Indians enough to expel from the land of their fathers' sepulchers, and to exterminate? What, in a prudential and military point of view, would be the addition of Texas to your domain? It would be weakness, and not power. Is your southern and southwestern frontier not sufficiently extensive? Not sufficiently feeble? Not sufficiently defenceless?—Why are you adding regiment after regiment of dragoons[6] to your standing army? Why are you struggling, by direction and indirection,

4. Michigan was a territory of the United States from 1796 to 1835. An acrimonious land dispute with the neighboring state of Ohio postponed Michigan's entry into the union as a state until 1837.

5. Land-jobbers bought and sold land.

6. Cavalrymen.

to raise per saltum[7] that army from less than six to more than twenty thousand men? Your commanding general, now returning from his excursion in Florida, openly recommends the increase of your army to that number.[8]

Sir, the extension of your sea-coast frontier from the Sabine to the Rio Bravo would add to your weakness tenfold: for it is now only weakness with reference to Mexico. It would then be weakness, with reference to Great Britain, to France, even, perhaps, to Russia, to every naval European power, which might make a quarrel with us for the sake of settling a colony: but, above all, to Great Britain. She, by her naval power, and by her American colonies, holds the keys of the Gulf of Mexico. What would be the condition of your frontier, from the mouth of the Mississippi to that of Rio del Norte, in the event of war with Great Britain? . . .

At this time circumstances have changed—popular revolutions both in France[9] and Great Britain,[10] have perhaps curbed the spirit of conquest in Great Britain, and France may have enough to do to govern her kingdom at Algiers.[11] But Spain is again convulsed with a civil war for the succession to her crown;[12] she has irretrievably lost all her colonies on both continents of America. It is impossible that she should hold much longer a shadow of dominion over the islands of Cuba and Porto Rico;[13] nor can these islands, in their present condition, form independent nations, capable of protecting themselves. They must for ages remain at the mercy of Great Britain or of these United States, or of both; Great Britain is even now about to interfere in this war for the Spanish succession. If by the utter imbecility of the Mexican confederacy, this revolt of Texas should lead immediately to its separation from that republic, and its annexation to the United States, I believe it impossible that Great Britain should look on, while this operation is performing, with indifference. She will see that it must shake her own whole colonial power on this continent, in the Gulf of Mexico, and in the Caribbean Seas, like an earthquake; she will see, too, that it endangers her own abolition of slavery in her own colonies. A war for the restoration of slavery where

7. All at once.

8. A reference to General Winfield Scott, one of the commanders who led U.S. forces in the Second Seminole War (1835–1842) and later in the war with Mexico. Scott called for increasing the size of U.S. forces on April 30, 1835, in order to effectively combat the Seminoles in Florida.

9. The July Revolution of 1830 deposed French King Charles X and replaced him with King Louis-Philippe, who ruled until 1848.

10. Through the Slavery Abolition Act of 1833, Britain ended slavery in its colonies.

11. Shortly before the July Revolution of 1830, King Charles X took possession of Algiers.

12. Upon the death of King Ferdinand in 1833, Spain found itself divided between supporters of his daughter Isabella and followers of his brother Charles V. Decades of civil war, known as the Carlist Wars, ensued.

13. An archaic alternate spelling of Puerto Rico.

it had been abolished, if successful in Texas, must extend over all Mexico; and the example will threaten her with imminent danger of a war of colors in her own island. She will take possession of Cuba and of Porto Rico by cession from Spain, or by the batteries from her wooden walls; and if you ask her by what authority she has done it, she will ask you in turn, by what authority you have extended your sea coast from the Sabine to the Rio Bravo? She will ask you a question more perplexing, namely—by what authority you, with freedom, independence, and democracy, upon your lips, are waging a war of extermination to force new manacles and fetters, instead of those which are falling from the hands and feet of man? She will carry emancipation and abolition with her in every fold of her flag! While your stars, as they increase in numbers, will overcast with the murky vapors of oppression, and the only portion of your banners visible to the eye will be the blood-stained stripes of the task master.

Mr. Chairman,[14] are you ready for all these wars? A Mexican War? A war with Great Britain, if not France? A general Indian war? A Servile war? And, as an inevitable consequence of them all, a civil war? For it must ultimately terminate in a war of colors as well as of races. . . .

## A Mexican Printer Lauds John Quincy Adams (1836)[15]

*It was not uncommon for Mexican journalists and commentators to reprint translations of speeches and writings by U.S. political figures who criticized U.S. policy toward Mexico. As noted by historian Gene Brack, Mexicans deeply admired and respected John Quincy Adams in particular, referring to him as "philanthropic," "respected," or "celebrated." In 1843, the administration of President Santa Anna instructed its minister to the United States, Juan Almonte, to cultivate a relationship with Adams. The following introduction to the translation of Adams' 1836 speech on Texas was not the only occasion on which Mexicans used the words of Adams to criticize the United States. In 1842, one of Mexico City's principal newspapers,* El Siglo Diez y Nueve, *reprinted a later speech by Adams that accused the United States of unjustly trying to provoke a war with Mexico. The text that follows is the preface to a Spanish language translation of Adams' May 25, 1836, speech in the House of Representatives, published in that same year in Mexico City.*

---

14. Ironically, the Speaker of the House of Representatives to whom Adams addresses his rhetorical questions is James K. Polk of Tennessee, who was later elected president in 1844 and led the United States during its war with Mexico.

15. John Quincy Adams, *Discurso del ex-presidente de los Estados Unidos, Mr. John Quincy Adams en la Cámara de Representantes de Washington, Miércoles, Mayo 25 de 1836* (Mexico City: 1836), 3–6. Translated by Gustavo Pellón.

The speech published below, delivered in the House of Representatives of the United States Congress by ex-president John Quincy Adams, is one of those documents that in the present circumstances should claim the attention of thinking men, not especially as a model of oratory, but as a model of the effusions of a noble soul that rises above the corruption of the times, dares to ask for the truth with purity and plead in defense of the principles of justice, so scandalously trampled in his country because of the Texas question.

Land speculators in New Orleans and New York have conceived the project of enriching themselves by grabbing from Mexico the territory of Texas, and since it was necessary to justify these low aims with a plausible pretext, they have trotted out an overused one, liberty. But there is yet another plan that threatens the political existence of Spanish-American nations and especially Central America and New Granada, who because of their geographical position and particular advantages in the commercial sphere ought to be considered the keys to the continent. This plan is the establishment of slavery. Therefore, if Anglo-Americans are successful in their attempt to appropriate Texas, tremble for your future lot, Mexicans, Central-Americans, and New Granadans,[16] because the day you least expect it you will fall prey to the insatiable Anglo-Saxon-American greed, and the ground you walk on will be sold in parcels in the exchanges of the United States to fill the pockets of your invaders and transfer your inheritance to the hands of a trafficking mob that is on the lookout for the moment to dominate you.

Mr. Adams' speech reveals important mysteries, discovers plans that he virtuously condemns, and publishes what many cannot see from afar. Mr. Adams is Anglo-American, knows well the character of his compatriots, and, guided by a pure zeal for the cause of humanity and justice, is not afraid to earn the hatred of his corrupted contemporaries, in order to save his personal honor at least, even if not that of his country, before the tribunal of the world and posterity, by giving to philanthropists, true liberals, and all good men, the pleasure of seeing the noble cause of the liberty of the human species defended with courage and energy. But Mexicans above all should know the lofty fate to which Providence calls them in the new world, entrusting to their care nothing less than the defense of this same liberty. What does it matter if journalists for hire and land merchants vociferate, if the whole world will witness the struggle and judge the justice of this noble cause? What does it matter if General Santa Anna has had an unfortunate encounter, if his personal lot, much as it is worthy of being lamented, is not the cause for which he fought? Is he, perchance, the one and only Mexican who loves his country, the only champion of liberty whom Mexico can send to the field to expel from the soil of the motherland those bandits who are trying to appropriate part of it in order to stain it immediately with the black blot of servitude? This war admits of no compromise; it is necessary for it to end in a triumph that will benefit the universal emancipation of the human lineage, or in the loss of liberty in all of America: the establishment of slavery where it had been abolished or

16. Colombia called itself the Republic of Nueva Granada between 1832 and 1857.

where it did not exist, imported by the degenerate branch of the English race that now occupies the part of the United States that extends from the Capitol to the border with Texas.

## Robert Walker's Argument for Reannexing Texas (1844)[17]

*The Pennsylvania-born Robert John Walker (1801–1869) was a Mississippi plantation owner and politician who rose to the office of senator (1836–1841), chairman of the National Democratic Committee, and Secretary of the Treasury under President Polk in 1844. Apart from having a close relationship with Polk, Walker was close to President Andrew Jackson (1767–1845) and President John Tyler (1790–1862). Walker's "Letter on the Annexation of Texas" was first published in the* Washington Globe *in 1844 and later reprinted and widely disseminated across the country as a pamphlet. In his influential tract, Walker criticized the Adams-Onís Treaty of 1819 for affirming that Texas belonged to Mexico and not to the Louisiana Purchase of 1803. To annex Texas now, he argued, was not to acquire "new" land but to restore Texas to its original and rightful place within the borders of the United States. The excerpts that follow illustrate the ideology of Manifest Destiny and pro-slavery arguments in favor of the annexation of Texas.*

This is no question of the purchase of new territory, but of the reannexation of that which once was all our own. It is not a question of the extension of our limits, but of the restoration of former boundaries. It proposes no new addition to the valley of the Mississippi; but of its reunion, and all its waters, once more, under our dominion. If the Creator had separated Texas from the Union by mountain barriers, the Alps or the Andes, these might be plausible objections; but He has planed down the whole valley, including Texas, and united every atom of the soil and every drop of the waters of the mighty whole. He has linked their rivers with the great Mississippi, and marked and united the whole for the dominion of one government and the residence of one people; and it is impious in man to attempt to dissolve this great and glorious Union. Texas is a part of Kentucky, a portion of the same great valley. It is a part of New York and Pennsylvania, a part of Maryland and Virginia, and Ohio, and of all the western states, whilst the Tennessee unites with it the waters of Georgia, Alabama, and Carolina. The Alleghany, commencing its course in New York, and with the Youghiogany, from Maryland, and Monongahela, from Virginia, merging with the beautiful

---

17. Robert J. Walker, *Letter of Mr. Walker, of Mississippi, relative to the annexation of Texas in reply to the call of the people of Carroll County, Ky., to communicate his views on that subject* (St. Louis: Missourian Office, 1845), 8–9.

Ohio at the metropolis of western Pennsylvania, embrace the streams of Texas at the mouths of the Arkansas and Red River, whence their water flow in kindred union to the gulf. . . . The treaty which struck Texas from the Union, inflicted a blow upon this mighty valley. And who will say that the West shall remain dismembered and mutilated, and the ancient boundaries of the republic shall never be restored? Who will desire to check the young eagle of America,[18] now refixing her gaze upon our former limits, and repluming her pinions for her returning flight? What American will say, that the flag of the Union shall never wave again throughout that mighty territory; and that what Jefferson acquired,[19] and Madison refused to surrender,[20] shall never be restored? Who will oppose the re-establishment of our glorious constitution over the whole of the mighty valley which once was shielded by its benignant sway? Who will wish again to curtail the limits of this great republican empire, and again to dismember the glorious valley of the West? Who will refuse to replant the banner of the republic upon our former boundary, or *resurrender* the Arkansas and Red River, and retransfer the coast of the gulf? Who will refuse to heal the bleeding wounds of the mutilated West, and reunite the veins and arteries, dissevered by the dismembering cession of Texas to Spain? To refuse to accept the reannexation, is to resurrender the Territory of Texas, and redismember the valley of the West. Nay, more: under existing circumstances, it is to lower the flag of the Union before the red cross of St. George,[21] and to surrender the Florida pass, the mouth of the Mississippi, the command of the Mexican gulf, and finally Texas itself, into the hands of England. . . .

Let us examine, now, some of the objections urged against the reannexation of Texas. And here, it is remarkable that the objections to the purchase of Louisiana are the same now made in the case of Texas;[22] yet all now acknowledge the wisdom of that great measure; and to have ever opposed it, is now regarded as alike unpatriotic and unwise. And so will it be in the case of Texas. The measure will justify itself by its results; and its opponents will stand in the same position now occupied by those who objected to the purchase of Louisiana. The objections we have said, were the same, and we will examine them separately. 1st. The extension of territory; and 2d., the question of slavery.

---

18. In 1782, the U.S. Congress designated the eagle a symbol of the United States.

19. The administration of Thomas Jefferson oversaw the Louisiana Purchase of 1803.

20. At the close of the War of 1812, in the peace negotiations that led to the Treaty of Ghent of 1814, President Madison's negotiators resisted British attempts to amend existing territorial boundaries in North America.

21. The red cross of St. George is a long-standing symbol of England. The modern Union Jack flag contains the red cross of St. George with Scotland's white St. Andrew's cross and the Irish red cross of St. Patrick.

22. The Federalists opposed the Louisiana Purchase, worrying about its effects on American democracy.

As to the extension of the territory, it applied with much greater force to the purchase of Louisiana. That purchase annexed to the Union a territory double the size of that already embraced within its limits; whilst the reannexation of Texas, according to the largest estimates, will add but one-seventh to the extent of our territory. . . . Indeed we may add both the Californias to Texas, and unite them all to the Union, and still the area of the whole will be less than that of the British North American possessions. And is it an American doctrine that monarchies or despotisms are alone fitted for the government of extensive territories, and that a confederacy of states must be compressed with narrower limits?[23] Of all the forms of government, our confederacy is most specifically adapted for an extended territory, and might, without the least danger, but with increased security, and vastly augmented benefits, embrace a continent. Each State, within its own limits, controls all its local concerns, and the general government chiefly those which appertain to commerce and our foreign relations. Indeed, as you augment the number of States, the bond of union is stronger; for the opposition of any one State is much less dangerous and formidable, in a confederacy of thirty states, than of three.[24] On this subject experience is the best test of truth. Has the Union been endangered by the advance in the number of states from thirteen to twenty-six? Look also at all the new States that have been added to the Union since the adoption of the constitution, and tell me what one of all of them, either in war or peace, has ever failed most faithfully to perform its duties; and what one of them has ever proposed or threatened the existence of the government, or the dissolution of the Union?

The only remaining objection is the question of slavery. And have we a question which is to curtail the limits of the republic—to threaten its existence—to aim a deadly blow at all its great and vital interests—to court alliances with foreign and with hostile powers—to recall our commerce and expel our manufactures from bays and rivers that once were all our own—to strike down the flag of the Union, as it advances toward our ancient boundary—to resurrender a mighty territory, and invite to its occupancy the deadliest (in truth, the only) foes

---

23. In his *Spirit of the Laws* (1748), a foundational text of political philosophy, Charles de Secondat, the Baron of Montesquieu (1689–1775), argued that there was a connection between the size of a kingdom and the kind of government most adequate for its rule. Small kingdoms favored republics and large, sprawling empires were conducive to despotic governments. Walker criticizes European received knowledge and begins to lay down an argument for American exceptionalism.

24. Walker's arguments echo some of those made in Federalist 10: "The smaller the society, the fewer probably will be the distinct parties and interests composing it; the fewer the distinct parties and interests, the more frequently will a majority be found of the same party; and the smaller the number of individuals composing a majority, and the smaller the compass within which they are placed, the more easily will they concert and execute their plans of oppression." See Scott J. Hammond, Kevin Hardwick, and Howard Lubert, eds., *Classics of American Political and Constitutional Thought,* vol. 1, *Origins through Civil War* (Indianapolis: Hackett Publishing, 2004), 466.

this government has ever encountered? Is Anti-Slavery to do all this? And is it so to endanger New Orleans, and the valley and commerce and outlet of the West, that we would hold them, not by our own strength, but by the slender tenure of the will and of the mercy of Great Britain? If anti-slavery[25] can effect all this, may God, in his infinite mercy, save and perpetuate the Union; for the efforts of man would be feeble and impotent. The avowed object of this party is the immediate abolition of slavery. For this, they traverse sea and land; for this, they hold conventions in the capital of England; and there they brood over schemes of abolition, in association with British societies; there they join in denunciations of their countrymen, until their hearts are filled with treason; and they return home. Americans in name, but Englishmen in feelings and principles. Let us all, then, feel and know, whether we live in North or South, that this party, if not vanquished, must overthrow the government, and dissolve the Union. This party proposes the immediate abolition of slavery throughout the Union. If this were practicable, let us look at the consequences. By the returns of the last census, the products of the slaveholding States, in 1840, amounted in value to $404,429,638. These products, then, of the South, must have alone enabled it to furnish a home market for all the surplus manufactures of the North, as also a market for the products of its forests and fisheries; and giving a mighty impulse to all its commercial and navigating interests. Now, nearly all these agricultural products of the South which accomplish all these great purposes, is the result of slave labour; and, strike down these products by the immediate abolition of slavery, and the markets of the South, for want of the means to purchase, will be lost to the people of the North; and North and South will be involved in one common ruin. Yes, in the harbours of the North (at Philadelphia, New York, and Boston) the vessels would rot at their wharves for want of exchangeable products to carry; the building of ships would cease, and the grass would grow in many a street now enlivened by an active and progressive industry. In the interior, the railroads and canals would languish for want of business; and the factories and manufacturing towns and cities, decaying and deserted, would stand as blasted monuments of the folly of man. One universal bankruptcy would overspread the country, together with all the demoralization and crime which ever accompany such a catastrophe. . . . Let us look at another result to the North. The slaves being emancipated, not by the South, but the North, would fly there for safety and protection; and three millions of free blacks would be thrown at once, as if by a convulsion of nature, upon the States of the North. They would come there to their friends to the North, who had given them freedom, to give them also habitation, food, and clothing; and, not having it to give, many of them would perish from want and exposure; whilst the wretched remainder would be left to live as they could, by theft or charity. They would still be a degraded caste, free only in name, without the reality of freedom.

---

25. Abolitionism and Great Britain are closely associated in the nineteenth century. Great Britain outlawed its slave trade in 1807 and abolished slavery in its colonies in 1833.

. . .

It is clear that, as slavery advanced in Texas, it would recede from the States bordering on the free States of the North and West; and thus, they would be released from actual contact with what they consider an evil, and as also from all influx from those States of a large and constantly augmenting free black population. As regards the slaves, the African being from a tropical climate, and from the region of the burning sands and sun, his comfort and condition would be greatly improved, by a transfer from northern latitudes to the genial and most salubrious climate of Texas. There he would never suffer from that exposure to cold and frost, which he feels so much more severely than any other race; and there, also, from the great fertility of the soil, and exuberance of its products, his supply of food would be abundant. If a desire to improve the condition and increase the comforts of the slave really animated the anti-slavery party, they would be the warmest advocates of the reannexation of Texas. Nor can it be disguised that, by the reannexation of Texas as the number of free blacks augmented in the slave-holding States, they would be diffused gradually through Texas into Mexico, and Central and Southern America, where nine-tenths of their present population are already of the colored races, and where, from their vast preponderance in number, they are not a degraded caste, but upon a footing, not merely of legal, but what is far more important, of actual equality with the rest of the population. . . . The process will be gradual and progressive, without a shock, and without a convulsion; whereas, by the loss of Texas, and the imprisonment of the slave population of the Union within its present limits, slavery would increase in nearly all the slaveholding States, and a change in their condition would become impossible. . . .

## James K. Polk's Inaugural Address (March 4, 1845)[26]

*The Democrat James Knox Polk (1795–1849) represented Tennessee in the U.S. Congress between 1825 and 1839, serving as Speaker of the House during his last two terms. After serving as governor of Tennessee, Polk unexpectedly became the candidate of the Democratic Party in 1844 when Martin Van Buren's antiannexation views proved unpopular with southern Democrats. Polk was inaugurated as the eleventh president of the United States on March 4, 1845. His foreign policy was characterized by intransigent positions on U.S. claims to the Oregon territory, which the U.S. and Great Britain had jointly occupied since 1818, and U.S. claims to the region of Texas between the Nueces River and the Rio Grande, which Mexico claimed as a part of its territory.*

---

26. U.S. Congress. House, *Abridgement of the Debates of Congress, from 1789 to 1856: Dec. 4, 1843–June 18, 1846* (New York: D. Appleton and Company, 1863), 236–41.

It is a source of deep regret that in some sections of our country misguided persons have occasionally indulged in schemes and agitations whose object is the destruction of domestic institutions existing in other sections—institutions which existed at the adoption of the Constitution and were recognized and protected by it.[27] All must see that if it were possible for them to be successful in attaining their object the dissolution of the Union and the consequent destruction of our happy form of government must speedily follow.

I am happy to believe that at every period of our existence as a nation there has existed, and continues to exist, among the great mass of our people a devotion to the Union of the States which will shield and protect it against the moral treason of any who would seriously contemplate its destruction. To secure a continuance of that devotion the compromises of the Constitution must not only be preserved, but sectional jealousies and heartburnings[28] must be discountenanced, and all should remember that they are members of the same political family, having a common destiny. To increase the attachment of our people to the Union, our laws should be just. Any policy which shall tend to favor monopolies or the peculiar interests of sections or classes must operate to the prejudice of the interest of their fellow-citizens, and should be avoided. If the compromises of the Constitution be preserved, if sectional jealousies and heartburnings be discountenanced, if our laws be just and the Government be practically administered strictly within the limits of power prescribed to it, we may discard all apprehensions for the safety of the Union.

With these views of the nature, character, and objects of the Government and the value of the Union, I shall steadily oppose the creation of those institutions and systems which in their nature tend to pervert it from its legitimate purposes and make it the instrument of sections, classes, and individuals. We need no national banks[29] or other extraneous institutions planted around the Government to control or strengthen it in opposition to the will of its authors. Experience has taught us how unnecessary they are as auxiliaries of the public authorities—how impotent for good and how powerful for mischief.

. . .

The republic of Texas has made known her desire to come into our Union, to form a part of our Confederacy and enjoy with us the blessings of liberty secured and guaranteed by our Constitution. Texas was once a part of our country—was unwisely ceded away to a foreign power—is now independent, and possesses an undoubted right to dispose of a part or the whole of her territory and to merge

27. A reference to slavery, commonly referred to by the defenders of slavery as "the peculiar institution."

28. Regional interests, most specifically with regard to the division between North and South.

29. After President Andrew Jackson refused to reauthorize the Bank of the United States in 1832, Democrats blocked Whig attempts to reinstitute it.

her sovereignty as a separate and independent state in ours. I congratulate my country that by an act of the late Congress of the United States the assent of this Government has been given to the reunion, and it only remains for the two countries to agree upon the terms to consummate an object so important to both.

I regard the question of annexation as belonging exclusively to the United States and Texas. They are independent powers competent to contract, and foreign nations have no right to interfere with them or to take exceptions to their reunion. Foreign powers do not seem to appreciate the true character of our Government. Our Union is a confederation of independent States, whose policy is peace with each other and all the world. To enlarge its limits is to extend the dominions of peace over additional territories and increasing millions. The world has nothing to fear from military ambition in our Government. While the Chief Magistrate and the popular branch of Congress are elected for short terms by the suffrages of those millions who must in their own persons bear all the burdens and miseries of war, our Government can not be otherwise than pacific. Foreign powers should therefore look on the annexation of Texas to the United States not as the conquest of a nation seeking to extend her dominions by arms and violence, but as the peaceful acquisition of a territory once her own, by adding another member to our confederation, with the consent of that member, thereby diminishing the chances of war and opening to them new and ever-increasing markets for their products.

To Texas the reunion is important, because the strong protecting arm of our Government would be extended over her, and the vast resources of her fertile soil and genial climate would be speedily developed, while the safety of New Orleans and of our whole southwestern frontier against hostile aggression, as well as the interests of the whole Union, would be promoted by it.

In the earlier stages of our national existence the opinion prevailed with some that our system of confederated States could not operate successfully over an extended territory, and serious objections have at different times been made to the enlargement of our boundaries.[30] These objections were earnestly urged when we acquired Louisiana. Experience has shown that they were not well founded. The title of numerous Indian tribes to vast tracts of country has been extinguished; new States have been admitted into the Union; new Territories have been created and our jurisdiction and laws extended over them. As our population has expanded, the Union has been cemented and strengthened. As our boundaries have been enlarged and our agricultural population has been spread over a large surface, our federative system has acquired additional strength and security. It may well be doubted whether it would not be in greater danger of overthrow if our present population were confined to the comparatively narrow limits of the original thirteen States than it is now that they are sparsely settled over a

---

30. Polk refers to the Federalist debates of the late eighteenth century and Federalist opposition to the Louisiana Purchase. For more information on this topic, see "Robert Walker's Argument for Reannexing Texas" in this section and accompanying notes.

more expanded territory. It is confidently believed that our system may be safely extended to the utmost bounds of our territorial limits, and that as it shall be extended the bonds of our Union, so far from being weakened, will become stronger.

None can fail to see the danger to our safety and future peace if Texas remains an independent state or becomes an ally or dependency of some foreign nation more powerful than herself.[31] Is there one among our citizens who would not prefer perpetual peace with Texas to occasional wars, which so often occur between bordering independent nations? Is there one who would not prefer free intercourse with her to high duties on all our products and manufactures which enter her ports or cross her frontiers? Is there one who would not prefer an unrestricted communication with her citizens to the frontier obstructions which must occur if she remains out of the Union? Whatever is good or evil in the local institutions of Texas will remain her own whether annexed to the United States or not.[32] None of the present States will be responsible for them any more than they are for the local institutions of each other. They have confederated together for certain specified objects. Upon the same principle that they would refuse to form a perpetual union with Texas because of her local institutions our forefathers would have been prevented from forming our present Union. Perceiving no valid objection to the measure and many reasons for its adoption vitally affecting the peace, the safety, and the prosperity of both countries, I shall on the broad principle which formed the basis and produced the adoption of our Constitution, and not in any narrow spirit of sectional policy, endeavor by all constitutional, honorable, and appropriate means to consummate the expressed will of the people and Government of the United States by the reannexation of Texas to our Union at the earliest practicable period.

Nor will it become in a less degree my duty to assert and maintain by all constitutional means the right of the United States to that portion of our territory which lies beyond the Rocky Mountains. Our title to the country of the Oregon is "clear and unquestionable,"[33] and already are our people preparing to perfect that title by occupying it with their wives and children. But eighty years ago our population was confined on the west by the ridge of the Alleghanies. Within that period—within the lifetime, I might say, of some of my hearers—our people, increasing to many millions, have filled the eastern valley of the Mississippi, adventurously ascended the Missouri to its headsprings, and are already engaged in establishing the blessings of self-government in valleys of which the rivers flow to the Pacific. The world beholds the peaceful triumphs of the industry of

---

31. Specifically, the fear was that Great Britain would become too close to Texas.

32. A reference to slavery in Texas.

33. Polk here quotes from the Democratic Party platform of 1844. The Treaty of the Joint Occupation of Oregon (1818) arranged for the United States and Great Britain to occupy Oregon. Polk refused to renew the treaty with Great Britain and was able to gain most of the territory for the United States in 1846.

our emigrants. To us belongs the duty of protecting them adequately wherever they may be upon our soil. The jurisdiction of our laws and the benefits of our republican institutions should be extended over them in the distant regions which they have selected for their homes. The increasing facilities of intercourse will easily bring the States, of which the formation in that part of our territory can not be long delayed, within the sphere of our federative Union. In the meantime every obligation imposed by treaty or conventional stipulations should be sacredly respected.

In the management of our foreign relations it will be my aim to observe a careful respect for the rights of other nations, while our own will be the subject of constant watchfulness. Equal and exact justice should characterize all our intercourse with foreign countries. All alliances having a tendency to jeopard the welfare and honor of our country or sacrifice any one of the national interests will be studiously avoided, and yet no opportunity will be lost to cultivate a favorable understanding with foreign governments by which our navigation and commerce may be extended and the ample products of our fertile soil, as well as the manufactures of our skillful artisans, find a ready market and remunerating prices in foreign countries.

## Mexican Politics and the Annexation of Texas (1845)

*Mexican politics on the eve of the U.S.-Mexican War was defined by two factions: federalists, who advocated a decentralized and more secular state, and centralists, who defended church privilege and rejected the federalist ideal of regional autonomy. Yet, the federalists were divided in separate camps as well; the* puros *were the more radical faction, and the* moderados *the more moderate one. Conflict between these factions could be as destabilizing as the antagonism between federalists and centralists. On December 6, 1844, a coalition of* puros *and* moderados *overthrew Santa Anna and placed the* moderado *José Joaquín de Herrera (1792–1854) in the presidency. Herrera's refusal to immediately reinstate the federalist constitution of 1824 and his conciliatory recognition of Texan independence alienated him from* puros *who tied the loss of Texas to the lack of regional autonomy for Mexico's states. In March 1845, Herrera's minister Luis Cuevas (1800–1867) sounded a cautionary note to the congress about the prospect of war with the U.S., sparking the anger of Mexican* puros, *such as the editors of the newspaper* La Voz del Pueblo, *who railed against his suggestion that Mexican recognition of the independence of Texas might be an acceptable policy. Below we excerpt Cuevas' speech and a subsequent article by the editors of* La Voz del Pueblo. *The final selection, from an anonymous pamphlet titled* The Texas War Unmasked, *is an attack on* puros *and their call to arms over Texas.*

## Minister Luis Cuevas on the Annexation of Texas (March 11–12, 1845)[34]

A minister of foreign affairs ought to consider the Texas question from the diplomatic point of view and examine it with regard to the greater or lesser influence it will have on the reputation and respectability of the nation. If he can also contemplate it from the point of view of internal security and the conservation of territorial integrity, from this viewpoint the conclusion is obvious and easy, since it cannot be doubted that it behooves every independent people not to lose any of the parts that make it up. Texas has in fact removed itself from national union; and this separation, for which our interior turmoil is responsible, has the definite support of the cabinet of the United States, and is recognized for reasons of pure commercial convenience by the most powerful nations of Europe. . . .

The war in Texas, which once the internal order has been consolidated may have a certain and glorious success, nevertheless presents difficulties that deserve to be considered thoroughly before it is undertaken in order to save the republic from sterile sacrifices and new commitments that would lengthen the resolution of this business. The entire population of Texas is made up of foreigners: they have no regard of any kind for the Mexican nation: their customs are not only different but opposite to ours; and furthermore in their political habits they differ in every way in which the Mexican character differs from that of the American race. To think of killing those inhabitants or make them abandon the territories they have usurped, would be to give to this campaign a character hardly in accordance with feelings of humanity and with the general principles of civilization. To think, on the other hand, that Texas, if the population that is there today were to remain, could continue to be united to Mexico would be an unforgivable error, and a fatal antecedent to the war that might be undertaken. The most resolute and disciplined army and the wisest policies would not suffice to keep Texas in a state of peace and sincere union with the republic, as long as the republic did not have sufficient means to introduce colonists from other nations who would neutralize the effect of those inhabitants and the hostile tendencies of its neighbors. The expense that the government would incur for the maintenance of the troops it might send, and in putting down the acts of aggression of that population, and that immediately to the North, would not be compensated by the advantages of suppressing a rebellious department that unfortunately does not have a single moral component to become an integral part of the Mexican Republic.

The difficulties that the recognition of the independence of Texas presents are not less grave, whether one considers the integrity of our territory, or the national honor, or the evils that may come from that part of our country that will be a center for smuggling, the constant threat of our borders, and the fulcrum of the enterprising and ambitious policy of the United States. Mexico has made protest

---

34. Luis Cuevas, *Reflexiones sobre la memoria del ministerio de relaciones en la parte relativa á Tejas* (Mexico City, 1845), 3–8. Translated by Gustavo Pellón.

to that government and has also declared that it is ready to go to war and that it will employ all its resources to carry it out. . . . Texas is a fertile and beautiful department where the elements necessary to agriculture, industry, navigation, and commerce abound, having therefore all the conditions to become a flourishing state in a few years. To lose it, therefore, is to dismember the territory of Mexico, abandoning one of the richest parts, and to undercut national dignity. Texas shall be the natural ally of the United States: it will acquiesce to all its demands and will also contribute as much as possible to harming our commerce and supporting disorder, principally in the departments in its immediate vicinity.

. . .

The independence of Texas is a misfortune that we shall always regret: its incorporation to the United States would be an even heavier blow, and with such fatal consequences that neither the government nor Congress can afford to stop thinking even for a moment about the energetic measures that ought to be adopted to crush this new aspiration that the government of the United States fortunately has not been able to carry out either last year or this. The political importance and significance of the independence of Texas must be subordinated to its annexation to that republic, and the Mexican government is in a position to consider the best course of action to impede that union, which would establish in that department the power and the immediate influence of the cabinet of the United States against the integrity of our territory. The reasons that come to mind are obvious and can be expressed in these few words. The independence of Texas does not imply its annexation to the United States, but the latter does suppose the former. The independence of Texas would perhaps not make a war with the American republic necessary: its annexation would make it inevitable. Texas as an independent state is recognized by the nations of Europe: perhaps they will oppose its becoming an integral part of the United States.

## *La Voz del Pueblo* Responds to Luis Cuevas (May 3, 1845)[35]

The admission of Texas as one of our departments ruled by exceptional laws is, therefore, our nation's last resort. Perhaps this will be the thread of Ariadne in the present labyrinth;[36] but the good effects that it might produce will depend exclusively on the way in which it is put into practice, because there are remedies that, applied in a certain manner, cure the illness and that, applied in another, aggravate rather than banish it. This is the admission we favor: we judge that

---

35. *"Federación y Tejas." Artículo publicado en "La Voz del Pueblo, Número 29." Reimpreso con algunas notas y adiciones* (Mexico City: Leandro J. Valdés, 1845), 24–28. Translated by Gustavo Pellón.

36. In Greek mythology, Theseus entered a labyrinth to kill the Minotaur and found his way back out with the aid of a spool of thread given to him by Ariadne.

Texans truly would return like another Joseph, to their father's bosom, if we guaranteed a local government adequate to their needs; but we have said that this admission cannot be effected by the present cabinet, as is evident from the following simple reasons.

The exception, with respect to Texas, that would result from permitting it to govern itself according to its laws, would in fact be a reward for its rebellion, and all the departments of the republic would have the right to protest against that hateful privilege that concedes to a rebellious subject what it denies to a faithful vassal, and the present cabinet, in particular, Señor Cuevas, whose political beliefs are well known,[37] would never concede to the departments the exemptions that would demolish his favorite system of centralization. Consequently, the admission of Texas would benefit the republic, but not at all the interests of a certain faction that never looks to the interests of the country, but to the advancement of their petty ideas, and would be willing to hand us over to a foreign power, to recall the government of General Santa Anna himself, rather than to yield to the impulse of liberal principles.

We have said several times, and we repeat it now with greater ardor than ever, that only the reestablishment of the federal system can save us from the woeful predicament in which Heaven in its high designs has seen fit to place us at present. It pains us to say that after the glorious movement of the 6th,[38] every day has brought new disappointments, and one by one we have seen wither all the hopes that the people harbored in their great uprising. . . .[39]

Perhaps someone will ask: what should we do if once the federal system is reestablished Texas does not want to return to the Mexican union? The answer is obvious: we have more than sufficient resources to make war on Texas and on the United States: let us do so and Victory will hover over our flags. EXTERMINATION AND DEATH UP TO THE SABINE was the cry of our conquering legions at the Alamo, Béjar, and the Salado. EXTERMINATION AND DEATH UP TO THE SABINE shall be the cry of the valiant army and the citizen militia that will march enthusiastically to the reconquest of Texas. May heaven grant that that day will never come, and that once the sacred code of 1824 is restored, all our differences will be settled in a manner peaceful and advantageous to the nation! These are the sincere and fervent wishes of the— Editors of *La Voz del Pueblo.*

---

37. Cuevas was a close associate of the centralist president Anastasio Bustamante (1780–1853), under whose authority he had served as minister of foreign relations (1837–1838). Cuevas was also close to the well-known conservative thinker Lucas Alamán (1792–1853).

38. On December 6, 1844, José Joaquín de Herrera (1792–1854) overthrew Antonio López de Santa Anna (1794–1876).

39. Mexican federalists, particularly the *puros,* were deeply disappointed by the cautious course taken by the policies of President Herrera, who did not reinstitute the federalist constitution of 1824 or take a more aggressive stance toward Texas and the United States.

## *The Texas War Unmasked* (1845)[40]

There was also a time when the war in Texas was invoked as an emblem of patriotism and as a word of concord. The years have passed and time, which discovers all, has torn away a veil that hid from us an abyss and a sinister future. Opinion is the queen of the world: if it is founded on truth, it promotes the happiness of nations; if it is based on error, it waylays and ruins them.

The moment has come to successfully rein in those liberticides who have exploited the honor of Mexicans in order to rob and oppress them. Today when the government has asked authorization ONLY TO HEAR Texans, they affect anger and cry *perfidy and treason.*

And whose voices stand out the most? Who are the ones who aspire to present themselves with the patriotic enthusiasm of Codrus[41] and Leonidas?[42] Those who vilified the republic by serving the tyrant whom we have just overthrown;[43] but do not think that it is all of them, nor even the majority of the servants of that abominable man, but rather it is the dregs of the party: the most cowardly ones, those who have never been near Texas; those who flattered the usurper, not out of conviction, not out of love for his person, not out of friendly complaisance, but out of pure calculation, to divide up the spoils of the people, and to steal without the risks incurred by highwaymen. It is necessary to call these men to judgment before the nation. . . .

## "Annexation" by John O'Sullivan (July–August 1845)[44]

*John L. O'Sullivan (1812–1895) was the editor of the* United States Magazine and Democratic Review *between 1841 and 1846. In the July–August issue of 1845, O'Sullivan coined the phrase "Manifest Destiny" in an article in favor of the annexation of Texas, a term that he used again in New York City's* Morning News *in December 1845. In early 1846, Congressman Robert C. Winthrop*

---

40. *La guerra de Tejas sin máscara,* (Mexico City: Imprenta de V. G. Torres, 1845), 3–4. Translated by Gustavo Pellón.

41. According to legend, Codrus was a king of Athens who sacrificed his life in 1068 B.C. to save his people.

42. King Leonidas led the vastly outnumbered Spartans at the Battle of Thermopylae in 480 B.C. against the Persians. Led by King Xerxes, the one hundred thousand strong Persian army slew Leonidas and his force of three hundred Spartans.

43. A reference to Antonio López de Santa Anna and the December 6, 1844, revolt that overthrew him.

44. John O'Sullivan, "Annexation," *The United States Magazine and Democratic Review* 17, no. 1 (July–August 1845): 5–10.

*of Massachusetts quoted O'Sullivan's phrase while opposing Polk's expansionist agenda. The ideology of Manifest Destiny refers to the belief that the Anglo-American peoples of the United States are destined to conquer and populate the North American continent, displacing the "inferior" races.*

Texas is now ours. Already, before these words are written, her Convention has undoubtedly ratified the acceptance, by her Congress, of our proffered invitation into the Union; and made the requisite changes in her already republican form of constitution to adapt it to its future federal relations. Her star and her stripe may already be said to have taken their place in the glorious blazon of our common nationality; and the sweep of our eagle's wing already includes within its circuit the wide extent of her fair and fertile land. She is no longer to us a mere geographical space—a certain combination of coast, plain, mountain, valley, forest and stream. She is no longer to us a mere country on the map. She comes within the dear and sacred designation of Our Country; no longer a "*pays,*" she is a part of "*la patrie;*"[45] and that which is at once a sentiment and a virtue, Patriotism, already begins to thrill for her too within the national heart. It is time then that all should cease to treat her as alien, and even adverse—cease to denounce and vilify all and everything connected with her accession—cease to thwart and oppose the remaining steps for its consummation; or where such efforts are felt to be unavailing, at least to embitter the hour of reception by all the most ungracious frowns of aversion and words of unwelcome. There has been enough of all this. It has had its fitting day during the period when, in common with every other possible question of practical policy that can arise, it unfortunately became one of the leading topics of party division, of presidential electioneering. But that period has passed, and with it let its prejudices and its passions, its discords and its denunciations, pass away too. The next session of Congress will see the representatives of the new young State in their places in both our halls of national legislation, side by side with those of the old Thirteen. Let their reception into "the family" be frank, kindly, and cheerful, as befits such an occasion, as comports not less with our own self-respect than patriotic duty towards them. Ill betide those foul birds that delight to file[46] their own nest, and disgust the ear with perpetual discord of ill-omened croak.

Why, were other reasoning wanting, in favor of now elevating this question of the reception of Texas into the Union, out of the lower region of our past party dissensions, up to its proper level of a high and broad nationality, it surely is to be found, found abundantly, in the manner in which other nations have undertaken to intrude themselves into it, between us and the proper parties to the case, in

45. *Pays* is French for "country"; *patrie* is "homeland." The meaning here is "Texas is no longer a separate country; it is now a part of our homeland."

46. To ruin or "defile."

a spirit of hostile interference against us, for the avowed object of thwarting our policy and hampering our power, limiting our greatness and checking the fulfillment of our manifest destiny to overspread the continent allotted by Providence for the free development of our yearly multiplying millions. This we have seen done by England, our old rival and enemy; and by France, strangely coupled with her against us,[47] under the influence of the Anglicism strongly tinging the policy of her present prime minister Guizot. . . .[48]

Nor is there any just foundation for the charge that Annexation is a great pro-slavery measure—calculated to increase and perpetuate that institution. Slavery had nothing to do with it. Opinions were and are greatly divided, both at the North and South, as to the influence to be exerted by it on Slavery and the Slave States. That it will tend to facilitate and hasten the disappearance of Slavery from all the northern tier of the present Slave States, cannot surely admit of serious question. The greater value in Texas of the slave labor now employed in those States, must soon produce the effect of draining off that labor southwardly, by the same unvarying law that bids water descend the slope that invites it. . . .

California will, probably, next fall away from the loose adhesion which, in such a country as Mexico, holds a remote province in a slight equivocal kind of dependence on the metropolis. Imbecile and distracted, Mexico never can exert any real governmental authority over such a country.[49] The impotence of the one and the distance of the other, must make the relation one of virtual independence; unless, by stunting the province of all natural growth, and forbidding that immigration which can alone develop its capabilities and fulfill the purposes of its creation, tyranny may retain a military dominion, which is no government in the legitimate sense of the term. In the case of California this is now impossible. The Anglo-Saxon foot is already on its borders. Already the advance guard of the irresistible army of Anglo-Saxon emigration has begun to pour down upon it, armed with the plough and the rifle, and marking its trail with schools and colleges, courts and representative halls, mills and meeting-houses. A population will soon be in actual occupation of California, over which it will be idle for Mexico to dream of dominion. They will necessarily become independent. All this without agency of our government, without responsibility of our people—in the natural flow of events, the spontaneous working of principles, and the adaptation of the tendencies and wants of the human race to the elemental circumstances in the midst of which they find themselves placed. . . .

---

47. In 1844, French and British diplomats expressed concern over the possibility that Texas might be annexed to the United States.

48. Francoise Pierre Guillame Guizot (1787–1874) was a French historian who occupied notable government positions in the first half of the nineteenth century, including prime minister, minister of foreign affairs, and ambassador to the British court.

49. Since the eighteenth century, European and American visitors to California noted both its natural riches and its weak military defenses.

Away, then, with all idle French talk of *balances of power* on the American Continent.[50] There is no growth in Spanish America! Whatever progress of population there may be in the British Canadas, is only for their own early severance of their present colonial relation to the little island three thousand miles across the Atlantic; soon to be followed by Annexation, and destined to swell the still accumulating momentum of our progress. And whosoever may hold the balance, though they should cast into the opposite scale all the bayonets and cannon, not only of France and England, but of Europe entire, how would it kick the beam against the simple, solid weight of the two hundred and fifty, or three hundred millions—and American millions—destined to gather beneath the flutter of the stripes and stars, in the fast hastening year of the Lord 1945!

## Mariano Paredes y Arrillaga

*On December 15, 1845, General Mariano Paredes y Arrillaga (1797–1849) overthrew President José Joaquín Herrera. Paredes was a lifelong centralist with monarchist sympathies who was deeply suspicious of the masses and of Mexican federalists. Although he was instrumental in the anti-Santa Anna coup that brought Herrera to power (1844), his conservatism made him an uneasy supporter of the new president, who was a* moderado. *When he rose up against Herrera, Paredes attacked Herrera for undermining the authority of the military, for recognizing Texan independence, and for contributing to the dissolution of society. The first document that follows is an excerpt of the memoirs of Guillermo Prieto (1818–1897), one of Mexico's most important nineteenth-century writers, about Paredes and his milieu. The second document is a nationalist circular by Paredes that prepares the nation for the outbreak of hostilities with the United States. The day after the release of this circular, Mexican forces skirmished with U.S. Dragoons, leading to Polk's formal declaration of war against Mexico on May 11.*

### Guillermo Prieto Remembers General Mariano Paredes y Arrillaga (1906)[51]

With General Paredes the anti-independence party was firmly enthroned in power. The party of the classes, the throne, and the altar was enthroned and

50. In 1840, Guizot said that all states in the Americas should remain independent of one another, without any one of them becoming unduly powerful and influential. Polk vehemently rejected this argument as having no application in the Americas.

51. Guillermo Prieto, *Memorias de mis tiempos* (Paris/Mexico City: Librería de la Viuda de Bouret, 1906), 178–79. Translated by Gustavo Pellón.

determined to implant the monarchical system with an organization that seemed indestructible.

Paredes, like almost all generals, was terribly ignorant; his admiration for the Spanish system was deep, and his hatred for the rabble, insurmountable.

Small of body, snub-nosed with small eyes and straight hair, stiff and pretentious, Paredes would not have been out of place collecting tickets at the entrance of a theater or leading a procession of penitents. But his reputation for valor was justly deserved, as was that of his rectitude.

Closely linked to the Condes del Valle, to the highest ecclesiastical authorities and related to the most noble houses of Spain, General Paredes had grounds to profess a profound veneration for Señor Alamán, Father Arrillaga, Father Nájera, Castillo Lanzas, Bonilla, Jauregui, Baldomero, Miranda, and other leaders of the conservative party.

Moreover, Señor Paredes' family was an exemplary family, renowned for its virtues as well as the most correct and exacting manners of high society. Señora Doña Josefa Cortés de Paredes was a most distinguished matron who belonged to a wealthy family of Guadalajara and had that tone of frankness typical of aristocratic families in that part of the republic.

But despite her reserve and her painstaking education, the lady was most intolerant, most devoted to the clergy, and most powerfully decisive in her influence on Sr. Paredes, not so much, in my opinion, on political matters, her family connections and interests, but rather on the subject of religious principles, which the lady thought were highly compromised by the liberals, who according to her were daily expanding the dominions of Satan against God and Heaven.

## Manifesto of April 23, 1846[52]

When at the beginning of the year I took upon myself the grave responsibility of guiding the nation's path for a short time, I determined with a resolute spirit to support and defend its rights and prerogatives, changing the weak and pernicious policy of accommodation that had been followed toward the government of the United States of America, despite the perfidy with which it prepared the occupation of Texas, the bad faith with which it violated the existing treaties that guaranteed the borders of the republic, and the treacherous act by which it added one of our departments to the states of its confederation. The Mexican nation did not conquer its independence by means of the most bloody and heroic sacrifices, nor take its seat among the civilized nations of the globe, to become the mockery of a neighboring power, who exploiting our quarrels, our painful upheavals, and the inordinate weakness that they produced, appeared with the instruments of

52. *Diario Oficial del Gobierno Mexicano*. April 24, 1846. Translated by Gustavo Pellón.

conquest and began to invade our territory, to flatter itself with the dream that it could wipe out the manly race to which we belong, apply to us the mark of the branding iron that the slaves of the South bear on their foreheads, extinguish our nationality, and abandon us to the humiliating misfortune of oblivion. Our magnanimous people who in an eleven-year bloody fight of extermination proved their valor no less than their constancy waited impatiently to hurl themselves again into another war to which they were summoned by the scandalous aggression of a government, who claimed to be our friend, and who in order to abase us resorted to its power and ignored the rights of equity and justice that all nations respect, that strengthen the hope of peace, and that maintain the harmony of the universe. This is why the nation sanctioned the movement that I started in San Luis Potosí,[53] not in order to seek the distressful exercise of power but so that my country's would shine with the triumph of a cause, which is that of the conservative principles of human societies.

The former injuries, the offenses that, since the year 1836, the United States government has incessantly repeated against the people of Mexico were crowned by the insult of sending us an ambassador to present his credentials to our government as a resident, as if relations between the two republics had suffered no alteration upon the definitive annexation of Texas.[54] At the same time that Mr. Slidell presented himself, the troops of the United States were occupying our territory,[55] their squadrons threatened at our door, and they were preparing for the occupation of the peninsula of the Californias, for which the Oregon question with England is only a preliminary; and I did not receive Mr. Slidell, because this new insult was repellent to the dignity of our nation.

Meanwhile the army of the United States camped in Corpus Christi and occupied Padre Vayín Island [Padre Island], went directly to the Frontón de Santa Isabel,[56] and unfurled the flag with the stars on the right bank of the Río Bravo del Norte, before the city of Matamoros, having previously taken control of navigation on the river with their warships. The town of Laredo was taken by surprise by a detachment of their troops, and a squad of our troops that was scouting there was disarmed. The hostilities, that have broken out because of

53. Paredes' December 1845 revolt against President Herrera began in San Luis de Potosí, where he published a proclamation of principles.

54. When Polk's agent John Slidell (1793–1871) arrived in Mexico in 1845, diplomatic relations between both countries had broken off. Mexican authorities refused to recognize Slidell's status as envoy extraordinary and minister plenipotentiary as opposed to that of mere commissioner ad hoc on the subject of Texas. The Mexicans believed that to recognize Slidell as anything other than a commissioner would have assumed the restoration of relations between both countries when that had not in fact occurred.

55. The corridor between the Nueces River to the north, which Mexico considered the boundary of Texas, and the Rio Grande to the south, which the United States and Texas claimed as the boundary.

56. A reference to the American fortifications at Point Isabel.

the United States, threaten Monterey in Alta California. There can be no doubt as to which of the two republics is responsible for a war that a feeling of equity and justice and the respect that civilization confers to the rights and property of all nations would have prevented. If Mexico were to suffer with indolence the repeated incursions of a power that already considers itself the owner and mistress of the American continent, not only would it lose the importance that its population and its resources and its privileged situation have given it since it became an independent nation, but it would fall into shameful contempt because when challenged to combat it allows the piecemeal loss of the parts that make up its territory. So many and such serious outrages could no longer be tolerated, and I have commanded the general in chief of the division of our northern border[57] to attack the army that is attacking us, to answer the enemy who makes war on us with war, and I invoke the God of Battles to preserve the valor of our soldiers, our unquestionable right to our territory, and the decorum of our arms that are going to be employed only in the defense of justice. Adhering to established procedure and in accordance with strict orders from my government, our general demanded that the general in chief of the American troops withdraw to the other bank of the Nueces River, the old border of Texas, and the demand was rejected.[58]

Nations interested in not seeing the peace of so many years disturbed, and whose trade relations with the Mexican Republic might be hurt, can grasp the difficult predicament to which the aggressive policy of the United States has reduced the republic and that it would succumb if it did not energetically defend its threatened existence. I solemnly announce that I am not declaring war on the United States of America, because it belongs to the august congress of our nation, and not to the executive, to resolve ultimately the reparation that so many offenses require.[59] But the defense of the Mexican territory invaded by United States troops is an urgent necessity, and my responsibility before the nation would be great if I did not order the repulse of the forces acting as enemies, and I have ordered it. The defensive war begins today, and any part of our territory that is invaded or attacked will be vigorously defended.

We have finally come to the situation that the administrations of the Mexican nation sought fruitlessly to forestall by debating our clear claims to justice; and trampled as they have been, we enter into a necessary fight, which shall win

57. General Mariano Arista (1802–1855), who led Mexican forces at Palo Alto and Resaca de la Palma (May 8–9, 1846).

58. On April 12, 1846, General Pedro Ampudia sent General Zachary Taylor a letter demanding that U.S. forces withdraw from the Rio Grande to the Nueces.

59. The Mexican congress never declared outright war on the United States. Instead, on July 6, months after the start of hostilities, it authorized Paredes to defend Mexico's territory from U.S. aggression. See Ramon Alcaraz et al., *The Other Side: Or, Notes for the History of the War between Mexico and the United States*, trans. Albert Ramsey (New York: John Wiley, 1850), 9–30. Also, see Karl Jack Bauer, *The Mexican War 1846–1848* (Lincoln: University of Nebraska Press, 1992), 76.

the empathy of the peoples and governments who condemn the usurpations of the powerful. We shall be victorious because of the sanctity of our purpose and because when everything is in peril, efforts rise to the demands of the occasion. Meanwhile, the Mexican nation is resolved to risk all to save all and will give an example of sublime dedication that will match the glory gained so many times by the peoples who through the centuries upheld their independence and liberties.

I am proud to have been chosen by Providence to be the instrument through which the energetic will of the Mexican Republic shall express itself. We shall prove in combat that the sons of the heroes and martyrs of our War of Independence are heartened by the memory of their pure glory, that valor has not degenerated in their breasts, and that they are ready to sacrifice themselves at the altar of their country.

Mexicans! On this memorable day, I raise the banner of independence, on which you can see inscribed the illustrious names of Hidalgo[60] and Iturbide.[61] Rally under this sacred ensign, postponing to a time of lesser peril our domestic issues and differences. I have assured you that the glory I seek, as the reward of my eventful career, is not that of the ambitious man who considers power as a prize. I have sworn to protect all the rights of the republic in the brief period of my government; and now as I urge you to fight and warn you that great sacrifices will be necessary, I also promise you that my blood will not be spared, if it is needed.

Mexicans! Your valiant army is going to fight, and will fight with the valor of heroes; send them your blessings and prepare to crown their noble brows, or their venerable tombs if they succumb, when destiny calls you to replace them in the ranks.

Mexico will conquer or cease to exist!

National Palace of Mexico, April 23, 1846

## Polk's War Message (May 11, 1846)[62]

*In 1845, the U.S. Congress passed a resolution annexing the republic of Texas to the United States. Texas agreed and joined the union in December 1845. After*

---

60. Miguel Hidalgo y Costilla (1753–1811) was one of Mexico's most important national heroes. He gave a speech called the "Grito de Dolores" on September 15, 1810, that began the War of Mexican Independence.

61. Agustín de Iturbide (1783–1824) consolidated Mexican independence and was emperor between 1822 and 1823.

62. United States. President (1845–1849: Polk), *Messages of the President of the United States, with the Correspondence, therewith communicated, between the Secretary of War and Other Officers of the Government, on the Subject of The Mexican War* (Washington, DC: Wendell and Van Benthuysen, 1848), 4–10.

*the annexation of Texas, Polk sought to adjudicate the claims issue with Mexico and purchase California. Most urgent, however, was the resolution of a border dispute between Texas and Mexico. For Mexico, the southern border of Texas was at the Nueces River, whereas Texas and the United States considered the border to be south of the Nueces at the Rio Grande. In November 1845, Polk sent John Slidell (1793–1871) to Mexico to resolve these issues, but the Mexican government refused to recognize Slidell's diplomatic credentials. Polk then ordered General Zachary Taylor to occupy the disputed area and protect it in the eventuality of a Mexican incursion. On May 11, after hearing news that sixteen U.S. Dragoons had died in a Mexican ambush, Polk declared war on Mexico. His claim that American blood had been shed on American soil is a controversial claim that was not unanimously accepted in its day, most notably by Congressman Abraham Lincoln.*

The existing state of the relations between the United States and Mexico renders it proper that I should bring the subject to the consideration of Congress. In my message at the commencement of your present session the state of these relations, the causes which led to the suspension of diplomatic intercourse between the two countries in March, 1845, and the long-continued and unredressed wrongs and injuries committed by the Mexican Government on citizens of the United States in their persons and property were briefly set forth.

As the facts and opinions which were then laid before you were carefully considered, I can not better express my present convictions of the condition of affairs up to that time than by referring you to that communication.

The strong desire to establish peace with Mexico on liberal and honorable terms, and the readiness of this Government to regulate and adjust our boundary and other causes of difference with that power on such fair and equitable principles as would lead to permanent relations of the most friendly nature, induced me in September last to seek the reopening of diplomatic relations between the two countries. Every measure adopted on our part had for its object the furtherance of these desired results. In communicating to Congress a succinct statement of the injuries which we had suffered from Mexico, and which had been accumulating during a period of more than twenty years, every expression that could tend to inflame the people of Mexico, or defeat or delay a pacific result, was carefully avoided. An envoy of the United States repaired to Mexico with full powers to adjust every existing difference.[63] But though present on the Mexican soil by agreement between the two Governments invested with full powers, and bearing evidence of the most friendly disposition, his mission has been unavailing. The Mexican Government not only refused to receive him or listen to his proposition

63. A reference to John Slidell's failed mission to Mexico. See Introduction and note 54 in this section.

but after a long continued series of menaces have at last invaded our territory and shed the blood of our fellow citizens on our own soil.[64]

. . .

The grievous wrongs perpetrated by Mexico upon our citizens throughout a long period of years remain unredressed, and solemn treaties pledging her public faith for this redress have been disregarded.[65] A government either unable or unwilling to enforce the execution of such treaties fails to perform one of its plainest duties.

Our commerce with Mexico has been almost annihilated. It was formerly highly beneficial to both nations, but our merchants have been deterred from prosecuting it by the system of outrage and extortion which the Mexican authorities have pursued against them, whilst their appeals through their own Government for indemnity have been made in vain. Our forbearance has gone to such an extreme as to be mistaken in its character. Had we acted with vigor in repelling the insults and redressing the injuries inflicted by Mexico at the commencement, we should doubtless have escaped all difficulties in which we are now involved.

Instead of this, however, we have been exerting our best efforts to propitiate her good will. Upon the pretext that Texas, a nation as independent as herself, thought proper to unite its destinies with our own, she has affected to believe that we have severed her rightful territory, and in official proclamations and manifestoes has repeatedly threatened to make war upon us for the purpose of reconquering Texas. In the meantime we have tried every effort at reconciliation. The cup of forbearance had been exhausted even before the recent information from the frontier of Del Norte. But now, after reiterated menaces, Mexico has passed the boundary of the United States, has invaded our territory and shed American blood upon the American soil. She has proclaimed that hostilities have commenced, and that the two nations are now at war.

As war exists, and notwithstanding all our efforts to avoid it, exists by the act of Mexico herself, we are called upon by every consideration of duty and patriotism to vindicate with decision the honor, the rights, and the interests of our country.

Anticipating the possibility of a crisis like that which has arrived, instructions were given in August last, "as a precautionary measure" against invasion or threatened invasion, authorizing General Taylor, if the emergency required, to accept volunteers, not from Texas only but from the States of Louisiana, Alabama,

64. The corridor between the Nueces and Rio Grande was never formally ceded to Texas, and its inhabitants were Mexicans. For more on Polk's claim, see "Abraham Lincoln's Spot Resolution" in Part IV.

65. U.S. claims against Mexico were over a million dollars and were the result of the loss of American capital and property in Mexico in the first half of the nineteenth century.

Mississippi, Tennessee, and Kentucky, and corresponding letters were addressed to the respective governors of those States.

These instructions were repeated, and in January last, soon after the incorporation of "Texas into our Union of States," General Taylor was further "authorized by the President to make a requisition upon the executive of that state for such of its militia force as may be needed to repel invasion or to secure the country against apprehended invasion." On the 2d day of March he was again reminded, "in the event of the approach of any considerable Mexican force, promptly and efficiently to use the authority with which he was clothed to call to him such auxiliary force as he might need." War actually existing and our territory having been invaded, General Taylor, pursuant to authority vested in him by my direction, has called on the governor of Texas for four regiments of State troops, two to be mounted and two to serve on foot, and on the governor of Louisiana for four regiments of infantry to be sent to him as soon as practicable.

In further vindication of our rights and defense of our territory, I invoke the prompt action of Congress to recognize the existence of the war, and to place at the disposition of the Executive the means of prosecuting the war with vigor, and thus hastening the restoration of peace. To this end I recommend that authority should be given to call into the public service a large body of volunteers to serve for not less than six or twelve months unless sooner discharged. A volunteer force is beyond question more efficient than any other description of citizen soldiers, and it is not to be doubted that a number far beyond that required would readily rush to the field upon the call of their country. I further recommend that a liberal provision be made for sustaining our entire military force and furnishing it with supplies and munitions of war.

The most energetic and prompt measures and the immediate appearance in arms of a large and overpowering force are recommended to Congress as the most certain and efficient means of bringing the existing collision with Mexico to a speedy and successful termination.

In making these recommendations I deem it proper to declare that it is my anxious desire not only to terminate hostilities speedily, but to bring all matters in dispute between this Government and Mexico to an early and amicable adjustment; and in this view I shall be prepared to renew negotiations whenever Mexico shall be ready to receive propositions or to make propositions of her own.

I transmit herewith a copy of the correspondence between our envoy to Mexico and the Mexican minister for foreign affairs, and so much of the correspondence between that envoy and the Secretary of State and between the Secretary of War and the general in command on the Del Norte as is necessary to a full understanding of the subject.

# III

# Scenes of War, 1846–1847

## U.S. and Mexican Views of the Battle of Palo Alto (May 8–9, 1846)

*The first major battles of the U.S.-Mexican War were fought on the outskirts of Matamoros north of the Rio Grande, in territory claimed by both the United States and Mexico. Under orders of President Polk, General Zachary Taylor (1784–1850) led the Army of Observation to the north banks of the Rio Grande in March 1846 where he built Fort Texas within sight of the town of Matamoros. On April 24, 1846, a squadron of sixty-three U.S. Dragoons on patrol near Fort Texas skirmished with Mexican forces, resulting in the death of sixteen U.S. soldiers and the capture of the rest. Upon receiving news of this engagement on May 9, President Polk called for war against Mexico, claiming that American blood had been shed on American soil. The Battles of Palo Alto (May 8) and Resaca de la Palma (May 9) took place after General Taylor took most of his men on a resupply mission from Fort Texas to Point Isabel on the Gulf Coast. General Mariano Arista (1802–1855) lay siege to Fort Texas and blocked Taylor's return. At the Battle of Palo Alto, the highly mobile U.S. artillery proved superior to Mexican cannon. The following day, in the chaparral-covered terrain of Resaca de la Palma, Mexican and U.S. forces fought hand to hand for the first time, inflicting many casualties. Taylor's forces succeeded in pushing Arista and his men back across the Rio Grande.*

### General Mariano Arista's Report on the Battle of Palo Alto (May 8, 1846)[1]

Determined to keep General Taylor from uniting the forces that he was bringing from Frontón de Santa Isabel[2] to those he left fortified before Matamoros, I left Tanques de Ramireño today . . . and headed for Palo Alto as soon as my spies informed me that the enemy had left Frontón with the intention of taking wagons laden with provisions and heavy artillery into their forts. I reached Palo Alto about one o'clock in the afternoon, and I observed that the enemy was entering

1. Emilio Castillo Negrete, *Invasión de los norte-americanos en México* (Mexico City: Imprenta del Editor, 1890), 191–93. Translated by Gustavo Pellón.

2. A reference to Taylor's position at Point Isabel. See note 56 in Part II.

Republic of Texas Dragoon. c. 1845 daguerreotype. Courtesy, Special Collections, The University of Texas at Arlington Library, Arlington, Texas.

said place. With all the forces at my disposal, I formed our line of battle in a great plain, with a wooded height protecting my right and a swamp that was difficult to cross on my left.

. . .

The forces under my command were three thousand men and twelve artillery pieces; those of the invaders were three thousand soldiers more or less, and they had superior artillery, as they had twenty, six, and eighteen caliber pieces.

The battle began so furiously that the cannon fire did not cease for a moment. During its course, the enemy wanted to continue toward Matamoros to raise the siege of its troops; for this purpose they set the grass on fire and formed such a thick cloud of smoke before their line of battle that they managed to hide from our view; but by virtue of maneuvering I impeded the enemy twice.

General Taylor maintained a rather more defensive than offensive attack, employing his best weapon, which is the artillery, protected by half the infantry and all the cavalry, keeping the rest fortified at Resaca, at about two thousand yards from the battlefield.

I was eager to charge because the cannon fire was wreaking havoc in our ranks, and I ordered General Don Anastasio Torrejón to execute it on our left flank with the greater part of the cavalry in order to attack at the same time on the right with a column of infantry and the rest of the cavalry.

I waited for the moment that the aforementioned general would execute the charge and for it to begin to have effect so as to make the push from the right, but the charge was contained by an enemy force that defended a bog hampering the attack.

Impatient because of the losses they suffered, some battalions asked to advance. I immediately had them charge with a column of cavalry at the command of Colonel Don Cayetano Montero, and the result of this operation was that these corps marched on the enemy, who given the distance of their location found it necessary to withdraw to their reserve, and as night fell the battle ended and our arms remained in command of the field.

. . .

The combat was long and bloody, as can be gauged from the calculation made by the commanding general of artillery, Don Tomás Resquena, who assures me that the enemy fired on us about three thousand artillery rounds from two in the afternoon, when the fighting began, until seven in the evening, when it ended, our side having fired 650 rounds.

The honor of our nation's armed forces was upheld because our soldiers did not retreat one hand span of ground, despite suffering great losses from the enemy's superior artillery.

Our troops lament the loss of 352 men missing, wounded, and dead. The latter are worthy of national remembrance and gratitude for the fearlessness with which they died, fighting for the most sacred of causes.

## General Zachary Taylor's Report on the Battle of Palo Alto (May 9, 1846)[3]

Sir: I have the honor to report that I was met near this place yesterday, on my march from Point Isabel, by the Mexican forces, and, after an action of about

3. T. B. Thorpe, *Our Army on the Rio Grande: Being a Short Account of the Important Events from the Time of the Removal of the "Army of Occupation" from Corpus Christi, to the Surrender of Matamoros with Description of the Battles of Palo Alto and Resaca de la Palma, the Bombardment of Fort Brown, and the Ceremonies of Surrender of Matamoros: With Descriptions of the City, etc. etc.* (Philadelphia: Carey and Hart, 1846), 85–86.

five hours, dislodged them from their position and encamped upon the field. Our artillery consisting of two eighteen-pounders and two light batteries, was the arm chiefly engaged, and to the excellent manner in which it was maneuvered and served is our success mainly due.

The strength of the enemy is believed to have been about 6000 men, with seven pieces of artillery and 800 cavalry. His loss is probably at least one hundred killed. Our strength did not exceed, all told, twenty-three hundred, while our loss was comparatively trifling: four men killed, three officers and thirty-seven men wounded, several of the latter mortally. I regret to say that Major Ringgold,[4] 2d Artillery, and Captain Page, 4th Infantry, are severely wounded. Lieutenant Luther, 2d Artillery, slightly so.

The enemy has fallen back, and it is believed has repassed the river. I have advanced parties now thrown forward in his direction, and shall move the main body immediately.

In the haste of this report, I can only say that the officers and men behaved in the most admirable manner throughout the action. I shall have the pleasure of making a more detailed report when those of the different commanders shall be received.

## Ulysses S. Grant Remembers the Battle of Palo Alto (1886)[5]

Early in the forenoon of the 8th of May as Palo Alto was approached, an army, certainly outnumbering our little force, was seen, drawn up in line of battle just in front of the timber. Their bayonets and spearheads glistened in the sunlight formidably. The force was composed largely of cavalry armed with lances. Where we were the grass was tall, reaching nearly to the shoulders of the men, very stiff, and each stock was pointed at the top, and hard and almost as sharp as a darning-needle. General Taylor halted his army before the head of column came in range of the artillery of the Mexicans. He then formed a line of battle, facing the enemy. His artillery, two batteries and two eighteen-pounder iron guns, drawn by oxen, were placed in position at intervals along the line. A battalion was thrown to the rear, commanded by Lieutenant-Colonel Childs, of the artillery, as reserves. These preparations completed, orders were given for a platoon of each company to stack arms and go to a stream off to the right of the command, to fill their canteens and also those of the rest of their respective companies. When the men were all back in their places in line, the command to advance was given.

---

4. Samuel Ringgold (1800–1846) was the son of a well-known U.S. senator and the grandson of General John Cadwalader (1742–1786), a notable veteran of the American Revolution. See "The Death of Ringgold" in the final section of this book.

5. Ulysses S. Grant, *Personal Memoirs of U. S. Grant* (New York: C. L. Webster and Co., 1885–1886), vol. 1, 66–69.

As I looked down that long line of about three thousand armed men, advancing towards a larger force also armed, I thought what a fearful responsibility General Taylor must feel, commanding such a host and so far away from friends. The Mexicans immediately opened fire upon us, first with artillery and then with infantry. At first their shots did not reach us, and the advance was continued. As we got nearer, the cannon balls commenced going through the ranks. They hurt no one, however, during this advance, because they would strike the ground long before they reached our line, and ricocheted through the tall grass so slowly that the men would see them and open ranks and let them pass. When we got to a point where the artillery could be used with effect, a halt was called, and the battle opened on both sides.

The infantry under General Taylor was armed with flint-lock muskets, and paper cartridges charged with powder, buck-shot and ball. At the distance of a few hundred yards a man might fire at you all day without your finding it out. The artillery was generally six-pounder brass guns throwing only solid shot;[6] but General Taylor had with him three or four twelve-pounder howitzers[7] throwing shell,[8] besides his eighteen-pounders before spoken of, that had a long range. This made a powerful armament. The Mexicans were armed about as we were so far as their infantry was concerned, but their artillery only fired solid shot. We had greatly the advantage in this arm.

The artillery was advanced a rod or two in front of the line, and opened fire. The infantry stood at order arms as spectators, watching the effect of our shots upon the enemy, and watching his shots so as to step out of their way. It could be seen that the eighteen-pounders and the howitzers did a great deal of execution.[9] On our side there was little or no loss while we occupied this position. During the battle Major Ringgold, an accomplished and brave artillery officer, was mortally wounded, and Lieutenant Luther, also of the artillery, was struck. During the day several advances were made, and just at dusk it became evident that the Mexicans were falling back. We again advanced, and occupied at the close of the battle substantially the ground held by the enemy at the beginning. In this last move there was a brisk fire upon our troops, and some execution was done. One cannon-ball passed through our ranks, not far from me. It took off the head of an enlisted man, and the under jaw of Captain Page of my regiment, while the splinters from the musket of the killed soldier, and his brains and bones, knocked down two or three others, including one officer, Lieutenant Wallen,—hurting them more or less.

---

6. Cannonballs.

7. A type of cannon with intermediate range that shot exploding projectiles.

8. Exploding projectiles.

9. In military terms, "execution" means to punish or damage a foe.

# U.S. and Mexican Views of the Conquest of New Mexico (1846)

*The Army of the West, commanded by General Stephen W. Kearny (1794–1848), took possession of New Mexico when it entered Santa Fe in August 1846 without encountering armed resistance. New Mexico's Governor Manuel Armijo (1801–1854) tried to organize a Mexican force to engage advancing U.S. forces, but he lacked the military support to mount an attack. Like California, most of New Mexico's population was composed of natives peoples and was militarily weak and politically divided. The most serious threat to U.S. authority in New Mexico was the Taos Revolt of 1847, when Mexican and Pueblo Indians rose up against U.S. officials and murdered New Mexico's first American governor, Charles Bent (1799–1847).*

## General Stephen W. Kearny at San Miguel (August 1846)[10]

The general made pretty much the same remarks to the Alcalde[11] and people that he had made to the people of the other villages. He assured them that he had an ample force and would have possession of the country against all opposition, but gave them assurances of the friendship and protection of the United States. He stated to them that this had never been given them by the government of Mexico, but the United States were able and would certainly protect them, not only in their persons, property, and religion, but against the cruel invasion of the Indians. That they saw but a small part of the force that was at his disposal. Many more troops were near him on another road (some of which he showed them a mile or two distant) and that another army would, probably, be through their village in three weeks.

After this, he said, "Mr. Alcalde, are you willing to take the oath of allegiance to the United States?" He replied that "he would prefer waiting till the general had taken possession of the capital." The general told him, "it was sufficient for him to know that he had possession of his village." He then consented and with the usual formalities, he said, "You swear that you will bear true allegiance to the government of the United States of America." The Alcalde said, "provided I can be protected in my religion." The general said, "I swear you shall be." He then continued, "and that you will defend her against all her enemies and opposers, in the name of the Father, Son, and Holy Ghost Amen."

---

10. Jeremiah Hughes, ed., "Diary of an Officer of the 'Army of the West'," *Niles' National Register* 71 (October 10, 1846): 91–92.

11. Mayor.

The general then said, "I continue you as the Alcalde of this village, and require you, the inhabitants of this village to obey him as such. Your laws will be continued for the present, but as soon as I have time to examine them, if any change can be made that will be for your benefit, it shall be done." The Padre then invited him to his house, and gave him and his staff refreshments; and after sundry hugs, jokes and professions of friendship, with an expression from the general, that, "the better they became acquainted the better friends they would be," and an invitation to the Padre to visit him at Santa Fe (which he promised), we left the village.

## General Manuel Armijo to Mariano Salas, President of Mexico (September 8, 1846)[12]

Through the communiqués that I have sent to Your Excellency by urgent mail, the Most Excellent General-in-Chief, who today holds the executive power of the nation, is no doubt informed that the United States, that treacherous and faithless power, had at its disposal a force of three to four thousand men to occupy the department in my command. I immediately formed companies of auxiliaries[13] with their respective commanders, all of them citizens who were armed in the department; I sent scouts to observe the enemy and keep me informed of everything, and I wrote to the commandant generals of Chihuahua and Durango, explaining that with the small military force that I had it was not possible to resist the forces of the United States that were coming to invade my department; that although there were some armed citizens, they all lacked ammunition, and I had no means of providing them with it, and that I counted on their patriotism to help me without delay to punish, in the most effective manner, the impudence of these usurpers who were coming to take possession of one of the most fertile departments of our nation. . . . On the ninth of this month, I received news that enemy forces were at Fort Bent; I gave orders for the auxiliary companies I had formed to move out. Lastly on the fourteenth, I was able to gather 1,800 men, not being able to do it earlier because they were dispersed through all the towns. . . . On the sixteenth I set out with said force, and on the same day I met up with the auxiliaries who were waiting for me. I immediately held a meeting of the officers and all the most influential people of the department who were accompanying me in order to make certain of my opinion, because I was informed that all the auxiliary companies did not want to offer any resistance. As soon as they were assembled I explained to them that the enemy forces were two leagues away, that the hour of combat was drawing near, and that their patriotism and the

12. Manuel Armijo, "Número 1," *El Republicano,* January 13, 1847, 2. Translated by Gustavo Pellón. Mariano Salas was president between August and December 1846.

13. Volunteer corps, auxiliaries to the military.

advantageous position we held led me to believe that we would win a complete victory; and finally, I tried to arouse their patriotism in every way I could think of; but unfortunately it was all in vain. The first declaration made by the captains of the auxiliary companies was that all the soldiers did not want to make any resistance because they had no provisions or ammunition, and that they did not want to sacrifice themselves in vain and bring calamities upon their country. When they finished making this declaration, they all withdrew, and the only men I had left were the two hundred who had accompanied me from Santa Fe. Then I held a meeting of the officers in which they resolved unanimously to retreat until we could meet up with the forces of the commandant general of Chihuahua, who we thought must be approaching our border towns. I accepted their resolution because I thought it wise under those circumstances, as I had sufficient reason to fear that the presidial companies[14] that made up the bulk of my force would make the same decision as the auxiliaries. And that is what happened, most of them deserted that night, and the next day the rest. . . . On the seventeenth, with my force reduced to sixty dragoons, with three artillery pieces and a howitzer, I set out, poorly equipped and badly mounted. . . .

## Manuel Armijo to His Compatriots (January 11, 1847)[15]

In New Mexico there has never been an adequate concentration of troops to protect that part of our frontier. The presidial companies and the citizens themselves made war on the barbarous tribes; and while it is clear that such forces could contain this type of enemy, who had no discipline, no artillery, no supplies, and only intent on pillage, they were inadequate to combat a numerous, well-equipped army under the direction of intelligent commanders and officers. The population of the capital, Santa Fe, barely comes to four thousand souls, and it is obvious that all of it as a whole could not compete with three thousand warriors such as those who have invaded her. New Mexico in its vast 5,709 square league territory scarcely has a population of sixty thousand people, scattered throughout *rancherías*[16] and small distant towns. Its inhabitants are poor, and in order to mitigate their hardships they have had to trade with the United States in order to transport their goods to Durango, Chihuahua, and Zacatecas, their largest markets. Given these circumstances and without outside help, in men, arms, and money, it was impossible, considering the natural resources of that country, to maintain and pay for a force competent to engage in a fight such as is presently taking place.

---

14. Army of the presidio or official military garrison.

15. Manuel Armijo, "El General Armijo a sus compatriotas," *El Republicano,* January 13, 1847, 1. Translated by Gustavo Pellón.

16. Small Indian settlements.

## Incidents of the Doniphan Expedition (1846–1847)[17]

*Col. Alexander W. Doniphan (1808–1887) led the one thousand strong First Regiment of Missouri Mounted Volunteers that served in General Stephen Kearny's Army of the West. He was instrumental in establishing a short-lived civil government of New Mexico through a set of laws called the Kearny Code, which was discontinued after the Taos Revolt in early 1847. Doniphan achieved fame and glory, however, for a grueling expedition through thousands of miles of arid, inhospitable terrain from Santa Fe into Northern Mexico and then northeast to Matamoros. Doniphan's Missouri Volunteers took El Paso after defeating Col. Antonio Ponce de León at the Battle of Brazito (December 25, 1846). They defeated General José Heredia at the Battle of Sacramento (February 28, 1847) and took Chihuahua City on March 2, 1847. Doniphan's exhausted men arrived in Matamoros in May 1847. The following excerpts, by a volunteer named Frank S. Edwards, document some of the experiences of Doniphan's men on their legendary march. The headings below do not appear in the original work; they have been inserted to assist the reader.*

### [Welcomed by the Pueblo Indians]

Our first encampment was at the village of San Domingo, which is inhabited by the Pueblo Indians, and supplies Santa Fé with the small amount of fruit it consumes. It has a very pretty appearance, every house being surrounded by small fruit trees. We were received here in Indian style. The inhabitants were dressed in their gayest trappings; all mounted and armed. They dashed down towards us at full speed, and only when almost touching us, wheeled to the right and left along our front, all the while discharging their few guns and pistols; and after separating into two parties, and going through a mimic battle, they formed around our officers, and escorted them into the place. These were the largest and finest Indians I saw, and were dressed in showy costume. I observed one particularly. It was a coat, or rather shirt of bright blue and red cloth, half of each color; the division running down the chest and back—the coat, as well as the buckskin leggings, being trimmed with blue and white beads very handsomely. Although they evidently liked to be noticed, yet they did not move a muscle of their painted faces, as we handled their dresses. They behaved hospitably; and were evidently satisfied with the change that had taken place in the government.

---

17. Frank S. Edwards, *A Campaign in New Mexico with Colonel Doniphan* (Philadelphia: Carey and Hart, 1847), 60–62, 69, 76–79, 140–43.

## [A Religious Procession]

Our men, while at the grazing camp at Galisteo, were kept two days accidentally without their regular supplies of food; and, therefore, were obliged to forage upon the corn-fields around, especially as the inhabitants had previously refused to sell any to us; and it had also been our constant habit to boil a pot of maize each night just before going to sleep, and, sitting round the fire, to eat and talk. The surrounding corn-fields began to look rather unproductive, much to the astonishment of the natives; so, to remedy this, the figure of the Virgin Mary was carried around the fields, in solemn procession—solemn, perhaps, to the poor Mexicans, but by no means so to us. The figure,[18] which was very fantastically dressed, was carried by a woman in the same manner as she would have carried a child, and over them was held an old red umbrella, the only one in the village, and reserved for great occasions like the present. At the head of the procession walked the priest, book in hand, sprinkling holy water on all sides, followed by two musicians with squeaking fiddles, and also by two men firing off continually a couple of old rusty fowling pieces, to the great admiration of the young folks. After them came the figure; and the procession was closed by all the rest of the inhabitants. At every twenty or thirty steps they would all kneel down and pray audibly. We smoothed our faces as best we could, not wishing to be supposed to know anything about the maize just then.

## [The Difficulties of Traveling *La Jornada del Muerto*]

At Fray Cristobal we encamped one day to cook for the two following, as, during this time, we were to be away from water—being about to cross the large bend which the river here takes. This dry stretch of road is called *La Jornada del Muerto,* or The (day's) Journey of Death. Although the word *Jornada* only means a day's journey, yet, from this day forward, our men called every long dry extent of road a *Jornada*. . . .

We first met on this part of the road, with the species of palm called by us Soap-weed,[19] from the fact that Mexicans use its root as a substitute for soap, for which it answers very well. . . . These plants have a singularly provoking quality; being from two to eight feet in height, they will assume to the eye, in the twilight, the most deceptive forms. To the sentinel, they will appear as forms of men; and

18. In eighteenth- and early nineteenth-century Mexico, processions with the Spanish icon of the Virgin of Remedios sought to bring rain. The Virgin of Remedios was the patroness of Spanish-born Mexicans (*peninsulars*) in the colonial period.

19. A variety of yucca plant. Mexicans used the roots to make soap.

many an unconscious soap-weed has run the chance of a sentry's shot, from not answering to the challenge of "Who goes there?"

Some of our men, thinking to avoid the usual suffering for water on this trip, got rather tipsy just before entering the *Jornada,* calculating that, with a canteen full of whisky, they could keep in that state all the way across. Some did so, but others having used their canteens too freely, exhausted their stock the first night, and suffered terribly from thirst.

## [Revenge]

One of our cannon drivers, a young and remarkably inoffensive man, who had been on the sick list for a week previous, had started, with two or three companions, to take a look at the town; but, after proceeding some way, he had found himself too weak to go further, and had separated from his companions to return to camp, when a thorn having entered his foot, he drew off his boot and sat down in the street. He was looking into his boot, when a stone struck him on the forehead, and knocked him down senseless. He supposed that the Mexicans then beat him on the face with stones, and left him for dead. On recovering his senses, he made his way down to camp; and I never saw a more horrible sight than his face presented; his forehead was broken through in two places, and the flesh all cut to pieces, and his lower jaw broken; besides, a fracture just below the eye. His wounds were dressed, and he seemed to be rapidly recovering at the time we left at Saltillo; but I afterwards heard that he died of lockjaw. The sight of our friend's bloody figure at once excited some of the soldiers; and they sallied into the town, and closed most of the shops. Vengeance was sworn and each felt that, after what had happened, it would not require much provocation to produce an outbreak. Nor did it. A short time afterwards, a Mexican sat down on the pole of one of our wagons. The driver, who was sitting near, and who, from having been prisoner among them for some time, spoke Spanish, told him, mildly, to get off as the hounds[20] were broken, and he was injuring the wagon by sitting on that part. The fellow insolently responded: "I shall not—this ground is as much mine as yours." Without another word, the teamster caught up his heavy iron-shod whip, and struck the Mexican on the left temple, fracturing the skull over four inches. He fell, but got up and staggered off. However, he died the same night.

---

20. According to the Oxford English Dictionary, "One of the wooden bars, of which there are two or more, connecting the fore-carriage of a springless wagon . . . with the splinter-bar or shaft; also occasionally applied to supports of the connexion of the perch with the hind-carriage."

## The Conquest of California (1846)

*California was prized by the administrations of Andrew Jackson, John Tyler, and James Polk because of U.S. competition with Great Britain. U.S. political and economic interests were also drawn to California's whaling ports, cowhide industry, and sea otter pelts, which were a precious commodity in Asia. When Lieutenant John Charles Frémont (1813–1890) of the U.S. Corp of Topographical Engineers arrived in California in December 1845 with a small band of armed men, ostensibly for the purpose of scientific exploration, the military commander of the territory, Colonel José Castro (1810–1860), tried to expel them. Anglo-American settlers of the Napa and Sacramento Valleys, who chafed under Mexican rule, feared that Castro meant to expel them as well. In June 1846, they captured Sonoma, took prisoners, and declared an independent republic under a banner that sported a bear, a star, and the phrase "California Republic." With the help of the Bear Flaggers, Colonel Frémont took the San Francisco presidio on June 5. Concurrently, Commodore John Sloat (1781–1867) and his successor Robert Stockton (1795–1866) of the U.S. Pacific Squadron claimed California for the United States. Colonel Stephen Kearny did the same when he and a small force arrived near San Diego in December 1846 after an arduous crossing of the Sierras. Military, guerilla, and popular resistance to U.S. occupation was scattered and ineffectual, lasting until January 1847, when the Mexican commander José María Flores surrendered to Frémont. The first document that follows is a proclamation by William B. Ide, an Anglo-American settler, explaining the causes of the Bear Flag Revolt. The second is Commodore Stockton's message to the people of California justifying U.S. seizure of the region.*

### Proclamation of the Bear Flag Revolt (June 14–15, 1846)[21]

To all persons, citizens of Sonoma, requesting them to remain at peace, and to follow their rightful occupations without fear of molestation.

The Commander in Chief of the Troops assembled at the Fortress of Sonoma, gives his inviolable pledge to all persons in California, not found under arms that they shall not be disturbed in their persons, their property or social relations one to another by men under his command.

---

21. Edwin Bryant, *What I Saw in California: Being a Journal of a Tour, by the emigrant route and South Pass of the Rocky Mountains, across the continent of North America, the Great Desert Basin, and through California. In the Years, 1846–1847* (New York: D. Appleton and Company, 1849), 290–91.

He also solemnly declares his object to be, first, to defend himself and companions in arms who were invited to this country by a promise of lands on which to settle themselves and families; who were also promised a Republican Government, who, when having arrived in California were denied even the privilege of buying or renting lands of their friends; who, instead of being allowed to participate in or being protected by a Republican Government were oppressed by a military despotism; who were even threatened, by proclamation, by the chief officers of the aforesaid despotism, with extermination if they would not depart out of the country, leaving all of their property, arms and beasts of burden, and thus deprived of the means of flight or defence, we were to be driven through deserts, inhabited by hostile Indians to certain destruction.[22]

To overthrow a government which has seized upon the property of the Missions for its individual aggrandizement; which has ruined and shamefully oppressed the laboring people of California, by their enormous exactions on goods imported into this country; is the determined purpose of the brave men who are associated under his command.

I also solemnly declare my object, in the second place, to be to invite all peaceable and good citizens of California who are friendly to the maintenance of good order and equal rights, and I do hereby invite them to repair to my camp at Sonoma without delay, to assist us in establishing and perpetuating a Republican Government, which shall secure to all civil and religious liberty; which shall encourage virtue and literature; which shall leave unshackled by fetters, agriculture, commerce, and manufactures.

I further declare that I rely upon the rectitude of our intentions, the favor of Heaven and the bravery of those who are bound to and associated with me, by the principles of self preservation, by the love of truth, and the hatred of tyranny for my hopes of success.

I furthermore declare that I believe that a government to be prosperous and happy, must originate with the people who are friendly to its existence; that the citizens are its Guardians, its officers are its Servants, and its glory their reward.

(Signed,) William B. Ide.
Headquarters, Sonoma, June 18th, 1846.

---

22. The California-born Colonel José Castro issued a proclamation in April 1846 ordering the expulsion of "all foreigners whose residence in the country was less than one year . . . on pain of death." See Hubert Howe Bancroft, *History of California* (San Francisco: The History Company, Publishers, 1886), vol. 5, 78.

## Commodore Robert Stockton to the People of California (July 29, 1846)

Californians:—The Mexican government and their military officers have, without cause, for a year past, been threatening the United States with hostilities.

They have recently, in pursuance of these threats, commenced hostilities by attacking, with 7000 men, a small detachment of 2000 United States troops, by whom they were signally defeated and routed.[23]

General Castro, the commander-in-chief of the military forces of California, has violated every principle of international law and national hospitality, by hunting and pursuing with several hundred soldiers, and with wicked intent, Captain Frémont, of the United States army, who came here to refresh his men, (about forty in number,) after a perilous journey across the mountains on a scientific survey.[24]

For these repeated hostilities and outrages, military possession was ordered to be taken of Monterey and San Francisco until redress could be obtained from the government of Mexico.

No let or hindrance was given or intended to be given to the civil authority of the territory, or to the exercise of its accustomed functions. The officers were invited to remain, and promised protection in the performance of their duties as magistrates. They refused to do so, and departed, leaving the people in a state of anarchy and confusion.

On assuming the command of the forces of the United States on the coast of California, both by sea and land, I find myself in possession of the ports of Monterey and San Francisco, with daily reports from the interior of scenes of rapine, blood, and murder. Three inoffensive American residents of the country have, within a few days, been murdered in the most brutal manner; and there are no Californian officers who will arrest and bring the murderers to justice, although it is well known who they are and where they are.

I must, therefore, and will, as soon as I can, adopt such measures as may seem best calculated to bring these criminals to justice, and to bestow peace and good order on the country.

In the first place, however, I am constrained by every principle of national honour, as well as a due regard for the safety and best interests of the people of California, to put an end at once, and by force, to the lawless depredations daily committed by General Castro's men upon the persons and property of peaceful and unoffending inhabitants.

---

23. At the Battles of Palo Alto and Resaca de la Palma near the banks of the Rio Grande.

24. Frémont and his men were not in California to rest or to explore; rather they were waiting for an opportunity to participate in its conquest by the United States.

I cannot, therefore, confine my operations to the quiet and undisturbed possession of the defenseless ports of Monterey and San Francisco, while the people elsewhere are suffering from lawless violence, but will immediately march against these boasting and abusing chiefs, who have not only violated every principle of national hospitality and good faith towards Captain Frémont and his surveying party, but who, unless driven out, will, with the aid of the hostile Indians, keep this beautiful country in a constant state of revolution and blood, as well as against all others who may be found in arms, or aiding or abetting General Castro.

The present general of the forces of California is a usurper,[25] has been guilty of great offences, has impoverished and drained the country of almost its last dollar, and has deserted his post now when most needed.

He has deluded and deceived the inhabitants of California and they wish his expulsion from the country.[26] He came into power by rebellion and force, and by force he must be expelled. Mexico appears to have been compelled, from time to time, to abandon California to the mercies of any wicked man who could muster one hundred men-in-arms. The distances from the capital are so great that she cannot, even in times of great distress, send timely aid to the inhabitants; and the lawless depredations upon their persons and property go invariably unpunished. She cannot or will not punish or control the chieftains who, one after the other, have defied her power and kept California in a constant state of revolt and misery.

The inhabitants are tired and disgusted with this constant succession of military usurpers and this insecurity of life and property. Therefore, upon them I will not make war. I require, however, all officers, civil and military, and all other persons, to remain quiet at their respective homes and stations, and to obey the orders they may receive from me, and by my authority; and, if they do no injury or violence to my authority, none will be done to them.

But notice is hereby given, that if any of the inhabitants of the country either abandon their dwellings or do any injury to the arms of the United States, or to any person within this territory, they will be treated as enemies and suffer accordingly.

No person whatever is to be troubled in consequence of any part he may heretofore have taken in the politics of the country, or for having been a subject of General Castro. And all persons who may have belonged to the government of Mexico, but who, from this day, acknowledge the authority of the existing laws, are to be treated in the same manner as other citizens of the United States, provided they are obedient to the law and to the orders they shall receive from me or by my authority.

---

25. Castro was a key player in the overthrow of Governor Manuel Micheltorena in 1845. Castro's role as military commander and his control over the port of Monterey made him the most powerful Mexican officer in California.

26. Stockton in part refers to discontent resulting from political divisions in California between a southern faction based in Los Angeles and a northern faction in Monterey.

Mexican Soldiers. c. 1850 daguerreotype. From the collection of Graham Pilecki.

The commander-in-chief does not desire to possess himself of one foot of California for any other reason than as the only means to save from destruction the lives and property of the foreign residents and the citizens of the territory, who have invoked his protection.

As soon, therefore, as the officers of the civil law return to their proper duties, under a regularly-organized government, and give security for life, liberty, and property, alike to all, the forces under my command will be withdrawn, and the people left to manage their own affairs in their own way.

## A Mexican Officer on the Difficulties of the Mexican Army (July–August 1846)[27]

*The civic militias and regular army that the Mexican armed forces were composed of during the U.S.-Mexican War could not effectively defend Mexico. The army was full of conscripts with little loyalty to the Mexican state. Pay was notoriously poor and military revolts were not uncommon on Mexico's frontier outposts—such as California—where supplies were hard to come by. Another problem was that the army and its officers were at the center of Mexico's unstable national politics in which federalists and centralists wrested power from each other through coup and countercoup. Moreover, Mexican armaments were outdated and less effective than those utilized by the United States. In the selection that follows, Artillery Lieutenant Manuel Balbontín relates the trials and tribulations of the Mexican army in 1846 as it advanced northward to battle the forces of General Zachary Taylor.*

### July 27

Our departure was marked by a bad omen; no sooner had we left behind the streets of the capital than the rain became a huge downpour that soaked us totally.

The road we followed was the one that leads from the Garita de Vallejo[28] to the town of Tlalnepantla. The surface, which is earth, and the construction, which is not very raised, make it extremely muddy; and the downpour had made it impassable. The soldiers walked with great difficulty; it can be asserted that few did not fall in the mud, a circumstance that of course, greatly disrupts progress.

Pulled by mules that were only half-broken, led by green drivers or teamsters, without training or military discipline, the artillery became stuck constantly, and it took great effort to dislodge it.

. . .

The state of drunkenness of the troops and the teamsters was unbearable.

### August 6

When the brigade was ready to march, it received orders to return to barracks.

---

27. Manuel Balbontín, *La invasión americana 1846 á 1848: Apuntes del subteniente de artillería Manuel Balbontín* (Mexico City: Tip. De Gonzalo Esteva, 1883), 12–18. Translated by Gustavo Pellón.

28. *Garita* means "city gate."

A little later the news spread that in Mexico City there had been a coup proclaiming "Federation and Santa Anna" and that General Don Simeón Ramírez[29] had received a communiqué from President Paredes, in which he ordered him to remain in Celaya, where he would join him.[30] The news received caused great alarm in the brigade; the whole day was devoted to huddles and secrets.

**August** 7

In view of what had happened, General Ramírez decided to call a meeting in his quarters with the chiefs and officers of the brigade. When orders were given to that effect, most of those named came to the appointment.

The general took the floor, briefly describing the worrisome circumstance to which the government in Mexico City was reduced. He said that he thought it advisable for the brigade to continue its march in order to join up with the ones ahead, so that forming a large body of troops, it could attack the revolution or obey the will of the nation if it declared itself in favor of the Plan de la Ciudadela. That proposition was rejected by the majority of the chiefs and officers, who sympathized with the revolution, and they asked the general to keep the brigade in Celaya to await further developments.

The general insisted and even begged that we continue the march to Guadalajara. Most of the chiefs and officers rejected this proposition, the opinion becoming more and more split as to what side we should take.

An officer declared that he thought the brigade should remain aloof from any revolutionary movement, marching, without wasting time, to the border to defend the republic.

As this idea was apparently accepted with enthusiasm, they began to write a statement to that purpose to be sent to Mexico City.

As this happened, several chiefs and officers gathered in groups and began to ponder the suffering and misery that awaited the army on the border and the fruitlessness of their sacrifice.

Those speeches had such an effect that when it came to signing the statement, few wanted to sign.

Annoyed, the general ordered that everyone's vote be registered in order to find out where the majority stood.

---

29. The commanding officer of the brigade to which Balbontín belonged was General Simeón Ramírez, who later fought U.S. forces as a colonel under the command of General Ampudia at the Battle of Monterrey and under Santa Anna at the Battle of Molino del Rey.

30. On August 4, 1846, in Mexico City, General Mariano Salas rose up against the Paredes regime, toppling it two days later. This revolt of the "*Ciudadela*" (Citadel) resulted in the reinstatement of the federalist constitution of 1824 and the return of Santa Anna to Mexico from exile on August 16.

This was done; but before the voting was concluded, Don Andrés Zenteno, who had just come from Querétaro, arrived at the meeting. He came with proclamations and communiqués and brought news that the city had rebelled and therefore invited the general and the brigade to join the uprising.

This new incident caused such chaos in the meeting that it became necessary to adjourn.

**August 8**

The appearance of Zenteno in Celaya made an impact. The municipal government joined the uprising and the Third Light Regiment sided with them that night.

Thus we have half the brigade siding with the uprising and the other half declaring its allegiance to the government. Nevertheless, we lived as good comrades, the Third Light obeying the general; but such a situation could produce disastrous results at any given moment.

**August 9**

We had news about the fall of General Paredes.

We marched from Celaya to Apaseo, on the orders of the new government.

D. N. Solares, second lieutenant of the ambulance corps, deserted. Later it was said that when he reported for duty in Mexico City he was promoted.

## Doña María de Jesús Dosamantes at Monterrey (September 19, 1846)[31]

*A significant portion of the Mexican army was composed of poor conscripts who were accompanied by their wives or female companions on long marches and even in battle. Such women are known in Mexican history as* soldaderas *(soldier-women), and they became nationalist and populist symbols after the Mexican Revolution of 1910. In December 1846, the* Niles Register *republished a first-person account from the* Louisville Journal *about a Mexican woman who was shot carrying food and water to U.S. and Mexican wounded alike. This anecdote provided the inspiration for John Greenleaf Whittier's poem, "The Angels of Buena Vista" and sustained romantic representations of self-sacrificing Mexican women as victims of war and idealized love objects in U.S. popular literature.*[32] *A few examples of*

---

31. "Bello Rasgo de Patriotismo," *El Republicano,* September 27, 1846, 3. Translated by Gustavo Pellón.

32. For more on this motif in U.S. literature about the war, see Whittier's poem in Part VI and this volume's title support page, which contains the poem "The Heroine Martyr of Monterey" by R. J. Lyons.

*upper-class Mexican women risking their lives to fight against the United States have passed into Mexican nationalist mythology and memory. Two young women in particular, María Josefa Zozaya and María de Jesús Dosamantes, about whom little is known, took an active role in the Battle of Monterrey. In the selection that follows, we include two contemporaneous accounts of how María de Jesús Dosamantes volunteered, dressed in a man's military uniform, to aid in the defense of the city of Monterrey. The city fell to General Zachary Taylor on September 25, 1846, after four days of intense fighting and the bombardment of the city.*

Ministry of War and Navy.—Army of the North.—General-in-Chief.—No. 89.—Dear Sir—The young lady Doña Jesús Dosamantes reported to me dressed as a captain and mounted to fight against the unjust invaders. I received her with the show of affection that her heroic behavior deserves and ordered her to ride the whole line so that all the corps that make up this army would see her, and furthermore I wrote her an order so that all would show the respect due to her.

Just now, I have received a note from Colonel Don José López Uraga, to whom I have entrusted the command of the citadel, which I enclose for Your Excellency for the approval of His Excellency the President.

God and liberty. General Headquarters in Monterrey, September 19, 1846—Pedro Ampudia.—to His Excellency the Minister of War.

Army of the North.—Third Brigade.—Dear Sir—Señorita Doña Jesús Dosamantes presented herself with a safe conduct from Your Excellency, expressing her desire to enter the ranks of the valiant men who are going to fight against the infamous usurpers. This event, rare in the annals of history, moved me to joy and enthusiasm, as it did all who are under my orders. I gave the relevant orders so that all the troops would know the intrepid heroine and accord her all the deference due to her sex and that such a patriotic conduct justly deserves. And although I explained to Señorita Dosamantes the privations and dangers to which she would expose herself in this citadel, seeing as another post might be better for her, she has refused to change her mind, because she wants to be where the enemy bullets will whistle first and where there will be more glory, even if greater risk.

I am grateful that this delicate señorita has chosen the position that has been entrusted to me, and I would not want an action as praiseworthy as that which occupies us to be buried in oblivion; with this object I make it known to Your Excellency, taking pleasure in relating an event that does so much honor to our dear country and that may have such an influence on the morale and enthusiasm of our valiant soldiers.

God and liberty. Fortín de la Independencia, Monterrey, September 19, 1846.—José L. Uraga.—to the General-in-Chief of the Army of the North.

## The Horrors of War at Buena Vista (February 22–23, 1847)[33]

*The Battle of Buena Vista (February 22–23, 1847), known in Mexican history as the Battle of Angostura, was the fourth major battle of the U.S.-Mexican War after Palo Alto, Resaca de la Palma, and Monterrey. It took place near the Hacienda of Buena Vista, south of the town of Saltillo in the Sierra Madre Oriental mountains of Mexico. In the battle, General Taylor's force of fewer than five thousand men defeated a Mexican force three times its size led by Santa Anna. U.S. casualties included hundreds of dead, and Santa Anna lost thousands. The following first-person account narrates the horrors of war at Buena Vista.*

We formed a line in front of three regiments of Mexico's oldest soldiers. It was an awful moment to face the thousands of veterans in solid column, with their gaudy uniforms and showy banners. But we had no time for admiration; for, before our line was formed, they had fired two rounds, which we soon returned in right good earnest. I was at my post in the rank of file closers, and was urging the men to form in their proper places, when Captain Sanderson cried out, "Never mind, Frank, fire away!" which I did, with all possible haste. About this time the battery on our left opened upon us a deadly fire of grape,[34] which raked our flank with terrible effect; still we stood front to front, and poured our fire upon the infantry, which did us but little injury, as they shot too high. But the battery on our left galled us exceedingly. It appeared as if we had purposely halted in their exact range, and the whole atmosphere resounded with the whizzing shot that came with increasing precision. Apollos Stephens was the first of the Grays[35] to fall. He received a grapeshot in the head, and fell back almost in my arms. O, how shall I describe the horror of my feelings? There lay quivering in death one of my comrades, with his eyes upturned, and the tears starting from them. It was a sad and touching scene—one that will never be effaced from my memory.

## Accounts of the Siege of Veracruz (March 22–March 26, 1847)

*The first large-scale amphibious assault by the U.S. military began on March 9, 1847, when more than ten thousand U.S. fighters commanded by General Winfield Scott (1786–1866) landed near Veracruz to begin the Mexico City campaign. Scott bombarded Veracruz for five days (March 22–March 26), destroying much*

---

33. *Camp Life of a Volunteer. A Campaign in Mexico, or a Glimpse at Life in Camp by "One Who Has Seen the Elephant"* (Philadelphia: Grigg, Elliot and Co., 1847), 60.

34. Grapeshot were very large bullets fired simultaneously from cannon.

35. Soldiers in the state volunteer corps often wore gray uniforms and were known as "Grays."

*of the city and demanding nothing less than the total surrender of the Mexican garrison defending it. Even for U.S. observers, the large civilian casualties that resulted from the indiscriminate bombing of Veracruz was one of the least heroic episodes of the war, especially because Scott had turned down a petition to allow noncombatants to leave the city during the siege. As accounts of the bombardment and fall of Veracruz filtered into Mexico City, Mexicans became outraged by Scott's actions. After the city's capitulation on March 28, Scott's army traveled the National Road toward the capital, defeating Mexican resistance at Cerro Gordo (April 18, 1847) near the city of Jalapa. In the selections that follow, we offer the observations of a U.S. soldier who participated in the siege, a first-person narrative by a foreign national residing in the city whose harrowing account was reprinted in one of Mexico City's most important newspapers, and Santa Anna's call for Mexicans to rise up to avenge Veracruz.*

## J. Jacob Oswandel of Co. C. First Regiment, Pennsylvania Volunteers (1885)[36]

### Monday, March 22, 1847

Gen. Worth has now got the range of his guns on the enemy and has commenced firing in earnest, and I tell you the way he is sending those nasty balls into the city is not slow. The thundering and roaring of the heavy cannons now tells us that the war has fairly commenced.

The Mexicans have now opened three batteries from the city on Gen. Worth's breastworks. The Castle[37] is assisting the city forts besides, and does everything in her power to protect the city from being destroyed by the Yankee. Oh! I tell you the bomb-shells and round shot[38] are flying like hail-stones into the city of the True Cross. Think of it, eighty-five bomb-shells were thrown into the city the first two hours, and over one hundred bomb-shells the next two hours. Everything is darkened from the clouds of smoke, and the city looks like Pittsburgh on a rainy day, all black with gunpowder smoke.

### Tuesday, March 23, 1847

Last night after 12 o'clock the Plaza de Toros bull pit was set on fire from our shells, which illuminated the whole city, and caused great excitement among the citizens.

---

36. J. Jacob Oswandel, *Notes on the Mexican War 1846–47–48* (Philadelphia, 1885), 85–94.

37. The Castle of San Juan Ulúa is a fortress on an island in the port of Veracruz.

38. Solid projectiles.

After a short pause this morning the Mexicans again opened their batteries on Gen. Worth's division and his battery, and of course Gen. Worth answered them bravely with his mortars.[39]

. . .

At noon while we were dragging up the cannons a sailor and one of the Tennessee Volunteers had a falling out, and it resulted in the sailor getting killed. He was shot dead by the Tennessean; rum was the whole cause of this sad affair, but it raised a great deal of ill-feeling between the tars[40] and the Tennesseans. There was also one man killed to-day by the bursting of one of the Mexican shells.

### Thursday, March 25, 1847

This morning all of our batteries were in full operation, they opened with terrible effect upon the city, and in fact we could sometimes hear our shells fall in the city and make a tremendous crash. Some of the fine buildings as well as the domes and steeples of churches were on fire and falling to the ground. The way things look now the city must either surrender or be burnt to the earth.

. . .

To-night I was put on picket-guard, stationed near the walls of the doomed city, and I could plainly hear the people cry out for to *rendiren tregar de cindad* (surrender the city)[41] before they were all killed off. That these Yankees won't give up firing. Also could hear the bells ringing and trumpets sounding to arms, to arms. It was really laughable to hear the Mexicans talk, and I heard enough to convince me that the city cannot hold out much longer, that something must be done soon or else the citizens would rebel against the government of Vera Cruz.

Our batteries to-night are throwing rocket after rocket into the city, which illuminated the sky as well as the whole city, and made it a most beautiful scene.

## Account by a Foreigner Residing in Veracruz (April 4, 1847)[42]

My dear friend: Today it is eight days since I wrote you a letter, the one Señor N. took to Medellín,[43] from where it must have gone out to Jalapa, and the object

39. Stubby cannon that fired at a higher angle than other guns.

40. Seamen.

41. Oswandel's vocabulary, spelling, and verbs in Spanish are incorrect. The phrase actually used may have been "*rindan la ciudad*" and/or "*entreguen la ciudad.*"

42. "Carta particular de un apreciable estranjero que con imparcialidad describe detalladamente todos los desastrosos acontecimientos," *El Monitor Republicano,* April 4, 1847, 2. Translated by Gustavo Pellón.

43. Village near Veracruz.

of the present letter is to inform you of everything that has happened since that date. On the twenty-second (Monday) at two-thirty in the afternoon, an officer of the enemy troops came before the walls of this city and asked General Morales[44] to surrender the city and said that if he refused to do so he would open fire. Sure enough, two hours later, that is to say at four thirty, without the least warning to the citizens, several bombs suddenly exploded over the city, destroying a great number of houses, among them that of Doña Ignacia Corral de Linares, which caught fire; only the walls were left standing. Since there are no working pumps or firemen in this city, it was impossible to save it; and although the people in N's house and we came immediately to do what we could do, we weren't able to do anything except to keep the flames from spreading to the neighboring houses. Toward dawn, the furor of the bombing slackened a bit; but when the city did not surrender at dawn, the projectiles began to fly again with a steadily increasing force. A strong storm from the north threatened to destroy what the bombs had not; and the flames of the house I mentioned placed that neighborhood in great confusion and danger; but thank God the engineers managed to put it out during the night. The longer the bombing lasted, the more destructive the bombs became as new batteries opened fire continuously. On the twenty-fourth the bombing was more atrocious than ever, and a fourteen-inch bomb entered our house and caused much damage. It burst exactly on the beams above the laths under which our friends A and T were lying; I was in the courtyard and the rest in the cellar, but no one was harmed; we all attended immediately to the fire that had started on the boards and grilles, but soon it was extinguished. Besides this, various other grenades and solid shot paid a visit to our house, leaving it in a rather sorry state. . . . All the bombardments that you have witnessed in this city are child's play in comparison to this one,[45] as you may infer from the fact that about four thousand bombs have fallen on a city that doesn't have more than 1,200 houses. The bombardment has been so destructive that Veracruz, at present, is no more than a pile of ruins, since the houses whose façades are still standing have suffered so much inside that few if any are inhabitable, and I can say without fear of contradiction that there is no house that has not suffered considerably. More than eight projectiles have fallen on some and in our block there is not a single one that has not received three or four. It would be futile to try to give you a description of the misfortunes of this unhappy population, its misery, and the barbarous manner in which the Americans have bombarded us, for which there isn't a single precedent in modern history.

---

44. On March 25, General Juan Morales (1802–1848) was replaced by General Juan Landero (1802–1869) as military commander of the Mexican forces defending Veracruz. On that same day, Landero surrendered the city to Scott.

45. Veracruz and the Castle of San Juan Ulúa had been bombarded previously during the war for independence and in a short-lived conflict with France in 1838.

Cowardly, they did not dare to expose themselves to the cannon fire of Ulúa nor the risks of an assault, while they completely destroyed an almost defenseless city in cold blood, and it seems that they purposely fired on San Agustín, where the powder magazine was, and on the hospitals where the wounded were all killed by the bombs while the doctors were treating them. To describe it is absolutely impossible, and the people who witnessed these scenes will remember, as long as they live, Scott's perfidy, baseness, and cruelty, which know no limits and fills every man with anger and horror. . . . The cannon fire lasted from four-thirty in the afternoon of the twenty-second until five in the morning of the twenty-sixth, with an interruption of only six hours, that is to say, eighty hours of massive fire, which almost seems incredible. That the general in charge of the city finally entered into negotiations with the enemy is due neither to the valor of the Americans nor the weakness of the Mexicans, but to his feelings of humanity, because he surrendered the city and castle when he saw that the resistance of either would cause the loss of both, and the ungenerous conduct of a general [Scott] who refused to let women and children leave the city. . . .

## Santa Anna Calls for Mexico to Fight to the Death (March 31, 1847)[46]

Mexicans! *Veracruz is already in the hands of the enemy.* It has succumbed, not under the weight of American valor, nor even under the influence of their good fortune. . . . We, ourselves, shameful as it may be to say it, *through our interminable discord, have brought this most disastrous misfortune upon ourselves.*

The government owes us the whole truth; you are the arbiters of our country's fate: if it is to be defended, you are the ones who must stop the victorious march of the enemy who occupies Veracruz; if they advance one more step, our national independence will sink into the abyss of the past; I am determined to meet the enemy. What is life ennobled by national gratitude if the fatherland suffers an affront whose stain will be on the forehead of every Mexican? My duty is to sacrifice myself and I will know how to do it. Perchance the American forces shall walk proudly through the capital of the Aztec empire. . . . I shall not witness such an injury, because I have decided to first die fighting.

The supreme moment has come for the Mexican Republic. It is as glorious to die fighting as it is infamous to declare yourself beaten without fighting and beaten by an enemy whose rapacity is as far from courage as it is from generosity.

Mexicans! Do you have a religion? Protect it. Do you have honor? Rid yourselves of infamy. Do you love your wives, your daughters? Free them from American brutality. But it is deeds, not vain pleas nor sterile wishes that must

---

46. Carlos María de Bustamante, *El nuevo bernal díaz del castillo* (Mexico City: Imprenta de Vicente García Torres, 1847), 154–56. Translated by Gustavo Pellón.

oppose the enemy. The national cause is infinitely just. Why does God seem to have abandoned it? His wrath will be placated if we offer as expiation for our crimes the feelings of sincere union and true patriotism. Then the Eternal will bless our efforts and we shall be impregnable because against the determination of eight million Mexicans, what are eight or ten thousand Americans worth when they are no longer the instrument of Divine Justice? Perhaps I am speaking to you for the last time, by God, believe me. Don't hesitate between death and slavery; and if the enemy conquers you, at least let him respect the heroism of your defense. It is time to stop thinking about anything except our common defense; the hour of sacrifices has tolled. . . . Awaken. . . . A tomb is gaping at your feet! At least conquer some laurel to place on it.

The nation is not dying yet; I swear it, I will still answer for Mexico's triumph if a unanimous and sincere effort seconds my wishes. A thousand times blessed the disaster of Veracruz if the burning of that city fills Mexican breasts with enthusiasm, dignity, and the generous ardor of true patriotism. The motherland shall indubitably be saved. But if she succumbs, she will bequeath her affront and injury to the egotists who did not want to defend her to the traitors who pursued their private combats, trampling the national flag. Mexicans! You hold the fate of your motherland. You, not the Americans, shall decide it: Veracruz cries out for vengeance; follow me to cleanse her dishonor.—Mexico City, March 31, 1847.—Antonio López de Santa Anna.

## Mexican Views of the Battle of Cerro Gordo (April 17–18, 1847)

*The two selections provided below speak to what combat was like on the Mexican side. Both narratives are set against the Battle of Cerro Gordo, which took place on April 18, 1847, when General Santa Anna tried to block General Scott's advance on Jalapa from Veracruz. The first selection is the first-person narrative of Pedro Vander Linden (1804–1860), the chief medical officer of the Mexican army. The Belgian-born Vander Linden's experience with military medicine began in the Dutch-Belgian War (1830–1832), and his service to the Mexican military began in 1837. When war with the United States broke out, he was Mexico's highest ranking and most respected military physician. Vander Linden's account of his capture at the Battle of Cerro Gordo, in the middle of an amputation surgery, was well known in its time and led to its re-creation in an early Mexican daguerreotype in 1847. The second selection is a personal account by a nameless Mexican officer who narrates Santa Anna's harrowing and dangerous retreat from Cerro Gordo.*

## Battlefield Medicine: Pedro Vander Linden's Report (April 19, 1847)[47]

As the enemy was advancing, circling Cerro Gordo, few of the wounded could reach my field hospital, and besides as two Congreve rockets[48] fell, one near my tent and the other, without bursting, in the artillery park, which was a pistol shot's distance away, I made up my mind, in order to avoid this danger and to be closer to the rearguard of our forces, to transport my field hospital farther up the national road, a distance of three rifle shots, to a reed hut, facing the commissariat, where at once several wounded soldiers came, and among others Artillery Sergeant Antonio Bustos, who had his left foot taken off by a four-pound cannon ball. All our cavalry was spread out along the national road: Sr. Ortega's infantry brigade was coming straight down at a quick pace, which made it difficult to get to the hut with my medical kit. Sr. Domínguez, who came with that force, presented himself, and I retained him to help me with Sergeant Busto's amputation. We laid out everything necessary for the amputation in the corridor of the house, as Señores Tarbe and Verde[49] held the patient, Domínguez and Rivadeneira[50] helping me with everything else. I began to cut the patient's flesh, when a rain of bullets, coming from the woods behind the little house and through its weak walls, made all our cavalry withdraw in the direction of Corral-Falso. A woman and an old man were wounded and a seven-year-old child in the kitchen of the house. The bullets continued in every direction, the soldiers of our cavalry continued their descent with impunity, and the presence of our horses tied to the columns of the corridor attracted the attention of the enemy and their bullets; but honor did not allow us to abandon the half-amputated sergeant, although our deaths seemed inevitable; nevertheless we were saved by Divine Providence. I continued to execute the different steps in my amputation in the midst of the bullets and the shouts of the enemy, and at last that operation, which to me had seemed to last a century, was over. The serenity and resignation of my comrades in this predicament was admirable and indescribable. . . . All remained around the wounded man, accomplishing the part of the operation that fell to them, amid the whistling of the bullets and the cries of death; and when we all raised our eyes to Heaven in thanksgiving, thinking we were saved, a new danger came

47. Pedro Vander Linden, "Interior. Distrito federal. Cuerpo Médico-Militar" [Letter from Vander Linden to D. Luis Carrion, inspector general of the medical corps], *El Republicano,* May 8, 1847, 2–3. Translated by Gustavo Pellón.

48. A type of exploding rocket invented by William Congreve (1772–1828) in 1806 and used in the first half of the nineteenth century.

49. Don Rafael Tarbe and Don Abundio Verde were medics who belonged to the First Medical Division (*La Ambulancia Principal*) under Vander Linden's command.

50. Don Ignacio Rivadeneira belonged to the Fourth Medical Division (*Cuarta Ambulancia*).

to terrify us. A few volunteers appeared in front of the corridor, and seeing our uniforms, shouted: "Death to the Mexican officers!" pointing their muskets at our breasts. I don't know what emotion influenced my decision to run before their rifles, showing them my hands still dripping with blood, and a piece of the mutilated leg, shouting: "Respect humanity, or a field hospital; we are surgeons!" My words were magical. At once an officer, whose name (as I later learned) was Captain Pion,[51] came between them and us and raised their muskets with his sword, and those men excited by victory, and made furious with a thirst for vengeance because their general had been mortally wounded, as I later learned, became from that moment our friends, our protectors! As this was happening in my unforgettable hut, our side had ceased firing, the troops in the redoubts, seeing themselves cut off by the national road, surrendered or capitulated; those in the skirts of Cerro Gordo withdrew through the ravine, and the enemy was left in possession of all our positions and a great deal of materiel. . . . The enemy volunteers began to bring to me, without distinction, their wounded and ours, and we treated them as humanity and our regulations require. We performed several amputations on some veritable athletes, and this won them over to the degree that they refused us nothing that was of use to our wounded and the performance of our duties.

Despite the fact that two of their surgeons had come, the corps I have the honor to command has the satisfaction that a doctor was chosen from our number to attend to several grave cases among their wounded, and even that of General Cheild,[52] who was pierced by grapeshot. . . .

## Letter by a Mexican Officer (April 23, 1847)[53]

Orizaba, April 23, 1847.—Dear Friend: As you will have seen from the official reports and some letters, on the 17th we were attacked by the Americans at our weakest point, Cerro Gordo. This hill lay to our left flank, behind the battery that defended the road, and all our positions on the right, the only side that was fortified and where they did not attempt any attack. Given the lack of time and workers, it was not possible to fortify this hill, the key to our position, nor cut down the forest that surrounds it and extends along the left slope and that favored so much the enemy's advance. Nevertheless, that day the enemy was totally repulsed, because after the firing started, which was around noon,

---

51. According to an article in the *New Orleans Medical and Surgical Journal* of 1847–1848, the captain in question was Captain Isaac Pugh of Company C Fourth Illinois Volunteers of Decatur, Illinois.

52. The correct name is Shields.

53. "Cerro-Gordo," *Boletín de Noticias,* May 1, 1847, 1–2. Translated by Gustavo Pellón.

General Santa Anna and all of us climbed to the summit, and our hurrahs and the presence of the general in the greatest danger, encouraged our troops, who fought with the greatest spirit until they silenced the enemy's fire and repulsed them completely.

It must have been around six the next day when the Americans opened fire again on the same hill, but without attempting an assault, and using only their artillery, hurling their usual projectiles, setting the woods on fire, and intimidating our poor Indians with their Congreve rockets, bar shots, etc., which make a lot of noise, although without much actual effect on the field. After two hours of this method, they launched an attack on all sides at the same time. The general's attention being thus distracted, he was not able, as on the previous day, to encourage the soldiers frequently, who furthermore unnerved by the death of General Vázquez,[54] who commanded that position,[55] abandoned it, leaving it in the hands of the Yankees, who substituted their infamous flag for ours. At the same time, a strong column gained possession of the road to our rear, repulsing the cavalry that was covering it, and we were enveloped completely. Then all was chaos, sword in hand we attempted vainly to regroup the scattered soldiers and make our way through the road to save the general. Instead of obeying, the soldiers rushed into the ravine that closed our right flank, and as the enemy encountered no resistance, we were quickly surrounded on all sides. No end of bullets made a not very pleasant music in our ears, as all were aimed at the general, on whose carriage they poured their fire, turning it into a sieve. Seeing that there was no choice, the general said: "There is nothing to be done, let us go," and we headed for a part of the ravine where the soldiers were escaping, almost breaking up with our swords the lines of Yankees who had stopped to murder the general's servants and whoever they could. No sooner had we reached the bottom than a shower of bullets fell all around us, carpeting our way with the bodies of dead and wounded men. They had taken the side of the ravine and were firing on us. But in the end, we escaped. Out of twenty-five of us who made up the president's general staff, we were the only ones who stayed by his side: General Argüelles, Romero, Vega, the brave and gentlemanly Feliz Galindo, and Pancho Schiafino, whose conduct during the two days was brilliant, for he encouraged the soldiers by his example and words. The rest, without exception, quickly got out of harm's way, forgetting their duty in order to save their soiled lives. Among his old aides, only Escobar was faithful to him, because after distinguishing himself in the danger experienced, the general honored him with the commission of saving his family, which he did immediately, departing for Jalapa.

Having escaped and now in a safer place, the general ordered Señor Ampudia to collect whatever infantry he could while he caught up to the cavalry. With

---

54. Ciriaco Vázquez (1797–1847).

55. Known in accounts of the Battle of Cerro Gordo as Telegraph Hill.

this object we headed for El Encero,[56] accompanied by the valiant General Don Francisco Pérez, the Honorable Don Ángel Trías, governor of Chihuahua, and Señores Urquidi and Armendariz, who were with us throughout the battle. When we learned that the cavalry was still in flight, now past Jalapa, and that a detachment of the enemy cavalry, which we actually saw, was pursuing it, nipping at its rearguard, we then changed course and headed to El Chico and from there to Orizaba.

The bad condition of the road and the fact that general did not have enough time to get his leg[57] made our journey extremely difficult. We finally reached the hacienda Tuzamapa, where we had thought to spend the night, but its owners fearing that they would be compromised pretended they had gotten a message from a nearby town, saying that a party of Americans was headed for the hacienda to capture the general. Although we knew this to be false, because it made clear how little they wanted to lodge us, we had to continue on our way and spend the rest of the night in the ruins of a mill a short distance from there, in whose courtyard we spread our capes and the general lay down. At dawn we continued our journey and reached a little town, I don't know what it's called; fortunately by now the general had his leg, because a servant caught up to us in a place called Las Juntas, where we stopped for a while because we had to cross a deep river and there was nothing but a raft that could take only one person and the steersman at a time.

The next day we slept in Huatusco, where I wrote you; this town, like all the towns in the Sierra, is very beautiful, and some other time I will describe it to you. Lastly, we reached Orizaba, where the general intends to reorganize the army and form guerrillas that will impede the enemy's communication with Veracruz; to this effect he has published an edict for all males between the ages of sixteen and forty, without exception, to take arms.

A wounded sergeant may come looking for you; I saved his life by giving him my horse so that he could cross the ravine, which I did on foot. The poor wretch's leg had been pierced through and the Yankees would have murdered him. When he returned my horse, he asked where my house was and I gave him my card; if he does come, help him.—Yours.

56. El Encero was one of Santa Anna's three country homes.

57. In 1838, Santa Anna revived his political fortune by successfully defending Veracruz against the French. On December 5, Santa Anna was seriously wounded by cannon fire, resulting in the amputation of his left leg below the knee. Santa Anna subsequently wore a prosthetic.

## Oath of Allegiance of the *La Insurgente Guadalupana Guerrilla* Fighters (April 23, 1847)[58]

*The word "guerrilla" is a diminutive form of* guerra, *meaning "war" in Spanish. The "little war" is a military strategy predicated on small bands of partisans who carry out hit-and-run attacks on larger, more traditional national or invading armies. After the defeat of Mexican arms at Buena Vista and Cerro Gordo, Santa Anna actively promoted the creation of guerrilla bands to harass the U.S. Army and disrupt its supply lines. The following document illustrates how guerrillas were advertised and organized in this period. The name of this guerrilla band refers to Mexico's most sacred national symbol, the Virgin of Guadalupe, who miraculously appeared to the Indian peasant Juan Diego in the sixteenth century. The band's leader, Miguel Orbe, is a village priest from the village of Huachinango. Throughout the nineteenth century, it was not uncommon for Mexican and Spanish priests to be guerrilla leaders. For example, Miguel Hidalgo y Costilla and Jose María Morelos y Pavón, two warrior priests, were central figures in Mexican independence. The most famous of all priest warriors of the U.S.-Mexican War was Padre Celestino Domeco de Jarauta (1814–1848).*

Huachinango, April 23.
The undersigned promises the following five articles:

1st To die defending and avenging our Lady of Guadalupe and the Catholic, apostolic, Roman religion he professes.
2nd To defend the integrity and independence of his nation.
3rd To pursue unto death Anglo-Americans, their followers, defenders, or allies, whoever they may be.
4th To abjure and detest any personal gain from all who have destroyed his country.
5th To respect all legitimate authorities, whoever they may be, in everything that does not conflict with the preceding articles.

These five articles shall be the fundamental regulations of your guerrilla that will be called *LA INSURGENTE GUADALUPANA*.—Miguel Orbe.

58. "Guerillas," *Boletín de Noticias,* April 25, 1847, 2. Translated by Gustavo Pellón.

# A Mexican Account of the U.S. Occupation of Jalapa (April 1847)[59]

*The following is an excerpt from José María Roa Bárcena's famous history and memoir of the U.S.-Mexican War,* Memories of the North American Invasion 1846–1848 by a Young Man of Those Times *(1883). Roa Bárcena (1827–1908) belonged to an affluent merchant family of Jalapa, which was near the site of the Battle of Cerro Gordo on the National Road to Mexico City from Veracruz. Roa Bárcena is one of the most important conservative writers in nineteenth-century Mexican literary and intellectual history. The prolific Roa Bárcena authored books of poetry, historical and geographical textbooks, short stories, and, later in life, translations of Virgil and Horace. In his memoir of the U.S. invasion of Mexico, he concludes that Mexico's racial inferiority, its weak social and political organizations, conscripted soldiers, poor armaments, and Mexican liberalism all contributed to the country's military defeat.*

There were widows and orphans who wept, the tongue of Prescott, of Daniel Webster, and Washington Irving,[60] lacked elegance and sonorousness in the mouths of our masters. The breezes in those gardens seemed to carry the plaints of a bloodied and sullied motherland. In the vicinity of hospitals the strident and almost continuous sound of the saws, the screams of the amputees, who were then not given chloroform,[61] and the sight of the bundles of legs and arms carried out to be cremated or buried, terrified the citizens. To lend some variety to their emotions, the citizens had the spectacle of funeral processions, where behind a simple pine coffin painted black and borne on shoulders, silent and downcast officers and soldiers marched to the tune of a symphony of wooden flutes—the saddest thing I have heard. . . .

Greater solace was undoubtedly offered by the motley mass of [U.S.] volunteers who vied with each other in the outlandishness of their garb. Many used the native palm sombreros in its multiple forms. On horseback or afoot they went in and out of the city, or walked through the streets congregating and lying down in benches wherever they felt tired; smoking their pipes or chewing Virginia tobacco; eating bread with tallow candles instead of butter, and eating pineapples

---

59. José María Roa Bárcena, *Recuerdos de la invasión norteamericana 1846–1848 por un joven de Entonces, V. II.* (Mexico City: Librería Madrileña de Juan Buxó y Ca., 1886), 92–95. Translated by Gustavo Pellón.

60. William Hickling Prescott (1796–1859) was the author of the widely read nineteenth-century classic *History of the Conquest of Mexico* (1843). Daniel Webster (1782–1852) was President John Tyler's Secretary of State and senator for Massachusetts during the U.S.-Mexican War. Washington Irving (1783–1859) was the celebrated author of the stories "The Legend of Sleepy Hollow" and "Rip Van Winkle."

61. Chloroform, an early anesthetic, was first used in 1847 in Edinburgh.

Col. Hamtramck, Virginia Volunteers. c. 1847 daguerreotype, artist unknown. Collection of Amon Carter Museum, Fort Worth, Texas.

and prickly pears, peels and all. They immediately became fond of the native foods and fruit, and to buy them they would sell the flour and bacon that the army distributed to them, but the greatest fondness they developed was decidedly for sugarcane liquor. Their abuse of it was undeterred by the restrictions and very high duties placed on its sale. A few sips of this liquid were enough to make them lose their minds, falling into fits of fury or weepy sentimentalism, and exposing them to losing their weapons and lives, because some of the lower element of the town did not scruple to take them one by one to the outskirts or the countryside and kill them there. . . .

Apart from this vice, in which we native sons had not yet advanced, there was nothing irregular in the conduct of the invaders. They abstained from bothering citizens, behaved appropriately in churches,[62] gave alms to beggars, and got along with the fruit and trinket vendors. As the last tried to make themselves understood and the former attempted to learn and speak the language of the country, a dialect arose whose vocabulary and idioms, if they were written down and collected, would make a most interesting book for philologists. The most striking thing about these people was their respect for women, which is traditional among the nations of their race. With the exception of some isolated cases of abduction, immediately and severely punished, the invaders could not be criticized for anything along these lines, and it can be said that prostitution was not in vogue among them. Desirous of female company and unable to visit any but a few private homes, they improvised parties attended only by women of licentious life, who, however, were treated and wooed according to the dictates of the most exquisite courtesy, which the young men of my day thought was hilarious.

## U.S. and Mexican Accounts of the Execution of the San Patricios (September 10–13, 1847)

*Mexico's Saint Patrick's Battalion, known as the* San Patricios *in Spanish, was composed of more than two hundred U.S. deserters who fought against the United States at many of the principal battles of the U.S.-Mexican War, such as Buena Vista (February 22–23, 1847), Cerro Gordo (April 18, 1847), and Churubusco (August 20, 1847). Many of the* San Patricios *were Irish, but there were also a number of English, German, and U.S. nationals among them. The leader and founder of the* San Patricios *was John Riley, an Irishman who had served in the British army before deserting and fleeing to the United States, where he enlisted in the army. Before the outbreak of the war in 1846, while stationed on the*

62. Footnote by José María Roa Bárcena: "At the beginning some of the volunteers entered with their caps on and smoking their pipes, but the ecclesiastical authorities complained, and these abuses ceased immediately. Apart from the Irish, there were few Catholics. Many Protestant soldiers carried their Bibles."

*Rio Grande, Riley deserted to Matamoros. Mexican generals such as Pedro de Ampudia, and later Santa Anna himself, actively encouraged the desertion of U.S. soldiers, promising protection and land in exchange for their service to Mexico. The* San Patricios *fought under a green banner that contained the symbols of Saint Patrick and a Mexican coat of arms and the mottoes "Liberty for the Mexican Republic" and "Erin go Bragh" (Ireland Forever). After the Battle of Churubusco, seventy-two* San Patricios *were captured and tried for treason by the U.S. military. Of the seventy who were convicted, fifty were executed by hanging in the villages of San Angel (September 10) and Mixcoac (September 13). General Scott pardoned five men and commuted the death sentence of fifteen others, including Riley, who were branded with the letter "D" (for deserter) on their faces. These men also received prison sentences and fifty lashes on their bare backs. At the end of the war, these* San Patricios *were released and rejoined the Mexican army, forming part of a newly constituted San Patricio Battalion in the summer of 1848. The* San Patricios *continue to be honored in Mexico as national heroes.*

## Account by Colonel George T. M. Davis, Captain and Aide-de-Camp of General Winfield Scott (1891)[63]

After their surrender to General Twiggs[64] a military commission was organized under a general order issued by General Scott for their trial as "deserters from the United States Army" in time of war, the penalty for which, under the "Articles of War," was death. The whole forty-two were tried, convicted and sentenced to be hung, subject, of course, to the approval of the general-in-chief; and the record of their conviction was transmitted to him for his approval, modification or rejection. The general held this under advisement several days, giving to the case of each of the condemned a rigid and impartial consideration. When his order was promulgated, carrying into effect the findings of the military commission, he had in part modified the findings as follows: 27 were ordered to be hung on the 10th of September, 1847; 14 were to be stripped to the waist of their pantaloons, and to receive fifty lashes each on their naked backs, and to be branded with the letter D high up on the cheek-bone, near the eye, but without jeopardizing its sight; 1 was unconditionally pardoned: 42 total.

Intense dissatisfaction, and an earnest remonstrance among the officers of the army in general, followed at the commutation of the sentences of the fourteen from death to whipping and branding, more particularly in the case of Riley, who was in command of the Mexican Battalion of St. Patrick, composed entirely of

63. George Turnbull Moore Davis, *Autobiography of the Late Col. Geo. T. M. Davis, Captain and Aide-de-Camp in Scott's Army of Invasion* (New York: Press of Jenkins and Son, 1891), 224–28.

64. General David E. Twiggs (1790–1862).

deserters from the United States Army, over one hundred strong; and who, from his rank at the time of his desertion, his general intelligence and influence, was believed by our officers to have been the principal cause of the desertion of the others. It was urged upon General Scott that it would be far preferable that every one of the rest of the forty-two condemned deserters should be pardoned rather than that Riley should escape death, more especially as we were in possession of the knowledge of the high estimate placed upon him as an officer by the enemy. The importance attached to saving his life was attested by the unwearied efforts that had been made by the whole Catholic priesthood within our lines to procure his liberty by exchange or ransom. It was held that if his life was spared from any cause it would, in their judgment, be attributed by the enemy to fear on our part, and its tendency would be to produce a more stubborn resistance, and increase our difficulties in taking the City of Mexico.

The facts upon which the action of General Scott was taken were simply these: Riley and his co-deserters, whose sentences he had commuted from death to whipping and branding, deserted during or immediately after the battle of Palo Alto, and before the United States had declared war against Mexico. Under the provisions of the "Articles of War," deserters in times of peace can receive no greater punishment than whipping and branding, as the penalty of such desertion; whereas in time of war the punishment of desertion is death upon conviction of the offender. And as Riley did not desert in time of war . . . to hang him in pursuance of the finding of the military court which tried and convicted him would have been nothing less than military judicial murder.

The fourteen that were to be whipped and branded were tied up to trees in front of the Catholic church on the plaza, their backs naked to the waistband of the pantaloons, and an experienced Mexican muleteer inflicted the fifty lashes with all the severity he could upon each culprit. Why those thus punished did not die under such punishment was a marvel to me. Their backs had the appearance of a pounded piece of raw beef, the blood oozing from every stripe as given. Each in his turn was then branded, and after digging the graves of those subsequently hung, the fourteen were drummed out of camp to the tune of the "Rogues' March."[65] I should have prefaced this revolting scene with the statement that all the generals, with their respective staffs, were required to be present, but for which order nothing on earth could have influenced my witnessing what I did.

. . .

The prisoner who was pardoned owed his deliverance from death to a singular and touching incident. He was an old man of three score years, and had been a loyal and faithful soldier for many years in the United States army until he was tempted and fell under the evil influence and example of Riley. In the same company with himself was his eldest son, who had attained the meridian of the

65. A military drumbeat used to announce the dishonorable discharge of a soldier and played as he marched away from his unit.

allotted period of man's life, and was still in the service of his country. The son had refused to desert, or to become a traitor to his flag. This circumstance was brought to the notice of General Scott mainly through my instrumentality, but without any expectation or design that it would in any way influence the action that followed. The deserter condemned to death was unconditionally pardoned, and the only reason assigned by General Scott for this act of unexpected clemency was given in these few words: "In the hour of the greatest temptation the son was loyal and true to his colors."

## Mexican Account (1906)[66]

I couldn't stand living in Mexico City, and I came to this town with my Aunt Angelita, whom you know I consider as a second mother.

My journey to San Angel was amid families of people who took shelter where they could, in huts, farmhouses, and shanties. There were unburied corpses, dead horses, broken wagons, wandering people who wept, ruins, blood, and all the traces of destruction and death.

Señor Mora's house in San Angel had become a field hospital, and there I saw Doctors Gabino Barrera and Juan N. Navarro treating the wounded with great diligence and charity.

When the Americans entered San Angel, the generous ladies of the family wanted to hide the wounded, and scissors in hand they urged the doctors to cut off their moustaches, but they refused and openly faced the danger. The Americans gave every kind of assistance to the doctors and wounded, which speaks highly of them as civilized and humane men.

What has left a terrible impression on me was the execution of the Irish San Patricio prisoners. As you know, these poor wretches belonged to the American army and were in large part won over for religious reasons, because they were all Christians, and by the most eloquent writings of Martínez de Castro Luis [sic],[67] directed by Don Fernando Ramírez[68] and Baranda.[69]

---

66. Guillermo Prieto, *Memorias de mis tiempos* (Paris/Mexico City: Librería de la Vda. de C. Bouret, 1906), 422–23. Translated by Gustavo Pellón. Prieto inserts this letter into his memoir without naming its author.

67. Luis Martínez Castro (1819–1847) was a journalist and writer who lent his services as a translator in the recruitment of U.S. deserters. He perished at the Battle of Churubusco. He is the subject of a short story by Niceto de Zamacois titled "Luis Martínez de Castro or The National Guard" (1847).

68. José Fernando Ramírez (1804–1871) was a *moderado* politician and writer who also collaborated in the recruitment of deserters from the U.S. Army.

69. Manuel Baranda (1789–1860?), former governor of the state of Guanajuato and minister of foreign affairs during the war, was instrumental in recruiting deserters.

The San Patricios had earned the esteem of the people due to their irreproachable conduct and the valor and enthusiasm with which they defended our cause.

When it was announced that the Irish would be executed, everyone was alarmed, and no stone was left unturned, money was offered, and all kinds of influences were brought to bear.

Lastly, the most distinguished and respectable ladies of the town made a moving plea to Scott, begging for the lives of his prisoners.

No one dared to take the request to the American general-in-chief, because of the cruel manner in which he had treated the bearers of similar petitions, but a friar . . . [sic] offered to take the message and to plead for those victims until the last moment, no matter what the danger.

Neither pleas nor tears nor respect for humanity were able to soften that man with the heart of a hyena, and he ordered that the terrible sentence of death be carried out.

Behind the Plaza de San Jacinto, in back of the houses that face east, they disposed at different intervals and installed thick posts with thick ropes stretched out horizontally on top, with other lassos hanging vertically at intervals.

The prisoners were placed into wagons distributed according to the open spaces between the posts; at a certain distance, amid shouts and the cracking of whips they tied the nooses to the necks of the prisoners . . . [sic] and shouting they made the horses that pulled the wagons run, leaving those defenders of our country swinging in the air, amid horrible convulsions and signs of pain. . . . [sic]

Of course, the death throes of those martyrs lasted a long time. The bodies of the victims were buried in the flowering little town of Tlaquepaque, located between Mixcoac and San Angel.

## U.S. and Mexican Accounts of the Fall and Occupation of Mexico City (1847)

*The attack on Mexico City began on September 13 with the bombardment and storming of Chapultepec Castle, an eighteenth-century structure built on a wooded hill overlooking the city. The defeat of Mexican forces at Chapultepec and at the city's gates forced Santa Anna and his forces to retreat from Mexico City. On September 14, the city surrendered to Scott, although a short-lived popular uprising took place when indignant Mexicans saw the U.S. raise its flag over the national palace. In the days that followed the fall of Mexico's capital, U.S. forces engaged the remnants of Santa Anna's forces at Huamantla, where the U.S. Mounted Rifles brutalized the civilian population after the death in battle of their commanding officer, Captain Samuel H. Walker. On September 16, Santa Anna resigned the presidency and fled Mexico, effectively ending major hostilities.*

*The Mexican government relocated to Querétaro, and peace negotiations with the United States began again in earnest. In the selections below, the occupation of Mexico City is described from different points of view, including that of* The American Star *newspaper, which served the U.S. military during its nine-month occupation of the city.*

## Account by Richard McSherry, M.D., U.S.N. (1850)[70]

[Scott] entered the city triumphantly early on the morning of the 14th; the stars and stripes were already waving over the national palace of Mexico; and we thought all contest was for a time at an end; not so, however. Santa Anna had opened the doors of the prisons, and turned out thousands of felons, who, arms in hands, opened an unexpected fire in all quarters on our troops in the streets, while the assassins were half concealed on the house-tops, and sheltered by parapets. The fire was quite destructive, and the more exasperating, as foul, unexpected, and cowardly. The villains were as unsuccessful as their army had been. In a little while our troops were on the house-tops; the unerring rifle was opposed to the murderous escopet.[71] The Mexicans were worsted, as they always had been; they were driven from house to house, and from square to square, leaving their dead and wounded behind them. Worth's division[72] surprised them, as at Monterey, by perforating the walls of the houses, and ascending upon them from below. Mountain howitzers were placed in lofty towers, which dismayed, as they dispersed, the felon army. It was a day's work, however, and even on the 15th and 16th, there was occasional skirmishing, receding from the centre to the outskirts of the city. General Scott issued a proclamation to the citizens, denouncing such warfare after the city had been fairly surrendered, and threatening the destruction of houses, and the execution of the occupants, wherever it was sanctioned or allowed. . . . The city authorities also published a proclamation, deprecating the attempts of the populace to oppose us. They declared that such warfare was only calculated to bring vengeance on peaceful and quiet citizens, and that the army having fled, such resistance was wholly unavailing.

---

70. Richard McSherry, *El Puchero: A Mixed Dish from Mexico, Embracing General Scott's Campaign with Sketches of Military Life, in Field and Camp of the Character of the Country, Manners and Ways of the People, etc.* (Philadelphia: Lippincott, Grambo and Co., 1850), 114.

71. A short-barreled gun, carbine.

72. Brigadier General William Jenkins Worth (1794–1849) fought at most of the principal battles of the war.

## Mexican Account of the Fall and Occupation of Mexico City (1906)[73]

A terrible night, that of the thirteenth; the city was completely dark, you could hear shooting in every direction, and three or four bombs burst, spreading terror.

At dawn on the fourteenth, the troops began to enter, the people went out to the flat rooftops and the street entrances, curious, threatening, and roaring.

You may remember that Tornel had ordered for the streets to be torn up and the cobblestones piled up on the rooftops, and this suited the intentions of the people to attack the invaders.

The forces began to enter at a steady rate between seven and eight in the morning. I only saw three of the main chiefs, Pillow,[74] tall, dry, ugly, and Twis, old, robust, white-haired, and short, with pale blue eyes that had an unsettling effect.[75] Scott, tall, dashing, graying, good-looking.

The regular troops, with their blue uniforms and their caps, although they marched in an ungainly, dummy-like manner, did not attract attention, but the volunteers, of whom there were many, presented a riotous, indecent carnival beyond imagination. Many had fashioned a sort of jacket with serapes and ponchos; others wore enormous boots over tattered trousers, and as far as their hats, their hats were inconceivable, indecipherable, with wrinkles, creases, drooping brims, grease, and holes; oh, and the tailcoats were an iniquity.

These demons with flaming hair, not blond, but almost red, swollen faces, noses like embers, marched like a herd, running, pushing each other, and carrying their muskets as they pleased. Bringing up the rear were what looked like galleys with wheels, with vaulted roofs made of canvas, they were full of provisions and drunken female camp followers, the most disgusting thing in the world.

The most notable thing about this entrance was the surrender of the city by the president of the municipal government, Licenciado Zaldivar, to Mr. Scott; this surrender was accompanied by a speech, so dignified, lofty, and patriotic that it will be a badge of honor for that official who in such unfortunate circumstances found a way to defend Mexico's rights.

Some motive or pretext that is neither easy nor necessary to discover aroused the crowd, and the fire of rebellion spread quickly, and in a matter of minutes,

---

73. Guillermo Prieto, *Memorias de mis tiempos* (Paris/Mexico City: Librería de la Vda. de C. Bouret, 1906), 417–19. Translated by Gustavo Pellón.

74. Major General Gideon Pillow (1806–1878) led the charge against the Castle of Chapultepec and was later arrested and court martialed for insubordination against Winfield Scott.

75. Translator's note: The original misspells the name of General David Twiggs (1790–1862). The original Spanish text reads: "*con unos ojos sirgos de malísimo efecto.*" Because *ojos sirgos* seems to be a typographical error, I have surmised that the author meant *zarcos,* meaning "light blue. "

burned and trampled everything it found in its way, growing into a stormy riot with all its attendant destruction.

Stones and bricks rained from the rooftops, the scum encouraged those who came by, at the intersections they provoked and attracted the soldiers who were dispersing. Those black drunkards who shouted and hurled themselves like beasts on women and children, killing and dragging them; it was horrible!

It is calculated that it was about fifteen thousand men, who weaponless, wild, and frenzied hurled themselves on the invaders, who truly seemed to be taking possession of a camp of savages.

Everywhere the wounded and the dead, bloody fights, and fearsome punishments all over.

They roamed like herds, setting fires wherever they wanted. The way they eat is unbelievable. They boil apples in the coffee they drink, they spread butter on watermelons, and sauté tomatoes, kernels of corn, and honey, they chew and make noise with their jaws like animals.

At first they kept the churches closed; later they opened a small door, and the sexton, because they didn't ring the bells, announced the hours of the masses. Later, when the churches were opened, the Yankees walked in with their hats on, and confessionals were their favorite places to sleep and snore like pigs.

They were quartered in many houses, and they turned them upside down. In the balconies, you could see rows of Yankee legs as they took their ease. Mexico City is a vast dunghill; everywhere there are piles of garbage and dogs harvesting filth.

## Another Mexican Account (1906)[76]

The officers walk through the streets holding in their hands, as if they were walking sticks, these very thin swords; with them they skewer the first person they run into, with frightening cold blood.

Foreigners keep to themselves; some, like a few Mexicans, have placed flags in their houses, as a sign of peace.

The hatred of the lower classes for the Yankees has not diminished yet, even when they give them money, and share their abundant provisions with the masses.

This is not an exaggeration; the corn was transported in wagons that left a trail of grain as they passed, and the crowds gathered to pick it up, without anyone uttering so much as a word of reprimand; so that in time people got used to the situation, much to the alarm of patriots.

They also handed out meat and bread.

---

76. Anonymous letters cited by Guillermo Prieto, *Memorias de mis tiempos,* 416–19. Translated by Gustavo Pellón.

They didn't bargain with the Indians, and they ran happily after the *daimes.*[77]

Women, in general, are hostile to them; but in my opinion, the distrust arises from the religious question, because of their disrespect to priests and churches. Their attitude would be different if the Yankees were sanctimonious and pretended to be believers.

The high society of Mexico City has not opened its doors to chiefs and officers, and Señor A's house, where Yankees have been received, is bitterly criticized and is, as it were, excommunicated.

## Selections from *The American Star* (October 1847)

### Assassinations[78]

We regret to say that the assassination of American soldiers, by Mexican hands, has recommenced in this city. Last evening, at about 3 o'clock, Sergeant Sutlife, of the Rifles, was stabbed in Calle de Plateros, but a few steps from our publication office. Life was extinct when his body was taken from the pavement, he having received a mortal wound near the heart. His purse was found empty upon the side-walk, though we learn that he had been seen, earlier in the evening, to have a hundred and fifty dollars in gold. It was probably the knowledge of his having this amount with him, that led to his assassination.

A private belonging to the infantry regiments, was also killed on the same evening, and no great distance from the same spot. We hear it stated, also that another, if not two other privates, were killed in another part of the city, but were unable to learn names or any particulars in regard to their death. . . .

### A Petition by Various Mexican Women[79]

"VARIAS MEXICANAS."—We must confess our surprise at the appearance of a small note in the *Eagle*[80] of the 2d, signed "Varias Mexicanas," and addressed to us. It came almost as unexpectedly upon us as did the earthquake of the same day, but thanks to our iron frame, we have survived them both. The note solicits us not to flatter them, for flattery from an enemy is an insult to their dear

77. In the original, misspelled as *damies. Daime* is a colloquial term for the U.S. dime coin. Elsewhere in his description of the occupation of Mexico City, one of Prieto's informants complains that the lower classes and Indians who collaborate with the invaders are more familiar with U.S. coinage than their own Mexican one.

78. "Assassinations," *The American Star,* October 16, 1847, 2.

79. "Varias Mexicanas," *The American Star,* October 5, 1847, 2.

80. A reference to *El aguila mexicana (The Mexican Eagle*), a Mexico City newspaper.

patriotism! Why, bless your sweet souls we are no enemy of yours! Nor are we enemies even of your countrymen, unless we meet them on the field of battle! We admire you, ladies, and will continue to do so, despite all the effusions you can send us through the columns of the *Eagle*. But stop—may we not be too fast—is it not possible that the editor of the *Eagle*, jealous of the compliments we have bestowed upon his fair countrywomen, has resorted to this scheme to stave us off . . . ?

### Advertisements from *The American Star*[81]

A GRAND BALL, to be given exclusively to the officers of the American Army, the gentlemen of the United States and of Mexico, at No. 7, 2d. street of San Francisco, on SUNDAY NIGHT, Tickets to be obtained at the principal hotels or coffee houses, and at the door. The price of tickets $2.00—admitting a gentleman and two ladies.

**Interesting to Students.**

A GRADUATE of Harvard University, Mass., whom a subsequent residence of many areas in various parts of Europe has familiarized with diverse modern tongues, proposes to open shortly in an apartment of the Palace, two classes of Spanish and French, for the benefit of such gentlemen of the army as may feel disposed to cultivate either of said languages, so important at the present day. Such as may be inclined will please inquire at Captain Naylor's quarters, in the National Palace, where daily from 8 to 9 in the morning, and from 3 to 5 in the afternoon will be found the professor.

**Eagle Coffee House.**

*Calle Coliseo Viejo, No. 5*

The undersigned proprietors have established the above Hotel on the American style for the accommodation of the officers of the army and citizens, and have spared no expense in procuring Wines, Liquors and Segars of the choicest brand. The table also will be supplied with the best the market affords. Gentlemen wishing private repasts can also be accommodated at the shortest notice. Steaks and chops constantly on hand and done up in the best and promptest manner.

N.B. There are TWO BILLIARD TABLES attached to the establishment.

H. B. Doane.
R. G. Ackley.
John Garrett.

---

81. From *The American Star*, October 10, 1847, 2.

## LIFE PILLS.

The celebrated Vegetable Life Pills (pildoras de la vida,) for the cure of Billious and Intermittent affections, Liver Complaints, Dispepsia,[82] Disentery, Impurities of the Blood, Headache, Costiveness,[83] pains in the back, loins and side; also in the cleansing the throat and stomach from phlegm, and an invaluable compound wherever an alternative or a purgative medicine may be required. Price one dollar and fifty cents per box.

Also for sale the American Hygeian Morisonian pills, [price one dollar and fifty cents], The Asiatic Tooth Wash, Windsor and Russian Soaps, Hair Dye, Bears Oil, and the famous septentrional Oil, for the growth of the hair, and black Writing Ink, all warranted genuine.

For sale at the American Eagle Coffee House, Calle Coliseo Viejo, and at Don Antonio de la Torre's bookstore. Portal de mercaderes.

82. Digestive disorders.
83. Constipation.

# IV

# The Politics of War

## Yucateco Separatism (January 2, 1846)[1]

*The Creole and mestizo elite of Mexico's southern state of Yucatán, populated primarily by Maya peoples, declared independence from Mexico on February 18, 1840, in protest of Santa Anna's high taxes and antifederalism. After rejoining Mexico in 1843, Yucatán affirmed its independence again in December 1845 and declared itself neutral during the U.S.-Mexican War. Political infighting and racial tensions in the region led to the destructive "Caste War" of 1847, which pitted Maya Indians against Creoles. The Creoles called for the assistance of Spain, Great Britain, or the United States and even went as far as offering sovereignty over Yucatán to any power that rescued it. Before the United States could act on the plan, which had piqued the interest of expansionist Democrats, Yucatán rejoined Mexico in 1848. The following excerpt is from a decree by Yucatecan Governor Miguel Barbachano (1807–1859) explaining the reason for the region's secession from Mexico in 1845. Yucatán's 1843 break from Mexico had been resolved by the signing of a treaty offering great autonomy to the state. Barbachano's document explains that the abrogation of that treaty by Mexico precipitated secession again.*

The legislative assembly of Yucatán, emboldened by the explicit vote of its constituents, believes the solemn moment has finally come to make a frank and express declaration of its true feelings. The fatherland [Yucatán] demands our undivided attention: the only pact of union that joined Yucatán to the rest of the republic[2] has been broken. Oaths have been violated, and there is no other option but to accept, such as the unjust government of Mexico presents it, the situation in which the peninsula once more finds itself. Those solely responsible

1. Miguel Barbachano, "Número 30," *Memoria de la primera secretaria de estado y del despacho de relaciones interiores y esteriores de los Estados Unidos mexicanos* (Mexico City: Imprenta de Vicente García Torres, 1847), 61–63. Translated by Gustavo Pellón.

2. On December 13, 1845, the Mexican congress refused to ratify the 1843 agreements between Mexico and Yucatán that had given the state great autonomy and ended her first secession. The Mexican congress declared that Yucatán should be organized according to the stipulations of the centralist constitution of Mexico, called the *Bases Orgánicas.*

for the evils and misfortunes that will befall the nation are the blind, ill-advised politicians who have brought matters to this extreme.

The assembly protested duly against any act that would tend to place a sacrilegious hand on the agreements of December 14, 1843, that established the just and imperative exceptions that the nature of things in Yucatán requires. The most powerful effort undertaken by Mexico as a nation since independence was not enough to make Yucatecans deviate one inch from the only path they had to follow. And those agreements, oh people!, were the fruit of the most bloody sacrifices, consumed in an irrational and savage aggression, in a war for which there is no name, because no epithet can hope to describe it appropriately.

Furthermore: from different reliable sources we have learned that against their literal tenor, these agreements have been subject to revision. That their nullity and invalidity have been discussed, and that when a proposal was made in the chamber of deputies to postpone the grave and delicate discussion of a subject of such vital importance, that body had rejected the proposal by an immense majority. Therefore, that pact is probably annulled by this date; and while the government of Mexico sells the honor of the nation to foreigners[3] and submits to the law of the strongest, it brashly vents its wrath against this virtuous people, who have been an integral part of a republic worthy of a better fate.

. . .

The assembly announces to the Yucatecan people that the moment of breaking the ties of union with the rest of the Mexican Republic draws near. All indications point to the coming consummation of that event. Meanwhile it must decree prudent measures to guarantee its happiness and future fate. It must, therefore, disown the Mexican government as a contracting party that has repeatedly violated those agreements. The assembly must, in pursuance of its rights, disown Mexico's authority and that of all the resolutions it may issue.

## Debate over the War in the House of Representatives (May 1846)

*The selections that follow illustrate differing responses in the U.S. House of Representatives to the outbreak of hostilities between the United States and Mexico. Ohio's Joshua Giddings (1795–1864) was a Whig (later a Free-Soiler and Republican) who served in the House of Representatives between 1838–1858. He opposed slavery and expansionism and later served in the administration of Abraham Lincoln. The Democrat Stephen Arnold Douglas (1813–1861) of Illinois*

3. The administration of President José Joaquín de Herrera, which was toppled in December 1845, had negotiated with Great Britain and Texas to recognize the independence of Texas and prevent its annexation to the United States.

*began his career in the House in 1843 and defeated Abraham Lincoln for a seat in the U.S. Senate in 1858 after the famous Lincoln-Douglas debates. Douglas was a defender of slavery and an expansionist who voted against the Treaty of Guadalupe Hidalgo that ended the U.S.-Mexican War because he considered its terms overly generous to Mexico.*

## Joshua Giddings of Ohio (May 12, 1846)[4]

Sir, I regard this war as but one scene in the drama now being enacted by this Administration. Our Government is undergoing a revolution no less marked than was that of France in 1792. As yet, it has not been characterized by that amount of bloodshed and cruelty which distinguished the change of government in France. When the Executive and Congress openly and avowedly took upon themselves the responsibility of extending and perpetuating slavery by the annexation of Texas, and by the total overthrow and subversion of the Constitution, and that, too, by the aid of Northern votes, my confidence in the ability of our institutions was shaken, destroyed. I had hoped that the free States might be aroused in time to save our Union from final overthrow; but that hope has been torn from me. The great charter of our political liberties has been tamely surrendered by our free States to purchase perpetual slavery for the South. Our Union continues, but our Constitution is gone. The rights of the several States and of the people now depend upon the arbitrary will of an irresponsible majority, who are themselves controlled by a weak but ambitious executive.

Sir, no man regards this war as *just. We know,* the country knows, and the civilized world are conscious, that it has resulted from a desire to extend and sustain an institution on which the curse of the Almighty most visibly rests. Mexico has long since abolished slavery.[5] She has purified herself from its crimes and its guilt. That institution is now circumscribed on the southwest by Mexico, where the slaves of Texas find an asylum. A gentleman from Matamoras [sic] lately assured me that there were in and about that city at least five hundred fugitives from Texan bondage. Experience has shown that they cannot be held in servitude in the vicinity of a free government. It has therefore become necessary to extend our dominions into Mexico in order to render slavery secure in Texas. Without this, the great objects of annexation will not be attained. We sought to extend and perpetuate slavery in a peaceful manner by the annexation of Texas. Now we are about to effect that object by war and conquest. Can we invoke the blessing

4. Joshua Reed Giddings, *Speeches in Congress* (Boston: John P. Jewett and Co., 1853), 177–201.

5. On September 15, 1829, President Vicente Guerrero emancipated all slaves in Mexico.

of Deity [sic] to rest on such motives? Has the Almighty any attribute that will permit Him to take sides with us in this contest?

. . .

This war is waged against an unoffending people, without just or adequate cause, for the purpose of conquest; with the design to extend slavery; in violation of the Constitution, against the dictates of justice, of humanity, the sentiments of the age in which we live, and the precepts of the religion we profess. I will lend it no aid, no support whatever. I will not bathe my hands in the blood of the people of Mexico, nor will I participate in the guilt of those murders which have been, and which will hereafter be committed by our army there. For these reasons I shall vote against the bill under consideration, and all others calculated to support this war.

## Stephen Douglas of Illinois (May 13, 1846)[6]

What reliance shall we place on the sincerity of gentlemen's professions that they are for the country, right or wrong, when they exert all their power and influence to put their country in the wrong in the eyes of Christendom, and invoke the wrath of Heaven upon us for our manifold crimes and aggressions? With professions of patriotism on their lips, do they not show that their hearts are against their own country? They appeal to the consciences and religious feelings of our countrymen to unite in execration of our Government, army, citizen soldiers, and country, for prosecuting what they denounce as an unholy, unrighteous, and damnable cause. They predict that the judgment of God will rest upon us; that sickness, and carnage, and death will be our portion; that defeat and disgrace will attend our arms. Is there not treason in the heart that can feel and poison in the breath that can utter such sentiments against their own country, when forced to take up arms in self-defense, to repel invasion by a brutal and perfidious enemy?

The Republic of Texas held the country [on the left bank of the Rio del Norte] by a more glorious title than can be traced through the old maps and musty records of Spanish and French courts. She held the country by the same title that our forefathers of the Revolution acquired our territory and achieved the independence of this Republic. She held it by virtue of her Declaration of Independence, setting forth the inalienable rights of man, by men who had hearts to feel and minds to comprehend the blessings of freedom; by principles successfully maintained by the irresistible power of her arms, and consecrated by the precious blood of her glorious heroes. These are her muniments of title to

6. Marion Mills Miller, ed., *Great Debates in American History,* vol. 2, *Foreign Relations: Part One* (New York: Current Literature Publishing Company, 1913), 360–62.

the empire which she has voluntarily annexed to our Union, and which we have plighted our faith to protect and defend against invasion and dismemberment. We have received the republic of Texas, with her entire territory, into this Union, as an independent and sovereign State, and have no right to alienate or surrender any portion of it.

## The Wilmot Proviso (1846–1847)[7]

*David Wilmot (1814–1868) of Pennsylvania began his career as a Democrat but later became a Free-Soiler and an influential Republican. He served in the U.S. House of Representatives (1845–1851) and in the Senate (1861–1863) and was the author of a controversial proviso that was added to a $2 million war appropriation bill. The proviso passed the House in 1846 but not the Senate.*

### The Wilmot Proviso (August 8, 1846)

Provided that, as an express and fundamental condition to the acquisition of any territory from the Republic of Mexico by the United States, by virtue of any treaty which may be negotiated between them, and to the use by the Executive of the moneys herein appropriated, neither slavery nor involuntary servitude shall ever exist in any part of said territory, except for crime, whereof the party shall first be duly convicted.

### Congressman David Wilmot on His Proviso (February 8, 1847)[8]

We ask but sheer justice and right. Sir, we ask the neutrality of this Government on this question of slavery. I have stood up at home and fought, time and again, against the abolitionists of the North. I stand by every compromise of the Constitution. I adhere to its letter and its spirit. And I would never invade one single right of the South. So far from it am I that I stand ready, at all times and upon all occasions, as do nearly the entire North, to sustain the institutions of the South as they exist, with our money and with our blood, when that day comes, as

---

7. U.S. Congress. House, *The Congressional Globe,* 29th Congress, First Session, vol. 15, 1217.

8. Marion Mills Miller, ed. *Great Debates in American History,* vol. 4, *Slavery from 1790 to 1857* (New York: Current Literature Publishing Company, 1913), 135–36.

many—many Southern men—fear it may come. When that day comes, sir, the North stands with them. We go for every compromise of the Constitution.

But, sir, this is another question—entirely another question. We ask that this Government preserve the integrity of free territory against the aggressions of slavery—against its wrongful usurpations. Sir, I was in favor of the annexation of Texas. I supported it with the whole influence which I possessed, and I was willing to take Texas in as she was. I sought not to change the character of her institutions. Texas was a slave country, and, although it was held out to us, that two slave and two free states might be made out of it, yet the whole of Texas was given up to slavery, every inch. . . . But, we are told, California is ours. And all we ask in the North is that the character of its territory be preserved. It is free, and it is part of the established law of nations, and all public law, that, when it shall come into this Union, all laws there existing, not inconsistent with its new allegiance, will remain in force. This fundamental law, which prohibits slavery in California, will be in force; this fundamental law, which prohibits slavery in New Mexico, will be in force. Shall the South invade it? Shall the South make this Government an instrument for the violation of its neutrality, and for the establishment of slavery in these territories, in defiance of law? That is the question. There is no question of abolition here, sir. It is a question whether the South shall be permitted, by aggression, by invasion of right, by subduing free territory and planting slavery upon it, to wrest this territory to the accomplishment of its own sectional purposes and schemes? That is the question. And shall we of the North submit to it? Must we yield this? It is not, sir, in the spirit of the compact; it is not, sir, in the Constitution.

## The Return of Santa Anna to Mexico (August 16, 1846)[9]

*By the summer of 1846, Mexican federalists led by Valentín Gómez Farías united to conspire against the centralist leadership of Mariano Paredes y Arrillaga, reaching out to Antonio López de Santa Anna, who was living in exile in Cuba. General Mariano Salas overthrew Paredes and his followers on August 6, 1846, and reinstated the federalist Constitution of 1824, paving the way for Santa Anna's return ten days later. Santa Anna was allowed passage through the U.S. naval blockade of Mexico because of secret negotiations with President Polk, in which the exiled leader suggested that he would respond favorably to U.S. territorial demands if he was allowed to return to power. Santa Anna did not follow through on those*

---

9. From "Esposición del General Antonio López de Santa Anna a sus compatriotas, con motivo del programa proclamado para la verdadera regeneración de la república." In *Memoria de la primera secretaria de estado y del despacho de relaciones interiores y esteriores de los Estados Unidos mexicanos* (Mexico City: Imprenta de Vicente Garcia Torres, 1847), 110–11, 114. Translated by Gustavo Pellón.

*assurances. After being elected president in December 1846, with Gómez Farías serving as his vice president, he led Mexican forces against the United States. The following excerpt is from a manifesto that Santa Anna released upon his return to Mexico from exile. In it, we see how Santa Anna represents President Mariano Paredes y Arrillaga as a monarchist threatening to reverse the gains of Mexican independence and himself as the standard bearer of Mexican republicanism.*

Meanwhile, I began to receive news of a revolution planned by General Paredes. The news did not fail to encourage my hope, because although he had been an obstinate enemy of any representative government of the people, I supposed that he must have modified his convictions, honoring him in the belief that he was incapable of sponsoring projects of European intervention in the domestic administration of the republic. The revolution finally broke out, and his manifesto adhering to the program proposed by the troops quartered in San Luis Potosí deeply troubled me, because I saw it as a diatribe against the nation's independence rather than the patriotic exposition of a Mexican general seeking in good faith to remedy the ills of his country.[10] Finally, his evil intentions were revealed to me by the proclamation of January 24, issued as a result of the aforementioned revolution, as well as by the newspapers that reported his government's design to establish in the republic a monarchy with a foreign prince.

As one of the principal leaders of our country's independence and a founder of the republican system, I became indignant that some of her sons would seek to expose the nation to the mockery of the world and to return to the ominous days of the conquest. I, therefore, firmly resolved to come to your aid to save her from such an affront and avoid the horrible consequences of a step that sought to sacrifice her glorious future for a return to what was and can never again be. To accomplish this vow, I was willing to sacrifice my blood to whomever would want to spill it in any unfortunate turn of events, in accordance with the terms of the barbarous decree that banished me from the republic; but I preferred to die in such a noble cause, rather than to remain indifferent to the country's ignominy, and allow the countless sacrifices it has cost us to conquer independence and the right to govern ourselves to come to nothing.

. . .

The protestations of republican sentiments, made by General Paredes, after so many irrefutable facts that condemn him, were they not perhaps a new perfidy to reassure the republic, to lull it to sleep, and exploit an opportunity in which his depraved intentions could be realized? He made the first protestations in the middle of March, when he saw that public discontent was turning against his power and sinister ideas. But, what happened? Didn't he, by chance, continue to

10. For more on Paredes and his politics, see Part II.

protect *El Tiempo,*[11] a newspaper established in the very capital, in order to render republican forms hateful and recommend the need for a monarchy, making use of whatever rumors were considered effective to waylay the good sense of the nation? . . . Meanwhile, he promoted by all means within his reach the meeting of the congress meant to bring his monarchical thoughts to fruition, concentrated his forces in order to repress the actions of the people who were alarmed at the proximity of such a disastrous event, and abandoned our invaded frontiers or, more accurately, handed them over to the exterior enemy, after our reversals, sought by him, in Palo Alto and Resaca de la Palma.[12]

No, Mexicans, no arrangement is possible with a party whose conduct has been a tissue of cruel lies for our fatherland—none, no matter how flattering their promises may be and whatever shape they may assume in the future. Amid the supreme convulsions of their death throes, they sought their health in their usual machinations, proclaimed principles they detested, rose up with bastard republicans, and pretended to be friends of liberty, hoping thereby to avoid their just punishment, stay in power, and continue to undermine the edifice erected on the illustrious blood of men such as Hidalgo and Morelos.[13]

## María de la Salud García, Mexican Patriot (August 31, 1846)[14]

*In Mexico's elite society, women did not generally participate in public life. In the first half of the nineteenth century, in Mexico as in the rest of Latin America, women were rarely given a forum to publish and disseminate their opinions. The following article, published on August 31, 1846, in the Mexico City newspaper* El Republicano, *is a revealing and invaluable exception to the rule. María Salud García sent the article to the editors with a cover letter dated August 16, in which she asked the editors to publish the article if they considered it worthy of seeing "public light." In her letter of introduction, García wrote: "As is natural, I distrust my limited understanding, and therefore I appeal to the judgement and prudence of your respectable talents." García's article puts a dramatic twist on the widespread, nationalist rhetoric that tied Mexican honor and virility to the protection of Mexico's women and the "motherland" in general.*

---

11. The conservative newspaper *El Tiempo* was founded in Mexico City in January 1846.

12. Santa Anna here misinterprets the action and intent of President Paredes in April and May 1846. See "Manifesto of April 23, 1846" in Part II.

13. Miguel Hidalgo y Costilla (1753–1811) and José María Morelos y Pavón (1765–1815) are foundational heroes of the Mexican War of Independence.

14. María de la Salud García, "Invitación a los mexicanos," *El Republicano,* August 31, 1846, 2. Translated by Gustavo Pellón.

Invitation to Mexicans

Mexicans: The day has come when impelled by my philanthropic feelings, by the sincere love that I bear my dear country, by the silence of the wise, who could have employed their eloquence to make known to you the need to fight, to defend this country, which must be dear to all of you. The day, I said, has come when you will hear a weak voice, a feminine voice, inspired by a feeling so noble and so sacred that it quells in my breast all others inherent to my sex. Yes, beloved compatriots, rush to the war that is today so necessary, so just. It would offend you if I were to think that a single Mexican would prefer slavery to the obligation to defend our homes invaded by an avaricious nation, brought to our soil by its thirst for the gold that abounds in our country. There is still time to repel them from our territory. All must heed the call, set aside your own opinions, put an end to those civil wars that have brought you so much ruin. You must no longer tear yourselves apart like furious tigers; may a fraternal bond join you to the same cause. Consider that your holy faith, your families, your interests, your persons, and your very country, everything, everything will fall into the hands of your enemies if you remain in your present culpable apathy. Your rest is reprehensible and shameful in the face of such an urgent need to try your mettle. To arms, Mexicans, make ready, fly to do your duty, a duty sacred to *hombres de bien*.[15] The Supreme Being sees the justice of your cause; He shall protect you. His Divine Providence shall watch over your well-being. Remember the glorious time of our independence; imitate those illustrious heroes, those famous leaders Hidalgo, Allende, Morelos, Iturbide, and others. In imitation of those noble and valiant founding fathers, dare to face the dangers of a just war, and like them you will cover the Mexican name with glory. Remember that following in their footsteps, your valor and constancy shook off the Spanish yoke that oppressed us. Keep in mind that in times past that same valor made you fearsome to France in Veracruz.[16] Therefore, let the Anglo-American cry out in shame: "Mexicans are brave, know their rights, and know how to defend them." Mexicans, may your noble valor make you fearsome to all the nations of the globe. Go wherever honor and liberty call you, that precious gift that the Eternal gave to man. Be not daunted by the numbers of your enemies. Become fearsome heroes, like those Lacedaemonian men, at whose name alone all nations trembled. Imitate the example of the fierce Leonidas, who with only three hundred Spartans dared, with a firmness that causes admiration, to await King Xerxes, who invaded

---

15. As Michael Costeloe writes, the *hombre de bien* was a virtuous, honorable gentleman and "ideal citizen" belonging to the middle class. The *hombres de bien,* not the old aristocracy, were the primary political players in Mexico in the middle of the nineteenth century. See Michael Costeloe, *The Central Republic in Mexico, 1835–1846: Hombres de Bien in the Age of Santa Anna* (Cambridge, UK: Cambridge University Press, 2002), 16–17.

16. During a short war with France in 1838 called "The Pastry War," Mexico resisted the French in Veracruz.

Greece with the formidable army of three hundred thousand Persians.[17] If you meet the fate of those famous warriors (who died betrayed by a wicked man), your names, like theirs, will be carved in marble, and posterity will repeat them with enthusiasm. Our widowhood and orphanhood will make us proud because of the noble cause from which it springs. We prefer the glory of your dying in the defense of our liberty to having you with us as vile slaves who would allow themselves to be chained in order to save their miserable and dishonored lives. Yes, Mexicans, liberty or death! The repose of the tomb is preferable to slavery!

Do not wait to hear, blushing, the just complaints from the lips of your families. Do not imitate that vile coward Boabdil, the last king of Granada, who preferred to run like a bandit than to sacrifice a life without honor to his fatherland. Do not expose yourselves to such an affront. The sultana, mother of this Moorish king, seeing him weep when he parted from the city, says to him: "Weep, coward, weep like a woman, since you knew not how to defend your fatherland and your crown like a man." Mexicans, what a lesson!

However, if you remain in your present inaction, observing with a serene face the imminent danger in which your republic finds itself, we, this weak sex, this part of the human race, this half of man, useless and weak as we are, we shall gather, and although used to leisure and household chores, we shall abandon them and sheathing ourselves in the valor that your sex should have, we shall know how to bear the fatigue of the road and the dangers of war. These delicate hands shall wield a sword.[18] Our love of country and liberty (like all virtuous feelings in noble and sensitive hearts) shall fill us with daring and, transformed into terrible Amazons, we shall combat, and this sword shall be as fearsome and fatal to the enemy as the Gaul's sword was to the Roman. We shall imitate that famous heroine of Argos, that noble and valiant Telesilla,[19] who when the warriors of her country had died in battle with the Lacedaemonians, and knowing that the enemy was coming to take the defenseless city, runs, hurries, gathers all her female friends, urges them to fight with valor, and to face a glorious death rather than bend the neck to the slavery that their enemies prepared for them. She places herself at the head of those brave women, and they attack the besiegers with such daring and fearlessness, that they conquer them in a few hours and put to shameful flight those fierce and terrible Spartans, those same warriors who filled all nations with terror, and who, until then, no army had dared attack, even when they were evenly matched. And if the love of liberty can work such miracles in the hands of some weak women, what can we not expect of brave Mexican men?

---

17. See note 42 in Part II.

18. For an example of a woman warrior of the U.S.-Mexican War, see "Doña María de Jesús Dosamantes at Monterrey (September 19, 1846)" in Part III of this book, as well as the short story "'Don Luis Martínez de Castro or The National Guard' by Niceto de Zamacois (1847)" in Part VI.

19. A poet who lobbied the people of Argos against Sparta; she was later memorialized with a statue at the Temple of Aphrodite in Argos.

Yes, compatriots: that daring, your concept of liberty and honor, makes us hope that you will rush to seek the glory with which you have so many times covered yourselves in the field of Mars. Victory will crown your noble brow with immortal laurels, and you will have the sweet satisfaction of having liberated your country from the vile chains of slavery. Mexicans, or slaves? No, never, rather die first!

## The Polkos Revolt (February–March 1847)

*While President Santa Anna was away on a military campaign, Mexico City was the scene of a short-lived armed insurrection against his vice president, the* puro *Valentín Gómez Farías (February 27–March 23). The revolt, led by* moderados *and supporters of church interests, was sparked by Gómez Farías' attempts to fund the war effort by expropriating church capital and property and his interference with a civic militia loyal to his political rivals. The insurgents were called "Polkos" because of their associations with the Mexican aristocracy, which enjoyed the polka dance. Santa Anna, who had approved of Gómez Farías' policy in writing, and at first rejected the revolt, later forced his vice president from office and installed General Pedro María Anaya as acting president. (Santa Anna was a consummate realist, and it was clear that Gómez Farías was too polarizing a figure to remain in office.) The revolt of the Polkos underscores the deep-seated divisions within the governing elite, even in the midst of a war. Below, we excerpt the manifesto of the Polko leader General Matías de la Peña y Barragán, who refused to follow an order by vice president Gómez Farías to lead his forces to Veracruz because he believed it was a ploy to defuse opposition to the expropriation of church property. Following Peña y Barragán's proclamation of revolt, we include the counterproclamation of General Valentín Canalizo, who supported vice president Gómez Farías. Subsequent documents in this section illustrate the impact and implications of the Polkos Revolt.*

### Plan for the Restoration of True Federalist Principles by Matías de la Peña y Barragán (February 27, 1847)[20]

The same congress, or its majority, composed of men blinded by emotion has followed the most tortuous and unwise path imaginable. The war that Mexico is forced to pursue, of course, demands prompt, sure, and efficacious succor. Our

20. Matías de la Peña y Barragán, "Plan para la restauración de los verdaderos principios federativos," *El Republicano,* February 27, 1847, 4. Translated by Gustavo Pellón.

representatives, instead of approaching other sources where such support could be securely and quickly obtained, instead of unifying and fostering public morale, instead of making good use of the ecclesiastical fund, without violating fairness and the rights of a class of the state, our congress has closed its eyes to any such consideration. Trampling the principles pertaining to the property of individuals and corporations, it has not wished to grasp the relationship between the wealth of the clergy and that of the other classes. It has not valued the observations that sought to frame the question in its true light, by demonstrating mathematically that the law of January 11[21] would only create the worst of all possible discords, which is that touching religious principles, also, and worst of all, that the desired resources would remain in the character of a mere project, and our worthy army would be exposed to die without glory in an immense desert.

. . .

Indeed the reins of state have been entrusted to a man incapable of guiding them wisely. His whim is the only guide for his acts, and his passion is out of control. He has surrounded his chair with all the most abject, despicable people, the scum of all parties, and his cabinet is so mutilated by the disrepute of the ministerial posts that even those who burn to occupy those posts refuse to do so. The whole offers the appearance of a corpse, at once evoking compassion and horror. Public distrust has reached its limit, and as an inescapable consequence, misery and despair are but the first features of this horrible but true picture.

## Proclamation of Valentín Canalizo (February 27, 1847)[22]

Comrades in arms, part of the national guard has risen against the republic at the critical moment in which its fate is being decided at the border. As our army faces dangers, treason and cowardice vie to proclaim anarchy in order to seek a disastrous destiny for Mexico. We have just established order and they proclaim disorder. The monarchist faction has barely been overthrown and it already rears its head. We must reinforce Veracruz, and these contemptible wretches who fear to face the foreign enemy dare to provoke a fratricidal war. It is our duty to strangle the uprising in its cradle, and your sincere friend exhorts you to do it.

---

21. This law sought to expropriate lands belonging to the church and was supported by Santa Anna himself in order to fund the armed forces during the war.

22. "El general en gefe, nombrado contra los sublevados de esta capital," *El Republicano,* February 27, 1847, 4. Translated by Gustavo Pellón.

### Excerpt from an Editorial from *El Republicano* (February 28, 1847)[23]

Amid all these sad circumstances, loyal to the principles we have always professed, we will not address flattering words to any side. Only the interest of our country guides our pen in such extraordinary circumstances: our position is to be *good Mexicans.* To us it seems inexcusable to light the flames of civil war when a foreign power threatens Veracruz, takes possession of Tuxpan, and is waiting to combat the army that will decide the fate of Mexico's independence. It is also inexcusable, now that the federal system has been restored and when our only salvation lies in not endangering the forms of the representative system, to return to settling political questions through armed force, to continue to impose sovereignty at the point of a bayonet. Our soul feels profound sorrow, seeing the national guard stubbornly fixed on this road to perdition.

### General Antonio López de Santa Anna to Vice President Valentín Gómez Farías (March 6, 1847)[24]

I am concerned about the results of that traitorous rising, and I hope that you will inform me of anything that happens. On the eighth I will be in San Luis Potosí, where I shall expect word from you. What is this curse that has befallen our unhappy fatherland? What will those who observe it from afar say? How can our enemies not be encouraged? No wonder Taylor said in Saltillo twenty days ago, "I'm not afraid of Santa Anna: in Mexico there will be a revolution very soon, and he will be deposed!" My friend, I protest to you that if the rule of law is not restored, if the merchants of these criminal risings are not punished, and if the leaders of this great scandal go unpunished, I will resign everything, and will prepare to leave a country where it is a crime to serve your fatherland well. There is no other choice.

## The All-Mexico Question (1847)

*By the end of 1847, complete U.S. victory on the battlefields of Mexico seemed inevitable. Many Democrats supported the annexation of Mexico in its entirety to the United States, an idea that Whigs rejected. In what follows, we include an*

---

23. "Tranquilidad pública," *El Republicano,* February 28, 1847, 4. Translated by Gustavo Pellón.

24. Antonio López de Santa Anna, "Comunicaciones del general Santa Anna." *El Republicano,* March 12, 1847, 4. Translated by Gustavo Pellón.

*excerpt from President Polk's December 1847 message to Congress, in which he proposes that Mexican land be claimed by the United States as indemnity for the costs of war and U.S. claims against Mexico. We also include excerpts of speeches for and against the annexation of Mexican territory by two well-known Democratic senators, John Caldwell Calhoun (1782–1850) of South Carolina and Daniel S. Dickinson (1800–1866) of New York. Calhoun had served as vice president under the administrations of John Quincy Adams (1767–1848) and Andrew Jackson (1767–1845). He had also served as secretary of state under President John Tyler (1790–1862), when plans for the annexation of Texas were formally drawn up. The final text presented is by Martin Robison Delany (1812–1885), a prominent African American activist, writer, and publisher who advocated African American emigration to Africa. Like his friend and collaborator Frederick Douglass (c. 1818–1895), Delany rejected the U.S.-Mexican War because he saw it as promoting slaveholding interests.*

## President Polk's Third Annual Message to Congress (December 7, 1847)[25]

The doctrine of no territory is the doctrine of no indemnity, and if sanctioned would be a public acknowledgement that our country was wrong and that the war declared by Congress with extraordinary unanimity was unjust and should be abandoned—an admission unfounded in fact and degrading to the national character.

. . .

Our arms having been everywhere victorious, having subjected to our military occupation a large portion of the enemy's country, including his capital, and negotiations for peace having failed, the important questions arise, in what manner the war ought to be prosecuted and what should be our future policy. I cannot doubt that we should secure and render available the conquests we have already made, and that with this view we should hold and occupy by our naval and military forces all the ports, towns, cities and provinces now in our occupation or which may hereafter fall into our possession; that we should press forward our military operations and levy such military contributions on the enemy as may, as far as practicable, defray the future expenses of the war.

Had the Government of Mexico acceded to the equitable and liberal terms proposed, that mode of adjustment would have been preferred. Mexico having declined to do this and failed to offer any other terms which could be accepted by the United States, the national honor, no less than the public interests, requires

25. U.S. Congress and Thomas Hart Benton, *Abridgement of the Debates of Congress, from 1789 to 1856,* vol. 16. (New York: D. Appleton and Company, 1868), 118–33.

that the war should be prosecuted with increased energy and power until a just and satisfactory peace can be obtained. In the meantime, as Mexico refuses all indemnity, we should adopt measures to indemnify ourselves by appropriating permanently a portion of her territory. Early after the commencement of the war New Mexico and the Californias were taken possession of by our forces. Our military and naval commanders were ordered to conquer and hold them subject to be disposed of by a treaty of peace.

These provinces are now in our undisputed occupation and have been so for many months, all resistance on the part of Mexico having ceased with their limits. I am satisfied they should never be surrendered to Mexico. Should Congress concur with me in this opinion, and that they should be retained by the United States as indemnity, I can perceive no good reason why the civil jurisdiction and laws of the United States should not at once be extended over them.

## Senator John C. Calhoun (January 4, 1848)[26]

We have conquered many of the neighboring tribes of Indians, but we have never thought of holding them in subjection, or of incorporating them into our Union. They have been left as an independent people in the midst of us, or been driven back into the forests. Nor have we ever incorporated into the Union any but the Caucasian race. To incorporate Mexico would be the first departure of the kind; for more than half of its population are pure Indians, and by far the larger portion of the residue mixed blood. I protest against the incorporation of such a people. Ours is the government of the white man. The great misfortune of what was formerly Spanish America, is to be traced to the fatal error of placing the colored race on an equality with the white. This error destroyed the social arrangement which formed the basis of their society. This error we have wholly escaped; the Brazilians, formerly a province of Portugal, have escaped also to a considerable extent, and they and we are the only people of this continent who made revolutions without anarchy. And yet, with this example before them, and our uniform practice, there are those among us who talk about erecting these Mexicans into territorial governments, and placing them on an equality with the people of these States. I utterly protest against the project.

. . .

The conquest of Mexico would add so vastly to the patronage of this Government, that it would absorb the whole powers of the States; the Union would become an imperial power, and the States reduced to mere subordinate corporations. But the evil would not end there; the process would go on, and

26. John C. Calhoun, *The Speeches of John C. Calhoun*, ed. Richard K. Crallé (New York: D. Appleton and Company, 1861), 410–12.

the power transferred from the Legislative Department to the Executive. All the immense patronage which holding it as a province would create,—the maintenance of a large army, to hold it in subjection, and the appointment of a multitude of civil officers necessary to govern it,—would be vested in him. The great influence which it would give the President, would be the means of controlling the Legislative Department, and subjecting it to his dictation, especially when combined with the principle of proscription which has now become the established practice of the Government. The struggle to obtain the Presidential chair would become proportionably great—so great as to destroy the freedom of elections. The end would be anarchy or despotism, as certain as I am now addressing the Senate.

## Senator Daniel S. Dickinson (January 12, 1848)[27]

And should our army now be withdrawn, leaving her deluded people the prey of the ferocious spirits who have hastened her downfall, we may expect to see some supernumerary of the House of Bourbon placed at their head to play automaton to the British Cabinet. The policy of extending our jurisdiction over any portion of Mexican territory, is a question between Europe and America—between monarchy and freedom—and not between the United States and the Republic of Mexico; and we should not hesitate to extend our protection to such provinces as are held by us in undisturbed possession now, and patiently await the development of the future. Should the progress of events, without injustice on our part, open to the enterprise of our citizens the rich mining and agricultural districts of that country, and infuse among this semi-barbarous people the blessings of civilization, should the valuable trade which has been monopolized by England be enjoyed by the States, and our mint coin the money of the world; and should a passage across the Isthmus be obtained, placing the mouth of the Columbia within two weeks sail of New Orleans, and valuable Pacific harbors be permanently secured, so indispensable to the protection of our vast trade in that sea, and our settlements upon that coast,—there would be no occasion for lamentation or alarm. The day is not far distant when all this and much more will be realized, through a process as fixed and unyielding as the laws of gravitation. And whenever the time which is to determine whether entire Mexico should shall come within the jurisdiction of the United States, or become a colonial dependent upon European power, the duty of this government will admit neither doubt or hesitation.

27. Daniel S. Dickinson, *Speeches, Correspondence, Etc., of the Late Daniel S. Dickinson of New York,* ed. John R. Dickinson (New York: G. P. Putnam and Son, 1867), 233–34.

## Martin Robison Delany to Frederick Douglass (February 11, 1848)[28]

The scheme, now freely and openly discussed, concerning the incorporation of Mexico with the United States, is a project the most frightful and monstrous within the pale of human conception. And even Dr. Bailey, of the *Era,* and some others who call themselves Abolitionists, favor and contend for a consummation of this project. They argue that it will facilitate the overthrow of American Slavery, and forsooth, bring the Mexicans under a more settled and stable government.

But what are the facts in this case? But a glance will suffice to show the fallacy and duplicity of this whole nefarious scheme.

Mexico is peopled by *ten millions* of inhabitants; but fifteen hundred thousand, or three-twentieths of whom are whites, the rest, seventeen-twentieths, or seven and a half millions, are Indians and mixed colors—from the black to the fairest quadroon. According to the *Christian* usages, laws and customs of this *free* republic, no colored person—that is to say, black, mulatto, or Indian—is eligible to the privileges secured to and enjoyed by the whites. Such being the case, should this high-handed project succeed, while it might in reality speed the overthrow of slavery, as such, in the South, yet in doing so, would bring with it degradation and servility to nearly eight millions of freemen, heretofore enjoying the rights and privileges of a free and equal people, common to all, of whatever origin; while but one and a half million would retain those rights, enjoyed in common heretofore by all! And this is what we are asked to subscribe to! How superlatively devilish is this whole scheme! Nay, rather than this, let all Mexico be engulfed in the horrors of an earthquake!

## Abraham Lincoln's Spot Resolution (December 22, 1847)[29]

*Before becoming the sixteenth president of the United States in 1861 as a member of the Republican Party, Abraham Lincoln (1809–1865) began his national political career in the Whig party by winning a seat in the U.S. House of Representatives in 1846. Lincoln literally disputed the grounds upon which Polk built his case for war against Mexico. On December 22, 1847, Lincoln submitted a series of resolutions querying the president about the circumstances that led to war.*

---

28. Martin Delany, "Letter to Frederick Douglass," *The North Star,* February 11, 1848, 2.

29. Abraham Lincoln, *Life and Works of Abraham Lincoln,* vol. 2, *Early Speeches 1832–1836,* ed. Marion Mills Miller (New York: Current Literature Publishing Company, 1907), 113–14.

*In February 1848, he expanded on his "Spot Resolutions" in a lengthy speech and accused Polk of being a "bewildered, confounded, and miserably perplexed man."*

WHEREAS, The President of the United States, in his message of May 11, 1846, has declared that "the Mexican Government not only refused to receive him [the envoy of the United States], or to listen to his propositions, but, after a long-continued series of menaces, has at last invaded our territory and shed the blood of our fellow citizens on our own soil."[30]

And again, in his message of December 8, 1846, that "we had ample cause of war against Mexico long before the breaking out of hostilities; but even then we forbore to take redress into our own hands until Mexico herself became the aggressor, by invading our soil in hostile array, and shedding the blood of our citizens."

And yet again, in his message of December 7, 1847, that "the Mexican Government refused even to hear the terms of adjustment which he [our minister of peace] was authorized to propose, and finally, under wholly unjustifiable pretexts, involved the two countries in war, by invading the territory of the State of Texas, striking the first blow, and shedding the blood of our citizens on our own soil."

AND WHEREAS, This House is desirous to obtain full knowledge of all the facts which go to establish whether the particular spot on which the blood of our citizens was so shed was or was not at that time our own soil; therefore,

RESOLVED, By the House of Representatives, that the President of the United States be respectfully requested to inform this House—

First. Whether the spot on which the blood of our citizens was shed, as in his message declared, was or was not within the territory of Spain, at least after the treaty of 1819 until the Mexican revolution.

Second. Whether that spot is or is not within the territory which was wrested from Spain by the revolutionary Government of Mexico.

Third. Whether that spot is or is not within a settlement of people, which settlement has existed ever since long before the Texas revolution, and until its inhabitants fled before the approach of the United States army.

Fourth. Whether that settlement is or is not isolated from any and all other settlements by the Gulf and the Rio Grande on the south and west, and by wide uninhabited regions on the north and east.

Fifth. Whether the people of that settlement, or a majority of them, or any of them, have ever submitted themselves to the government or laws of Texas or the United States, by consent or by compulsion, either by accepting office, or voting at elections, or paying tax, or serving on juries, or having process served upon them, or in any other way.

---

30. From "Polk's War Message (May 11, 1846)" in Part II. The wording in the quote is Lincoln's, not Polk's.

Sixth. Whether the people of that settlement did or did not flee from the approach of the United States army, leaving unprotected their homes and their growing crops, before the blood was shed, as in the message stated; and whether the first blood, so shed, was or was not shed within the enclosure of one of the people who had thus fled from it.

Seventh. Whether our citizens, whose blood was shed, as in his message declared, were or were not, at that time, armed officers and soldiers, sent into that settlement by the military order of the President, through the Secretary of War.

Eighth. Whether the military force of the United States was or was not so sent into that settlement after General Taylor had more than once intimated to the War Department that, in his opinion, no such movement was necessary to the defense or protection of Texas.

## Frederick Douglass on the War (June 8, 1849)[31]

*Frederick Douglass (c. 1818–1895) grew up under harsh conditions as a slave in Maryland before escaping to Philadelphia and New York in 1838, where he began a lifelong career as an orator and writer who advocated freedom for the slaves. Apart from editing notable African American abolitionist newspapers, such as* The North Star, *he published a landmark memoir,* Narrative of the Life of Frederick Douglass, an American Slave, Written by Himself *(1845). Undoubtedly the most recognized African American of his time, Douglass helped recruit African Americans for the Union army during the Civil War and served as an advisor to President Abraham Lincoln.*

Someone has asked me to say a word about General Worth. I only know General Worth by his acts in Mexico and elsewhere, in the service of this slaveholding and slave-trading government. I know why that question is put: it is because one of your city papers, which does not rise to the dignity of being called a paper—a sheet of the basest sort—has said that my tongue ought to be cut out by its roots because, upon hearing of the death of that man, I made use of the remark—(it is not stated in what connection I made it, or where)—that another legalized murderer had gone to his account. I say so yet! I will not undertake to defend what I then said, or to shop up his character or history. You know as well as I do, that Faneuil Hall has resounded with echoing applause of a denunciation of the Mexican war, as a murderous war—as a war against the free states—as a war against freedom, against the Negro, and against the interests of workingmen of this country—and as a means of extending that great evil and damning curse,

31. Frederick Douglass, "Great Meeting at Faneuil Hall," *The Liberator* 29, no. 23 (June 8, 1849): 90.

negro slavery. Why may not the oppressed say, when an oppressor is dead, either by disease or by the hand of the foeman on the battlefield, that there is one the less of his oppressors left on earth? For my part, I would not care if, to-morrow, I should hear of the death of every man who engaged in that bloody war in Mexico, and that every man had met the fate he went there to perpetrate upon unoffending Mexicans. A word more. There are three millions of slaves in this land, held by the United States Government, under the sanction of the American Constitution, with all the compromises and guaranties contained in that instrument in favor of the slave system. Among those guaranties and compromises is one by which you, the citizens of Boston, have sworn, before God, that three millions of slaves shall be slaves or die—that your swords and bayonets and arms shall, at any time at the biding of the slaveholder, through the legal magistrate or governor of a slave State, be at his service in putting down the slaves. With eighteen millions of freemen standing upon the quivering hearts of three millions of slaves, my sympathies, of course, must be with the oppressed. I am among them, and you are treading them beneath your feet. The weight of your influence, numbers, political combinations and religious organizations, and the power of your arms, rest heavily upon them, and serve at this moment to keep them in their chains. When I consider their condition—the history of the American people—how they bared their bosoms to the storm of British artillery, in order to resist simply a three-penny tea tax, and to assert their independence of the mother country—I say, in view of these things, I should welcome the intelligence to-morrow, should it come, that the slaves had risen in the South, and that the sable arms which had been engaged in beautifying and adorning the South were engaged in spreading death and devastation there. There is a state of war at the South at this moment. The slaveholder is waging a war of aggression on the oppressed. The slaves are now under his feet. Why, you welcomed the intelligence from France, that Louis-Philippe had been barricaded in Paris[32]—you threw up your caps in honor of the victory achieved by Republicanism over Royalty—you shouted aloud—"Long live the republic!"—and joined heartily in the watchword of "Liberty, Equality, Fraternity"—and should you not hail, with equal pleasure, the tidings from the South that the slaves had risen, and achieved for himself [sic], against the iron-hearted slaveholder, what the republicans of France achieved against the royalists of France?

## Jane Grey Swisshelm Remembers the War (1880)

*A feminist and an abolitionist, Jane Grey Swisshelm (1815–1884) was one of the most politically engaged and controversial nineteenth-century women writers in the*

32. The Revolution of 1848 ended the reign of King Louis-Philippe (1773–1850) and began the French Second Republic.

*United States. Most of her writings can be found in the newspapers that she edited, such as the* Pittsburgh Saturday Visiter *(1847–1851), the* Minnesota St. Cloud Visiter *(1857), and the* Reconstructionist *(1865), as well as articles she published in the* New York Tribune *(1850). The same year she began publishing in the* Tribune, *Swisshelm received national attention and lost her post at the New York paper when she published a much reprinted story accusing presidential candidate Daniel Webster (1782–1852), the Whig senator of Massachusetts and former secretary of state, of being sexually promiscuous and a drunkard. In 1857, after Swisshelm had left her husband and moved to Minnesota, her controversial articles resulted in an angry mob burning the printing press of her paper the* St. Cloud Visiter. *Apart from her journalism, Swisshelm also authored* Letters to Country Girls *(1853) and an autobiography titled* Half of a Century *(1881). During the Civil War, Swisshelm volunteered as a nurse for the Union, distinguishing herself in the care of a large number of wounded men at Fredericksburg (1862).*

## From *Half a Century*[33]

Samuel Black, a son of my pastor, dropped his place as leader of the Pittsburg bar and rushed to the war. . . . Samuel returned with a colonel's commission, and one day I was about to pass him without recognition, where he stood on the pavement talking to two other lawyers, when he stepped before me and held out his hand. I drew back, and he said: "Is it possible you will not take my hand?"

I looked at it, then into his manly, handsome face, and answered:

"There is blood on it; the blood of women and children slain at their own altars, on their own hearthstones, that you might spread the glorious American institution of woman-whipping and baby-stealing."

"Oh," he exclaimed, "This is too bad! I swear to you I never killed a woman or a child."

"Then you did not fight in Mexico, did not help to bombard Buena Vista."[34]

His friends joined him, and insisted that I did the Colonel great wrong, when he looked squarely into my face and, holding out his hand, said:

"For sake of the old church, for sake of the old man, for sake of the old times, give me your hand."

I laid it in his, and hurried away, unable to speak, for he was the most eloquent man in Pennsylvania. He fell at last at the head of his regiment, while fighting in the battle of Fair Oaks, for that freedom he had betrayed in Mexico.[35]

---

33. Jane Grey Swisshelm, *Half a Century* (Chicago: Jansen, McClurg and Company, 1880), 95–96.

34. Swisshelm confuses the siege of Veracruz for the Battle of Buena Vista.

35. The Battle of Fair Oaks took place on June 27, 1862.

# V

# Legacies of War

## Selection from the Treaty of Guadalupe Hidalgo (1848)[1]

*The Treaty of Guadalupe Hidalgo ended the U.S.-Mexican War and resulted in the Mexican surrender of more than five hundred thousand square miles of its territory to the United States, an area comprising the present-day U.S. states of California, Nevada, Arizona, Utah, and New Mexico and parts of Colorado and Wyoming. The treaty was signed on February 2, 1848, in the village of Guadalupe Hidalgo and later amended and ratified by the U.S. Congress on March 10. The Mexican senate ratified the amended treaty on May 7, 1848. The treaty consists of twenty-three articles, covering topics such as the end of hostilities, the withdrawal of U.S. forces from Mexico, the drawing of new borders, and the payment of nearly $15 million for the purchase of territory and the cancellation of Mexican debts to the United States. Articles VIII, IX, and X, included below, are of particular interest because of their impact on the legal and economic status of Mexicans residing in the territories ceded by Mexico to the United States. The U.S. government amended article IX to make guarantees of Mexican rights more vague and struck out article X, which had forcefully provided protection for Mexican land rights, especially in Texas. Throughout the nineteenth century and into the twentieth, the legal status of Mexicans in the ceded territories and their property rights were the subject of vigorous litigation. In spite of the protections of the treaty, large numbers of Mexicans and their descendants lost property to an influx of land-hungry white settlers.*

### ARTICLE V

The boundary line between the two Republics shall commence in the Gulf of Mexico, three leagues from land, opposite the mouth of the Rio Grande, otherwise called Río Bravo del Norte, or opposite the mouth of its deepest branch, if it should have more than one branch emptying directly into the sea; from thence up the middle of that river, following the deepest channel, where it has more than one, to the point where it strikes the southern boundary of New Mexico; thence,

1. U.S. Congress. Senate, *Compilation of Treaties in Force* (Washington, DC: Government Printing Office, 1904), 514–27.

westwardly, along the whole southern boundary of New Mexico (which runs north of the town called Paso[2]) to its western termination; thence, northward, along the western line of New Mexico, until it intersects the first branch of the river Gila; (or if it should not intersect any branch of that river, then to the point on the said line nearest to such branch, and thence in a direct line to the same); thence down the middle of the said branch and of the said river, until it empties into the Rio Colorado; thence across the Rio Colorado, following the division line between Upper and Lower California, to the Pacific Ocean.

The southern and western limits of New Mexico, mentioned in the article, are those laid down in the map entitled *Map of the United Mexican States, as organized and defined by various acts of the Congress of said republic, and constructed according to the best authorities. Revised edition. Published at New York, in 1847, by J. Disturnell;* of which Map a Copy is added to this Treaty, bearing the signatures and seals of the Undersigned Plenipotentiaries. And, in order to preclude all difficulty in tracing upon the ground the limit separating Upper from Lower California, it is agreed that the said limit shall consist of a straight line drawn from the middle of the Río Gila, where it unites with the Colorado, to a point on the coast of the Pacific Ocean, distant one marine league due south of the southernmost point of the port of San Diego, according to the plan of said port made in the year 1782 by Don Juan Pantoja, second sailing-master of the Spanish fleet, and published at Madrid in the year 1802, in the atlas to the voyage of the schooners Sutil and Mexicana; of which plan a copy is hereunto added, signed and sealed by the respective Plenipotentiaries.

In order to designate the boundary line with due precision, upon authoritative maps, and to establish upon the ground land-marks which shall show the limits of both republics, as described in the present article, the two Governments shall each appoint a commissioner and a surveyor, who, before the expiration of one year from the date of the exchange of ratifications of this treaty, shall meet at the port of San Diego, and proceed to run and mark the said boundary in its whole course to the mouth of the Río Bravo del Norte. They shall keep journals and make out plans of their operations; and the result agreed upon by them shall be deemed a part of this treaty, and shall have the same force as if it were inserted therein. The two Governments will amicably agree regarding what may be necessary to these persons, and also as to their respective escorts, should such be necessary.

The boundary line established by this article shall be religiously respected by each of the two republics, and no change shall ever be made therein, except by the express and free consent of both nations, lawfully given by the General Government of each, in conformity with its own constitution.

2. El Paso.

## ARTICLE VI

The vessels and citizens of the United States shall, in all time, have a free and uninterrupted passage by the Gulf of California, and by the river Colorado below its confluence with the Gila, to and from their possessions situated north of the boundary line defined in the preceding article; it being understood that this passage is to be by navigating the Gulf of California and the river Colorado, and not by land, without the express consent of the Mexican Government.

If, by the examinations which may be made, it should be ascertained to be practicable and advantageous to construct a road, canal, or railway, which should in whole or in part run upon the river Gila, or upon its right or its left bank, within the space of one marine league from either margin of the river, the Governments of both republics will form an agreement regarding its construction, in order that it may serve equally for the use and advantage of both countries.

## ARTICLE VII

The river Gila, and the part of the Río Bravo del Norte lying below the southern boundary of New Mexico, being, agreeably to the fifth Article, divided in the middle between the two Republics, the navigation of the Gila and of the Bravo below said boundary shall be free and common to the vessels and citizens of both countries; and neither shall, without the consent of the other, construct any work that may impede or interrupt, in whole or in part, the exercise of this right; not even for the purpose of favoring new methods of navigation. Nor shall any tax or contribution, under any denomination or title, be levied upon vessels or persons navigating the same or upon merchandise or effects transported thereon, except in the case of landing upon one of their shores. If, for the purpose of making the said rivers navigable, or for maintaining them in such state, it should be necessary or advantageous to establish any tax or contribution, this shall not be done without the consent of both Governments.

The stipulations contained in the present article shall not impair the territorial rights of either Republic within its established limits.

## ARTICLE VIII

Mexicans now established in territories previously belonging to Mexico, and which remain for the future within the limits of the United States, as defined by the present Treaty, shall be free to continue where they now reside, or to remove at any time to the Mexican Republic, retaining the property which they possess in the said territories, or disposing thereof, and removing the proceeds wherever they please, without their being subjected, on this account, to any contribution, tax, or charge whatever.

Those who shall prefer to remain in the said territories may either retain the title and rights of Mexican citizens, or acquire those of citizens of the United States. But they shall be under the obligation to make their election within one year from the date of the exchange of ratifications of this Treaty: and those who shall remain in the said territories after the expiration of that year, without having declared their intention to retain the character of Mexicans, shall be considered to have elected to become citizens of the United States.

In the said territories, property of every kind, now belonging to Mexicans not established there, shall be inviolably respected. The present owners, the heirs of these, and all Mexicans who may hereafter acquire said property by contract, shall enjoy with respect to it guarantees equally ample as if the same belonged to citizens of the United States.

## ARTICLE IX

The Mexicans who, in the territories aforesaid, shall not preserve the character of citizens of the Mexican Republic, conformably with what is stipulated in the preceding article, shall be incorporated into the Union of the United States and be admitted at the proper time (to be judged of by the Congress of the United States) to the enjoyment of all the rights of citizens of the United States, according to the principles of the Constitution; and in the mean time, shall be maintained and protected in the free enjoyment of their liberty and property, and secured in the free exercise of their religion without restriction.

## ARTICLE X [Stricken out (Land Grants).]

All grants of land made by the Mexican Government or by the component authorities, in territories previously appertaining to Mexico, and remaining for the future within the limits of the United States, shall be respected as valid, to the same extent that the same grants would be valid, if the said territories had remained within the limits of Mexico. But the grantees of lands in Texas, put in possession thereof, who, by reason of the circumstances of the country since the beginning of the troubles between Texas and the Mexican Government, may have been prevented from fulfilling all the conditions of their grants, shall be under the obligation to fulfill said conditions within the periods limited in the same respectively; such periods to be now counted from the date of exchange of ratifications of this treaty: in default of which the said grants shall not be obligatory upon the State of Texas, in virtue of the stipulations contained in this Article.

The foregoing stipulation in regard to grantees of land in Texas, is extended to all grantees of land in the territories aforesaid, elsewhere than Texas, put in possession under such grants; and, in default of the fulfillment of the conditions of any such grant, within the new period, which, as is above stipulated, begins with the day of the exchange of ratifications of this treaty, the same shall be null and void.

# Mexican Views of the Treaty of Guadalupe Hidalgo (May 1848)

*The Mexican government in 1848 was divided over whether or not the Treaty of Guadalupe Hidalgo should be ratified. Manuel Gómez Pedraza (1789–1851), who had been an influential and prominent* moderado *liberal, argued that despite the magnitude of Mexican concessions to the United States, Mexico was too weak to reject the treaty. The* puro *liberal Manuel Crescencio Rejón (1799–1849) ardently opposed the treaty on nationalist grounds. On May 25, the treaty was ratified in both the chamber of deputies and the senate of the Mexican congress, with votes of 51–35 and 33–4, respectively.*

## Manuel Crescencio Rejón (April 17, 1848)[3]

Now that the borders of our conquerors have been brought closer to the heart of our country, with them occupying the entire length of our border from sea to sea, with such a resolute merchant marine, well accredited in the system of colonization with which they attract numerous proletarians from the old world, what can we, who are so behind in everything, do to stop their swift conquests, their future invasions? Thousands of men will come daily to establish themselves under their auspices in the new limits that we shall agree on, they will develop their commerce there, they will build large warehouses for the goods that they will smuggle, will flood us with them, and our treasury, once miserable and in decline, will subsequently be insignificant and null. We will gain nothing then by lowering the maritime tariffs, with the disappearance of customs houses in the interior, the suppression of trade restrictions: the Anglo-Americans, who by then will be established near our populous provinces, will provide them with all the wonders of the world, and these will pass from our bordering states to our southern states, and against us they will have the advantage of the self-interest of our own merchants, of our own consumers who will favor them in this regard, by virtue of the low prices for which they will buy their merchandise. Because even if we only imposed a 20 percent tariff on the goods brought through our ports, which will be difficult to effect, we will never be able to compete in our markets with North American importers, who will be able to offer for a cheaper price the merchandise they bring to sell us since they will not have paid any or

3. Manuel Crescencio Rejón, *Observaciones del Diputado Saliente Manuel Crescencio Rejón, contra los Tratados de Paz firmados en la Ciudad de Guadalupe el 2 del próximo pasado febrero* (Mexico City: Imprenta de J. M. Lara, 1848), 33–36. Translated by Gustavo Pellón.

almost any duties. The Drawback[4] alone, well known in that republic, would be enough to give them an advantage that would destroy our frontier and maritime customs, and we would not have enough revenue to face even the costs for the upkeep of the border.

And, what protection would be enough, what troops would be sufficient to guard such an extensive border and avoid the introduction of fraudulent goods? On the other hand what fights, what disputes, what quarrels with the bold smugglers of that republic, what constant claims, what lawsuits for compensation amounting, in the long run, to vast sums that would provoke another war in which they would take away, without resistance, the rest of the territory we still hold! Why do we forget so quickly what has just happened to us in New Mexico, the Californias, and Chihuahua, where large armed parties have shown up, sometimes even with artillery pieces, to bring in their goods without paying any duty and without adherence to our laws and regulations? Are we hoping perhaps that what happened in those places will not occur because our neighbors have brought their border closer to us? Gentlemen, what these fatal treaties propose is our sentence of death, and I wonder that there are Mexicans who negotiated, signed, and considered them of benefit to our unfortunate country. This circumstance alone makes me worry and makes me despair for the life of the republic.

. . .

After this treaty is approved, it will no longer be possible for us to derive the great benefits that are now proposed, because even supposing that we could easily overcome the resistance, the petty, contemptible ideas that even those men reputed to be the most eminent in the so-called party of intelligence have opposed to the friends of progress, how could we overcome the obstacles to deal with the policy and the overwhelming resources of the United States, seeing that they are in possession of our most precious territories? Having established in the Old World their reputation for hospitality, with a knowledge of the type of industry of which we are totally ignorant, with a merchant marine that competes with that of Great Britain and which makes it so easy for them to bring to their country the exuberant population of teeming Europe, what means can we adopt to take away from them at least a part of the emigration in order to overcome the preference given to them due to the high opinion in which its civilization and wealth are held? With the most fertile lands that they are taking from us, with such sweet climates as they have never had before, with brilliant positions for maritime commerce, such as those offered by that inestimable jewel, Alta California, gentlemen, they will empty Europe. They will amalgamate Europe to themselves, and

4. According to John Wharton's *The Law Lexicon, or Dictionary of Jurisprudence* (1848), a drawback is "a term used in commerce to signify the remitting or paying back of the duties previously paid on a commodity on its being exported. A drawback is a device resorted to for enabling a commodity affected by taxes to be exported and sold in the foreign market on the same terms as if it had not been taxed at all."

they will champion the settlements that they will establish over us, and in less than fifteen years perhaps we shall no longer be masters of the land they let us keep. Then our race, our poor people will have to roam foreign lands in search of hospitality, only to be cast out later to other places.

## Manuel Gómez Pedraza (May 24, 1848)[5]

Why speculate on what did not happen? What is important is to try to foresee what may happen to us, so as to plan our future conduct wisely. Furthermore, the senate is going to make its decision after the fact. Its point of departure is the present state of things, and the past is not its concern. We have before us a treaty, and we need to vote on its desirability or undesirability.

Having presented the issue before us, I shall examine briefly the arguments for peace and those put forth for war. I have noticed that those in favor of war direct their efforts at arousing emotion rather than reason. The memory of injustice, duplicity, and felony and the exposition of insults are matters that should in no way influence our resolution, as our means of reprisal are ineffectual. Every invasion entails this retinue of insults, but impotent resentment is not the means to avenge them. Desirability and the likelihood of success are the only factors that should influence our decision. Let us, therefore, examine those motives.

Some gentlemen who have had the floor before me have said that if we continue the war, some nation is bound to denounce the abuse we have suffered; that the enemy will not be able to bear the growing expense of an indefinite campaign; that the peace party in the United States will prevail over the war party; that the next president of that nation, who supposedly will be the illustrious Clay,[6] will return the disputed territory to us; and finally, that our nation will be able to awaken from its lethargy. Their argument comes down to these allegations.

To the first allegation, I answer that people in general are less sensitive to the misfortunes of others than to their own. The deeds of violence in Algiers and China[7] have been read about in the newspapers and forgotten. Nations, unless

5. Manuel Gómez Pedraza, "Discurso pronunciado por el Sr. D. Manuel G. Pedraza, Presidente de la Cámara de Senadores, el 24 de Mayo de 1848, en la Discusión Sobre Aprobar o no el Tratado Celebrado entre el Gobierno de México y el de los Estados Unidos de América," in *Galería de oradores de México en el siglo XIX,* ed. Emilio del Castillo Negrete, vol. 1 (Mexico City: Tipografía de Santiago Sierra, 1877), 337–56. Translated by Gustavo Pellón.

6. The Kentuckian senator, secretary of state, and Whig leader Henry Clay (1777–1852) ran for president for a fifth time in 1848, losing to General Zachary Taylor.

7. He refers to the French occupation of Algiers, which began in 1830, and the Anglo-Chinese Opium War of 1839–1842.

their own major interests require it, do not launch crusades in favor of victims of aggression. . . .

I will respond to the second one by saying that if the war continues, the enemy will seek to defray its cost at the expense of the occupied country and reduce their own expenses to a minimum.

To the third, I will say that the party that declared itself in favor of peace in the United States acted like any party. There as here, parties seize opportunities to advance their goals, but there (unlike here) parties yield to expediency and law. A few years ago the country that has invaded us confronted France and made its king agree to the payment of twenty-five million francs that the United States demanded.[8] Subsequently, it threw down the gauntlet at England in the Oregon question, and Great Britain did not hurry to take it up.[9] Having started the war with Mexico, the future of our neighboring republic perhaps depends on its triumph. What would Europe say of a nation by which it feels intimidated and will feel threatened before long, if it were defeated by another nation, which in the opinion of the aggressors themselves, is worth little? On this point the feeling of all Americans must be uniform. . . . Colonel Carlos Smith,[10] who is lodged in my house in Mexico City, is a just gentleman who sympathizes with us, but this affection in no way impedes his carrying out the duties imposed on him by his position.

To the fourth allegation, I will say that the illustrious Clay, if he obtains the presidency of his nation, will have to sacrifice his inclinations and even his affections to the eventualities of politics. It is naïve to imagine that statesmen are ruled by personal sympathies.

Regarding the last point, I will say that the paralysis into which a nation falls is the effect of numerous causes that have been at work for a long time and that getting out of that condition is a slow and lengthy process. The evils of war are near at hand and imminent. The solution of an energetic uprising, even if it were possible, would be belated and tardy. That unfounded hope must not enter into our reckoning. . . .

The agreement, or treaty, before us is, in my opinion, a summons or an ultimatum, but what else have pacts between the victor and the vanquished ever been? The conqueror imposes his will at the point of the sword, and Cyrus,

---

8. In 1831, France agreed to compensate the United States 25 million francs for damages inflicted on U.S. interests during the Napoleonic Wars. After a drawn out diplomatic dispute, France began its payments in 1836.

9. A reference to President Polk's refusal to renew the Treaty of the Joint Occupation of Oregon with Great Britain in 1846, which resulted in the United States taking sole control of most of the Oregon territory.

10. Charles F. Smith (1807–1862) of Philadelphia fought with distinction under both Taylor and Scott in the war with Mexico and died as a result of a serious leg injury and its subsequent medical treatment while commanding a Union force in Tennessee during the Civil War.

Alexander, and Tamerlane did nothing less than that. . . .[11] What would be the consequences of rejecting the ultimatum we have on the table? Inevitable war, which is to say the immediate occupation of the six or seven state capitals we still hold; the imposition of a new and heavy tribute demanded with the rigor of those who dominate; the destruction of the buildings occupied by their soldiers; the insecurity and ill-treatment of the inhabitants of the occupied cities; the moral degradation to the greatest degree of the best of our cities; the corruption of our youth; the predominance, in short, of an army without restraint, and whose savage conduct in the areas that have already been subjected to its power is nothing but an imperfect prelude to its subsequent behavior.

What would happen in the rest of our occupied country would not be less horrible: towns sacked by bandits who call themselves guerrillas, fields trampled by roving bands who in the name of patriotism will allow themselves every kind of excess. Theft, arson, murder, and all the crimes of a vandalistic and unbridled assault would be the consequences of the uprising that is desired. There is no use in lulling ourselves with illusions. The present generation is not the innocent and well-behaved generation of 1810; and if that one, despite its good habits, was perverted shortly after the insurrection, what can we expect of the masses who are already corrupted?

. . .

I have reflected slightly about the dire consequences that the continuation of the war would bring to us; but from this it should not be inferred that I consider peace an absolute good. In our difficult situation we should not expect anything favorable. Nevertheless, I accept peace as a relative good, and I accept it because it can become a benefit if we know how to use it. Peace means a truce, a temporary recess from our grave misfortunes. Let us take advantage of this small benefit that fortune offers us, but that great task, oh, senators! depends largely on us. One of our disadvantages is the topographical position that our republic occupies on the continent. Since we are neighbors to an enterprising and active people who inhabit the glacial land to our north and who are just as prone as their parents to emigrate to better climates, we shall be perpetually threatened by their incursions if we do not hurry to build a dike to hold back this torrent. Emigrations have perpetually and constantly taken place from the north to the south of continents, and this rule embraces men, animals, and even plants. The Tartars spilled over China, the Scythians over Italy and Spain, and the Scandinavians over the British Isles. The Americans of the North will spread to the Isthmus of Panama unless they are stopped.

. . .

The way to avoid the incursions of our neighbors is to truly open our doors to them and to European immigration; to invite them to come and establish

11. Cyrus the Great, founder of the Persian Empire (c. 500 B.C.); the Macedonian Alexander the Great (356–323 B.C.); and Tamerlane (1336–1405), a Mongol conqueror.

themselves in our pleasant lands; guarantee their lives, property, and whatever pleasures a man expects from society; to assure them of ample protection under the law and the benevolence of the government; to introduce them to our national character, which we must preserve at all costs; to have them adopt it by speaking our beautiful language, becoming used to our customs, acquiring our habits, mixing with our families, in short, assimilating and forming together with us the body of a nation. In this manner, after a few generations, the heterogeneity of our population will disappear, and that strong, numerous, and regenerated population will be a firm bulwark against the enterprises of our enemies. The United States has grown in this manner; let us rise to their level, and an equilibrium will be established.

## Considerations on the Political and Social Situation of the Mexican Republic in the Year of 1847 (1848)

*In June 1848, Mexico City's* El Monitor Republicano *reprinted a pamphlet authored by "various Mexicans" but now attributed to the* moderado *federalist Mariano Otero (1817–1850). The excerpts that follow illustrate the federalist view of Mexican political, cultural, and economic underdevelopment after the war.*

### Introduction[12]

The fact that a foreign army of ten to twelve thousand men has penetrated from Veracruz to the capital of the republic and that, with the exception of the bombardment of that port, the action at Cerro Gordo, and the small skirmishes it had with Mexican troops in the vicinity of the capital, it can be said that it has not found enemies with which to fight in its long journey across three of the most important and most highly populated states of the Mexican federation with more than two million inhabitants is an event of such a nature that it cannot but give rise to the most serious reflections.

Shallow men, those who judge events only according to facts, without delving into the causes that produce them, usually commit serious errors. It is, therefore, not strange that, as we have already seen in some foreign newspapers, the Mexican people are described as an effeminate people, as a degenerate race, who have not known how to govern or defend themselves.

But the thinking man who, not content to admire the effects before his eyes, seeks to delve into the causes from which they come will easily find in Mexico the

12. Anonymous, *Consideraciones sobre la situación política y social de la república mexicana, en el año 1847* (Mexico City: Valdés y Redondas Impresores, 1848), 3–4, 5–8, 32, 37, 42–43. Translated by Gustavo Pellón.

reasons for which its people, far from taking an active part in the present struggle, remain, so to speak, as cold spectators of the conflict. Once those reasons are found, only the blindest partiality can insist on claiming that they are defects peculiar to the Mexican race, as they are nothing but the necessary results of certain, determinate causes.

## First Part: Indians

Indians are disseminated over the entire territory of the republic, grouped in small villages, really forming a family apart from the white and the mixed races. Their miserable way of life today differs not at all or very little from that of the subjects of the great emperor Moctezuma. The only notable variation between the latter and the former is the extinction of idolatry with its barbarous sacrifices of human blood; because Indians nowadays have been taught to adore their saints *their way* and to expect happiness in the other life, something that we must suppose they have come to believe in through the school of hard knocks, being thoroughly convinced that they can expect nothing good in this vale of tears. Neither at the time of the viceregal government nor after independence has an effective system of education been adopted for this race that would better the condition of individuals, taking them out of their present stultified state while making them useful to society. Neither before nor after have they been taught anything but to fear God, the priest, and the mayor; and the ignorance in which they live is such that we can assert that three-quarters of the Indians have not yet received the news of our having achieved our independence. It is all the more understandable that they are still ignorant of this, as in many places they are still charged tribute for the king of Spain, in the same manner and for the same reason that they are asked to give alms for the ransoming of captives and for the holy places in Jerusalem.

. . .

In order to apply the last brushstroke to this true painting of the sad experience of Indians, we shall only add that the only active part that they take in the public order of the country is by serving as soldiers in the army, which they are compelled to do by force. In this form of service, more than the fatherland, they serve as instruments for the promotion of their officers, who in time of peace give them little bread and plenty of beatings and in war frequently abandon them at the moment of danger. Given this, it is easy to understand the total lack of interest that this important part of the population of the republic has in the conservation of an order of things in which it is the victim. The Indians surely saw the entry of the North American army with the same indifference that they formerly saw the entry of Spanish armies when they dominated the country and with the same equanimity that, after our independence, they saw the comings and goings of our troops in our continuous internal revolution. . . .

## Commerce

The import commerce, with very few exceptions, is in the hands of foreigners, who, thanks to our petty and intolerant ideas, which derive directly from the monastic education we inherited from our good parents, neither take nor can take any interest in the welfare of our country. They only devote themselves to their business, and as soon as they amass the sum commensurate with their desires, they leave to enjoy it elsewhere. The import trade comes to some sixteen million pesos yearly, and there is no hope that it will increase as long as we lack a large population that will consume European goods and as long as we also do not have other goods to give in exchange. As long as Mexico has no other export than money, the importation of goods will always approximately equal the value of the silver that can be mined.

## The Clergy

Let us move to an examination of the clergy, who by virtue of being the greatest real estate owner of the republic, which explains the great and fatal influence they have had on our society, could naturally be expected to undertake with ardor the defense of our country, that is to say, the defense of its own property. The clergy must surely realize that any other moderately enlightened government that might establish itself in the country will strip it of all its vast property and reduce it to the simple exercise of its purely spiritual mission on earth. It should, therefore, have made every effort with all its resources to hinder the advance of the enemy army, because as this army represents a people where absolute freedom of religion is one of the fundamental bases of the social system, it should have been evident that if Mexico succumbed in the struggle, the clergy here must fear not only the loss of its interests but also that of the unique and absolute power that it exercises without opposition in a country like this where the practice of any religion other than its own is not tolerated.

. . .

Those guilty of this crime, in our opinion, are only and principally the persons who constitute the so-called high clergy and all others who trade and make a living from the management of those vast properties so inappropriately called Church properties. These men not only are criminals because of their selfishness in the present circumstances but are in great measure the origin of all the misfortunes of the nation. They have successively controlled the personnel of all our governments since our independence was won, impeding any fundamental reform that would endanger their absurd power. They have exercised their perverse influence on society to keep it stationary, ignorant, and stultified because that is the only way they can continue to enjoy undisturbed all their abuses and privileges. They have employed part of that wealth, which they say is God's and for the worship of God, to foment the immorality of the nation, provoking various revolutions to overthrow any government that did not serve their selfish interests.

**Conclusion**

Therefore, it seems totally useless for foreign writers to overwork their brains, seeking an explanation for the indifference that the nation has demonstrated in the present war in the "feminization or degeneration of the Mexican race," just as it is ridiculous for Mexicans to insist on blaming each other for what has happened. We, on the other hand, believe that it is all explained by these brief words: IN MEXICO THERE IS NOT, NOR COULD THERE BE WHAT IS CALLED A NATIONAL SPIRIT, BECAUSE THERE IS NO NATION. Indeed, if a nation deserves that name only when it contains in itself all the elements to make its own happiness and welfare at home and be respected abroad, Mexico cannot properly be called a nation.

. . .

A nation is nothing but a large family, and for this to be strong and powerful, it is necessary for all its members to be intimately joined by common interest and other feelings of the heart. In Mexico that union is not possible, and in order to convince ourselves of that, it is enough for us to take a quick glance at the different classes that make up this unfortunate society. Furthermore, civil war, which has been permanent here for a space of thirty-seven years, has demoralized all classes and has thereby destroyed the only element of order that this country had when it achieved its independence, that is to say, the respect and blind obedience to authority that formed the basis of the colonial system.

## The Mexican Cession and the Slavery Question

*The Missouri Compromise of 1820 stipulated that slavery could not extend north of the southern boundary of Missouri, at the 36°30′ parallel. The acquisition of Mexican lands after the U.S.-Mexican War, however, intensified debate over the future of slavery. Supporters of the Wilmot Proviso argued that slavery could not extend to any land acquired from Mexico, whereas others argued that the freedom to possess slaves was protected by the Fifth Amendment of the Bill of Rights or that each future state should decide the question for itself (the doctrine of "popular sovereignty"). In 1850, the status of the territories acquired from Mexico, especially with regard to the future of slavery, came to a head in the U.S. Congress. Senator Henry Clay of Kentucky (1777–1852) introduced a set of resolutions to tackle all of the issues and unite the nation in 1850. Although his resolutions at first failed, they provided the foundation for a set of separate bills called the Compromise of 1850, passed in September of that year. Under the compromise, California entered the union as a free state, the territorial governments of Utah and New Mexico were established under the doctrine of popular sovereignty, a border dispute between Texas and New Mexico was resolved, the slave trade in the District of Columbia was abolished, and a restrictive slave act that denied freedom to slaves who fled slavery was passed.*

*This section presents four documents. The first is an abolitionist argument by the poet Walt Whitman, who was a passionate advocate of the war and of U.S. expansion. The remaining documents address the Compromise of 1850. These include the full text of Clay's original resolutions that led to the compromise and excerpts of two opposing views of the slavery and territory question.*

## "American Workingmen, versus Slavery" by Walt Whitman (September 1, 1847)[13]

The question whether or no there shall be slavery in the new territories which it seems conceded on all hands we are largely to get through this Mexican war, is a question between *the grand body of white workingmen, the millions of mechanics, farmers, and operatives of our country,* with their interests on the one side—and the interests of the few thousand rich, "polished," and aristocratic owners of slaves at the South, on the other side. Experience has proved, (and the evidence is to be seen now by any one who will look at it) that a stalwart mass of respectable workingmen, cannot exist, much less flourish, in a thorough slave State. Let any one think for a moment what a different appearance New York, Pennsylvania, or Ohio, would present—how much less sturdy independence and family happiness there would be—were slaves the workmen there, instead of each man as a general thing being his own workman. We wish not at all to sneer at the South; but leaving out of view the educated and refined gentry, and coming to the "common people" of the whites, everybody knows what a miserable, ignorant, and shiftless set of beings they are. Slavery is a good thing enough, (viewed partially,) to the rich—the one out of thousands; but it is destructive to the dignity and independence of all who work, and to labor itself. An honest poor mechanic, in a slave State, is put on a par with the negro slave mechanic—there being many of the latter, who are hired by their owners. It is of no use to reason abstractly on this fact—farther than to say that the pride of a North American freeman, poor though he be, will not comfortably stand such degradation.

The influence of the slavery institution is to bring the dignity of labor down to the level of slavery, which, God knows! is low enough. And this it is which must induce *the workingmen of the North, East, and West, to come up, to a man, in defense of their rights, their honor, and that heritage of getting bread by the sweat of the brow, which we must leave to our children.*

. . .

13. Walt Whitman, "American Workingmen, versus Slavery," *Brooklyn Daily Eagle,* September 1, 1847, 2.

. . . But now, in the South, stands a little band, strong in chivalry, refinement and genius—headed by a sort of intellectual Saladin[14]—assuming to speak in behalf of sovereign States, while in reality they utter their own idle theories; and disdainfully crying out against the rest of the Republic, for whom their contempt is but illy concealed. The courage and high tone of these men are points in their favor, it must be confessed. With dexterous but brazen logic they profess to stand on the Constitution against a principle whose very existence dates from some of the most revered framers of that Constitution! And these—this band, really little in numbers, and which could be annihilated by one pulsation of the stout free heart of the North—these are the men who are making such insolent demands, in the face of the working farmers and mechanics of the free States—the nine-tenths of the population of the Republic. We admire the chivalric bearing (sometimes a sort of impudence) of these men. So we admire, as it is told in history, the dauntless conduct of kings and nobles when arraigned for punishment before an outraged and too long-suffering people. . . . [sic] But the course of mortal light and human freedom (and their consequent happiness,) is not to be stayed by such men as they. Thousands of noble hearts at the North—the entire East—the uprousing giant of the free East—will surely, when the time comes, sweep over them and their doctrines as the advancing ocean tide obliterates the channel of some little brook that erewhile ran down the sands of its shore. Already the roar of the waters is heard; and if a few short-sighted ones seek to withstand it, the surge, terrible in its fury, will sweep them too in the ruin.

## Henry Clay's Resolutions (January 29, 1850)[15]

It being desirable, for the peace, concord, and harmony of the Union of these States, to settle and adjust amicably all existing questions of controversy between them arising out of the institution of slavery upon a fair, equitable and just basis: therefore,

1. Resolved, That California, with suitable boundaries, ought, upon her application to be admitted as one of the States of this Union, without the imposition by Congress of any restriction in respect to the exclusion or introduction of slavery within those boundaries.

---

14. Here Whitman is referring to John C. Calhoun. Saladin led the Saracens against Richard the Lionheart during the Crusades in the twelfth century. The association between Calhoun and Saladin stems from an anecdote comparing the brute strength of Richard the Lionheart to the agility of Saladin. In this frame, Calhoun was Saladin to Daniel Webster's Richard the Lionheart.

15. U.S. Congress. House, *Abridgment of the Debates of Congress, from 1789 to 1856: Dec. 7, 1846–September 30, 1850* (New York: D. Appleton and Company, 1861), 391.

2. Resolved, That as slavery does not exist by law, and is not likely to be introduced into any of the territory acquired by the United States from the Republic of Mexico, it is inexpedient for Congress to provide by law either for its introduction into, or exclusion from, any part of the said territory; and that appropriate territorial governments ought to be established by Congress in all of the said territory, not assigned as the boundaries of the proposed State of California, without the adoption of any restriction or condition on the subject of slavery.
3. Resolved, That the western boundary of the State of Texas ought to be fixed on the Rio del Norte, commencing one marine league from its mouth, and running up that river to the southern line of New Mexico; thence with that line eastwardly, and so continuing in the same direction to the line as established between the United States and Spain, excluding any portion of New Mexico, whether lying on the east or west of that river.
4. Resolved, That it be proposed to the State of Texas, that the United States will provide for the payment of all that portion of the legitimate and bona fide public debt of that State contracted prior to its annexation to the United States, and for which the duties on foreign imports were pledged by the said State to its creditors, not exceeding the sum of _______ dollars, in consideration of the said duties so pledged having been no longer applicable to that object after the said annexation, but having thenceforward become payable to the United States; and upon the condition, also, that the said State of Texas shall, by some solemn and authentic act of her legislature or of a convention, relinquish to the United States any claim which it has to any part of New Mexico.
5. Resolved, That it is inexpedient to abolish slavery in the District of Columbia whilst that institution continues to exist in the State of Maryland, without the consent of that State, without the consent of the people of the District, and without just compensation to the owners of slaves within the District.
6. But, resolved, That it is expedient to prohibit, within the District, the slave trade in slaves brought into it from States or places beyond the limits of the District, either to be sold therein as merchandise, or to be transported to other markets without the District of Columbia.
7. Resolved, That more effectual provision ought to be made by law, according to the requirement of the constitution, for the restitution and delivery of persons bound to service or labor in any State, who may escape into any other State or Territory in the Union. And,
8. Resolved, That Congress has no power to promote or obstruct the trade in slaves between the slaveholding States; but that the admission or exclusion of slaves brought from one into another of them, depends exclusively upon their own particular laws.

## Speech by John C. Calhoun (March 4, 1850)[16]

The question then recurs: What is the cause of this discontent? It will be found in the belief of the people of the Southern States, as prevalent as the discontent itself, that they cannot remain, as things now are, consistently with honor and safety, in the Union. The next question to be considered is: What has caused this belief?

One of the causes is, undoubtedly, to be traced to the long-continued agitation of the slave question on the part of the North, and the many aggressions which they have made on the rights of the South during the time. I will not enumerate them at present, as it will be done hereafter in its proper place.

There is another lying back of it—with which this is intimately connected—that may be regarded as the great and primary cause. This is to be found in the fact that the equilibrium between the two sections in the government as it stood when the Constitution was ratified and the government put in action has been destroyed. At that time there was nearly a perfect equilibrium between the two, which afforded ample means to each to protect itself against the aggression of the other; but, as it now stands, one section has the exclusive power of controlling the government, which leaves the other without any adequate means of protecting itself against its encroachment and oppression. . . .

. . .

The result of the whole is to give the Northern section a predominance in every department of the government, and thereby concentrate in it the two elements which constitute the federal government: a majority of States, and a majority of their population, estimated in federal numbers. Whatever section concentrates the two in itself possesses the control of the entire government.

But we are just at the close of the sixth decade and the commencement of the seventh. The census is to be taken this year, which must add greatly to the decided preponderance of the North in the House of Representatives and in the Electoral College. The prospect is, also, that a great increase will be added to its present preponderance in the Senate, during the period of the decade, by the addition of new States. Two Territories, Oregon and Minnesota, are already in progress, and strenuous efforts are making to bring in three additional States from the Territory recently conquered from Mexico; which, if successful, will add three other States in a short time to the Northern section, making five States, and increasing the present number of its States from fifteen to twenty, and of its senators from thirty to forty. . . . On the contrary, there is not a single Territory in progress in the Southern section, and no certainty that any additional State will be added to it during the decade. The prospect then is, that the two sections

---

16. Richard K. Crallé, ed., *The Works of John C. Calhoun,* vol. 4 (New York: D. Appleton and Company, 1888), 542–44, 556.

in the Senate, should the efforts now made to exclude the South from the newly acquired Territories succeed, will stand, before the end of the decade, twenty Northern States to fourteen Southern (considering Delaware as neutral), and forty Northern senators to twenty-eight Southern. This great increase of senators, added to the great increase of members of the House of Representatives and the Electoral College on the part of the North, which must take place under the next decade, will effectually and irretrievably destroy the equilibrium which existed when the government commenced.

. . .

Unless something decisive is done, I again ask, what is to stop this agitation before the great and final object at which it aims—the abolition of slavery in the States—is consummated? Is it, then, not certain that if something is not done to arrest it, the South will be forced to choose between abolition and secession? Indeed, as events are now moving, it will not require the South to secede in order to dissolve the Union.

## Speech by Daniel Webster (March 7, 1850)[17]

Mr. President, I wish to speak to-day, not as a Massachusetts man, nor as a Northern man, but as an American, and a member of the Senate of the United States. It is fortunate that there is a Senate of the United States; a body, not yet moved from its propriety, not lost to a just sense of its own dignity and its own high responsibilities, and a body to which the country looks, with confidence, for wise, moderate, patriotic, and healing counsels. It is not to be denied that we live in the midst of strong agitations, and are surrounded by very considerable dangers to our institutions and government. The imprisoned winds are let loose. The East, the North, and the stormy South, combine to throw the whole ocean into commotion, to toss its billows to the skies, and disclose its profoundest depths. . . . I have a part to act, not for my own security or safety, for I am looking out for no fragment upon which to float away from the wreck, if wreck there must be, but for the good of the whole, and the preservation of all; and there is that which will keep me to my duty during this struggle, whether the sun and the stars shall appear, or shall not appear, for many days. I speak to-day for the preservation of the Union. "Hear me for my cause." I speak, to-day, out of a solicitous and anxious heart, for the restoration to the country of that quiet and that harmony which make the blessings of this Union so rich and so dear to us all. These are the topics that I propose to myself to discuss; these are the motives, and the sole motives, that influence me in the wish to communicate my opinions to the Senate and the country.

---

17. U.S. Congress and Thomas Hart Benton, *Abridgement of the Debates of Congress, from 1789 to 1856,* vol. 16 (New York: D. Appleton and Company, 1868), 415–34.

. . .

In 1803, Louisiana was purchased from France, out of which the States of Louisiana, Arkansas, and Missouri have been framed, as slaveholding States. In 1819, the cession of Florida was made, bringing in another region of slaveholding property and territory. . . . And lastly, sir, to complete those acts of men which have contributed so much to enlarge the area and the sphere of the institution of slavery, Texas—great, and vast, and illimitable Texas—was added to the Union as a slave State in 1845; and that, sir, pretty much closed the whole chapter, and settled the whole account. That closed the whole chapter—that settled the whole account—because the annexation of Texas, upon the conditions and under the guaranties upon which she was admitted, did not leave within the control of this Government an acre of land, capable of being cultivated by slave labor, between this Capitol and the Rio Grande or the Nueces, or whatever is the proper boundary of Texas—not an acre, not one. From that moment, the whole country, from this place to the western boundary of Texas, was fixed, pledged, fastened, decided to be slave territory forever, by the solemn guaranties of law.

. . .

Now, as to California and New Mexico, I hold slavery to be excluded from those Territories by a law, even superior to that which admits and sanctions it in Texas. I mean the law of nature, of physical geography, the law of the formation of the earth. That law settles forever, with a strength beyond all terms of human enactment, that slavery cannot exist in California or New Mexico. Understand me, sir; I mean slavery as we regard it; slaves in gross, of the colored race, transferable by sale and delivery, like other property. I shall not discuss the point, but leave it to the learned gentlemen who have undertaken to discuss it; but I suppose there is no slave of that description in California now. I understand that peonism, a sort of penal servitude, exists there, or rather a sort of voluntary sale of a man and his offspring for debt, as it is arranged and exists in some parts of California and some provinces of Mexico. But what I mean to say is, that African slavery, as we see it among us, is as utterly impossible to find itself, or to be found in California and New Mexico, as any other natural impossibility. California and New Mexico are Asiatic in their formation and scenery. They are composed of vast ridges of mountains of enormous height, with broken ridges and deep valleys. The sides of these mountains are barren, entirely barren; their tops capped by perennial snow. There may be in California, now made free by its constitution, and no doubt there are, some tracts of valuable land. But it is not so in New Mexico. Pray, what is the evidence which every gentleman must have obtained on this subject, from information sought by himself or communicated by others? I have inquired and read all I could find, in order to acquire information on this important question. What is there in New Mexico that could, by any possibility, induce anybody to go there with slaves? There are some narrow strips of tillable land on the borders of the rivers; but the rivers themselves dry up before midsummer is gone. All that the people can do is to raise some little articles—some little wheat for their tortillas—and all that by irrigation. And who expects to see a hundred black men cultivating tobacco, corn, cotton, rice, or anything else, on lands in New Mexico, made fertile only by irrigation? I look upon it, therefore, as a fixed fact, to use an expression current at this day, that both California and New Mexico are destined to be free, so far as they are settled at all, which I believe, especially in regard to New Mexico, will be very little for a great length of time; free by the arrangement of things by the Power above us. I have therefore to say, in this respect also, that this country is fixed for freedom, to as many persons as shall ever live in it, by a less repealable law than the law that attaches to the right of holding slaves in Texas; and I will say further, that if a resolution, or a law, were now before us to provide a territorial Government for New Mexico, I would not vote to put any prohibition into it whatever. The use of such a prohibition would be idle, as it respects any effect it would have upon the Territory; and I would not take pains uselessly to re-affirm an ordinance of Nature, nor to re-enact the will of God. And I would put in no Wilmot proviso for the mere purpose of a taunt or a reproach. I would put into it no evidence of the votes of superior power, for no purpose but to wound the pride, even whether a just pride, a rational pride, or an irrational pride, to wound the pride of the gentlemen who belong to Southern States. I have no such object, no such purpose. They would think it a taunt, an indignity; they would think it to be an act taking away from them what they regard a proper equality of privilege; and whether they expect to realize any benefit from it or not, they would think it at least a plain theoretic wrong; that something more or less derogatory to their character and their rights had taken place.

. . .

Mr. President, I should much prefer to have heard from every member on this floor declarations of opinion that this Union could never be dissolved, than the declaration of opinion by anybody that, in any case, under the pressure of any circumstances, such a dissolution was possible. I hear with pain, and anguish, and distress, the word "secession," especially when it falls from the lips of those who are patriotic, and known to the country, and known all over the world, for their political services. Secession! Peaceable secession! Sir, your eyes and mine are never destined to see that miracle. The dismemberment of this vast country without convulsion! The breaking up of the fountains of the great deep, without ruffling the surface! Who is so foolish, I beg everybody's pardon, as to expect to see any such thing? Sir, he who sees these States, now revolving in harmony around a common centre, and expects to see them quit their places and fly off without convulsion, may look the next hour to see the heavenly bodies rush from their spheres, and jostle against each other in the realms of space, without causing the crush of the universe. There can be no such thing as a peaceable secession. Peaceable secession is an utter impossibility. Is the great Constitution under which we live, covering this whole country, is it to be thawed and melted away by secession, as the snows on the mountain melt under the influence of a vernal sun? disappear almost unobserved, and run off? No, sir! No, sir! I will not state what might produce the disruption of the Union; but, sir, I see as plainly as I see the sun in heaven, what that disruption itself must produce; I see that it must produce war, and such a war as I will not describe, in its two-fold character.

## Racial Conflict in California (1855–1856)

*The Treaty of Guadalupe Hidalgo required that Mexicans who remained on the U.S. side of the newly drawn borders between the United States and Mexico be given U.S. citizenship as long as they did not opt to return to Mexico instead. Mexican property claims were also to be respected. In reality, new settlers and land speculators flooded the U.S. Southwest and dispossessed many Mexicans and American Indians. In 1855, the California legislature passed an Anti-Vagrancy Act that specifically targeted Mexicans. The act used a racist term to refer to Mexicans, "Greasers," although this term was later removed from the act. The act criminalized any person who seemed suspicious or idle and facilitated the arbitrary persecution of the rural and urban poor, specifically Mission Indians and Mexicans. Another symptom of the state of affairs between Mexicans and North American Anglos can be found in the murder of Antonio Ruiz in Los Angeles by a former deputy constable named William Jenkins on July 19, 1856. The murder led to skirmishing between hundreds of Mexicans and a force of Anglos intent on defending the town from Mexican reprisals. Below we excerpt the original California Anti-Vagrancy Act of 1855 as well as a mosaic of voices relating to the case of the murder of Ruiz, drawn from the Los Angeles Spanish-language newspaper* El Clamor Público.

### The California Anti-Vagrancy Act of 1855[18]

Sec. 1. All persons except Digger Indians,[19] who have no visible means of living, who in ten days do not seek employment, nor labor when employment is offered to them, all healthy beggars, who travel with written statements of their misfortunes, all persons who roam about from place to place without any lawful business, all lewd and dissolute persons who live in and about houses of ill-fame; all common prostitutes and common drunkards may be committed to jail and sentenced to hard labor for such time as the court, before whom they are convicted shall think proper, not exceeding ninety days.

---

18. Theodore H. Hitell, ed., *The General Laws of the State of California, 1850–1864* (San Francisco: A. L. Bancroft Company, 1872), 1076–77.

19. A derogatory term for the American Indians of California, whose foods included the roots and seeds of the Digger Pine (*Pinus sabiniana*).

Sec. 2.[20] All persons who are commonly known as "Greasers" or the issue of Spanish and Indian blood, who may come within the provision of the first section of this act, and who go armed and are not known to be peaceable and quiet persons, and who can give no good account of themselves, may be disarmed by any lawful officer, and punished otherwise as provided in the foregoing section.

Sec. 3. It shall be the duty of any justice of the peace, on knowledge or on written complaint from any creditable person of the State, to issue his warrant to apprehend such person or persons, and upon due conviction to send such person or persons to jail, as prescribed in section first of this act; and on a second conviction for the same offense any offenders may be sentenced to the county jail for such additional time as the court may deem proper, not exceeding one hundred and twenty days; and in case of a conviction for either of the offenses aforesaid, an appeal may be taken to the court of sessions, in the same manner as provided for by the law in criminal cases in this State.

## The Murder of Antonio Ruiz (July 19, 1856)

### María Candelaria Pollorena's Deposition[21]

María Candelaria Pollorena, having sworn, declared as follows: that she knew Antonio Ruiz. The defendant went to the house of the deceased last Saturday; and without saying a word went into the room and took out a guitar. She and Ruiz followed him into the room. Then he came and sat down, and taking out a piece of paper from the bag gave it to the deceased. He left with the guitar and after he left the deceased said to her: "I remember that a letter of yours is inside the guitar," and he left the room. They returned immediately, and she said to the defendant, "Please allow me to remove a letter from the guitar," and the defendant said no; but she again said, "What do you want to do with that letter, it's mine, give it to me." The deceased also said to the defendant: "Give her that letter, what do you want to do with it." The defendant refused to hand it over. Then she approached him and took the guitar. When the defendant got up and took out his pistol, the defendant pointed it at me. The deceased immediately grabbed the defendant by the arm. The latter pointed the pistol back and fired.

20. On February 19, 1856, this section was amended to remove the word "Greaser," as follows: "All persons who may come within the provisions of the first section of this act, and who go armed, and are not known to be peaceable and quiet persons, and who can give no good account of themselves, may be disarmed by any sheriff, constable, or police officer, and punished otherwise, as provided in the foregoing section."

21. María Candelaria Pollorena, "Examen de William W. Jenkins," *El Clamor Público,* July 26, 1856, 2. Translated by Gustavo Pellón.

The deceased fell to the ground. The defendant immediately left the house. The deceased was unarmed; he was sewing when the accused entered.

MARÍA CANDELARIA POLLORENA

Witness: William Dryden

### Editorial by *El Clamor Público*[22]

This week has been a week as we have never seen in California, at least not since the war between Mexico and the United States. No one speaks of anything except the bad conditions that exist in this community. Commerce has suffered considerable reverses, and everyone is armed. There is no doubt that the news about what happened will be received in the North with little surprise. All were already prepared for a revolution to take place. For more than six years this city has been the theater of the most atrocious murders. The criminals have always managed to escape. Justice hardly ever fulfills its obligations. Disorder and confusion have been the fruits of all these faults. The Spanish people have always wanted to maintain public order and peace, have submitted blindly to the laws they do not know, and have tried in every way to obey them. Time and circumstances have influenced the regrettable events that have taken place in these days. We do not wish to mitigate nor justify the disturbances that took place on the memorable Tuesday night. The conduct of the persons who made up that gathering was sufficiently ambiguous. They have not thought well if they want to attack the Americans, who have made themselves strong in the walls of the city. They will never be able to do it safely, because while they incur grave responsibilities, the lives of their families are also placed in danger and their property suffers. The death of Don Antonio Ruiz has exasperated the spirit of all Mexicans. It is becoming a very common custom to murder and insult Mexicans with impunity. The latter are therefore tired of the many abuses and injustices they have suffered, but to take up arms to find a remedy to their ills is not a reasonable approach. We desire that peace be restored, that justice fulfill its obligations, that the Mexicans who are now wandering around will return as soon as possible to their homes, and we hope that reforms will take place immediately.

---

22. "Sábado, ....... Julio 26, 1856," *El Clamor Público,* July 26, 1856, 2. Translated by Gustavo Pellón.

## Juan Cortina's Proclamation to the Mexicans of Texas (1859)[23]

*Juan Cortina (1824–1894) was a Mexican veteran of the U.S.-Mexican War who settled near Brownsville, Texas, and harbored deep resentments about how U.S. settlers and lawmen mistreated* Tejanos *(Texans of Mexican descent) and Mexicans. On July 13, 1859, in a fit of rage over how Marshall Robert Shears was mistreating a* Tejano, *Cortina shot the lawman and started a short-lived revolt against the United States. On September 28, Cortina and a small band of men took Brownsville. At its peak, Cortina's army numbered in the hundreds, but the U.S. Army and Texas Rangers defeated his men in December 1859. In the 1870s Cortina continued to raid the U.S. side of the border, sparking violent incursions by the Texas Rangers into northern Mexico. The following excerpt from one of Cortina's proclamations is presented in the anonymous nineteenth-century English translation that was published by the U.S. Congress.*

Mexicans! When the State of Texas began to receive the new organization which its sovereignty required as an integral part of the Union, flocks of vampires, in the guise of men came and scattered themselves in the settlements, without any capital except the corrupt heart and the most perverse intentions. Some, brimful of laws, pledged to us their protection against the attacks of the rest; others assembled in shadowy councils, attempted and excited the robbery and burning of the houses of our relatives on the other side of the river Bravo; while others, to the abusing of our unlimited confidence, when we entrusted them with our titles, which secured the future of our families, refused to return them under false and frivolous pretexts; all, in short, with a smile on their faces, giving the lie to that which their black entrails were meditating. Many of you have been robbed of your property, incarcerated, chased, murdered, and hunted like wild beasts, because your labor was fruitful, and because your industry excited the vile avarice which led them. A voice infernal said, from the bottom of their soul, "kill them; the greater will be our gain!" Ah! This does not finish the sketch of your situation. It would appear that justice had fled from this world, leaving you to the caprice of your oppressors, who become each day more furious towards you; that, through witnesses and false charges, although the grounds may be insufficient, you may be interred in the penitentiaries, if you are not previously deprived of life by some keeper who covers himself from responsibility by the pretense of your flight. There are to be found criminals covered with frightful crimes, but they appear to have impunity until opportunity furnish them a victim; to these monsters

23. U.S. Congress. House, *Difficulties on the Southwestern Frontier.* 36th Cong., 1st sess. H. Exec. Doc. 52, April 2 1860, 70–82. The translation presented here dates from 1860.

indulgence is shown, because they are not of our race, which is unworthy, as they say, to belong to the human species. But this race, which the Anglo-American, so ostentatious of its own qualities, tries so much to blacken, depreciate, and load with insults, in a spirit of blindness, which goes to the full extent of such things so common on this frontier, does not fear, placed even in the midst of its very faults, those subtle inquisitions which are so frequently made as to its manners, habits, and sentiments; nor that its deeds should be put to the test of examination in the land of reason, of justice, and of honor. This race has never humbled itself before the conqueror, though the reverse has happened, and can be established; for he is not humbled who uses among his fellow-men those courtesies which humanity prescribes; charity being the root whence springs the rule of his actions. But this race, which you see filled with gentleness and inward sweetness, gives now the cry of alarm throughout the entire extent of the land which it occupies, against all the artifice interposed by those who have become chargeable with their division and discord. This race, adorned with the most lovely disposition towards all that is good and useful in the line of progress, omits no act of diligence which might correct its many imperfections, and lift its grand edifice among the ruins of the past, respecting the ancient traditions and the maxims bequeathed by their ancestors, without being dazzled by brilliant and false appearances, nor crawling to that exaggeration of institution which, like a sublime statue, is offered for their worship and adoration.

Mexicans! Is there no remedy for you? Inviolable laws, yet useless, serve, it is true, certain judges and hypocritical authorities, cemented in evil and injustice, to do whatever suits them, and to satisfy their vile avarice at the cost of your patience and suffering; rising in their frenzy, even to the taking of life, through the treacherous hands of their bailiffs. The wicked way in which many of you have been often-times involved in persecution, accompanied by circumstances making it the more bitter, is now well known; these crimes being hid from society under the shadow of a horrid night, those implacable people, with the haughty spirit which suggests impunity for a life of criminality, have pronounced, doubt ye not, your sentence, which is, with accustomed insensibility, as you have seen, on the point of execution.

## The Navajo Long Walk (1863)

*The Navajos, who called themselves the* Diné *(the people), had lived in the U.S. Southwest since the end of the fourteenth century. The cession of Mexican lands to the United States after the war transformed the society and culture of the* Diné, *as it did for other American Indian groups residing in the Southwest and West, such as the Comanche, Apache, and Mission Indians. In 1864, after almost twenty years of conflict with the authorities and settlers of New Mexico, the famed frontiersman Christopher "Kit" Carson (1809–1868) and the first New Mexico volunteers violently expelled the* Diné *from their sacred, ancestral home at Canyon de Chelly in eastern Arizona, burning crops and thousands of peach trees that had provided sustenance to generations. Carson's forces then drove eight thousand of the* Diné *on a three hundred mile march to a reservation in northeastern New Mexico. This terrible journey, remembered as the "Long Walk" by the* Diné, *has parallels to the Trail of Tears (1838–1839), when the Cherokee were forced to march from their ancestral homes in Georgia and Tennessee to lands west of the Mississippi. Although the* Diné *were later allowed to return to some of their ancestral lands, the "Long Walk" ended their era of active and organized resistance to U.S. settlement.*

## Kit Carson's Letter to Captain B. C. Cutler (January 23, 1864)[24]

While en route on my return to camp I was joined by three Indians with a flag of truce, requesting permission to come in with their people and submit. I told them, through my interpreter, that they and their people might come unmolested, to my camp up to 10 o'clock A.M. next day, but that after that time if they did not come my soldiers would hunt them up, and the work of destruction recommence. Accordingly, next morning, before the time appointed, sixty Indians arrived. They had made known to them the intention of the Government in regard to them, and expressed their willingness to immigrate to the Bosque Redondo. They declare that owing to the operation of my command they are in a complete state of starvation, and that many of their women and children have died from this cause. They also state that they would have come in long since, but they believed it was a war of extermination, and that they were agreeably surprised and delighted to learn the contrary from an old captive whom I had sent back to them for this purpose. I issued them some meat and they asked permission to return to their haunts and collect the remainder of their people. I directed them to meet me at this post in ten days. They have all arrived here according to promise, and many of them with others joining and traveling in with Capt. Carey's command. This command of seventy-five men, I conferred upon Capt. Carey at his own request, he being desirous of passing through this stupendous cañon.[25] I sent the party to return through the cañon from west to east, that all the peach orchards, of which there were many, should be destroyed, as well as the dwellings of the Indians. . . .

We have shown the Indians that in no place, however formidable or inaccessible in their opinion, are they safe from the pursuits of the troops of this command; and have convinced a large portion of them that the struggle on their part is a hopeless one. We have also demonstrated that the intentions of the Government toward them are eminently humane, and dictated by an earnest

---

24. Ralph Emerson Twitchell, *Leading Facts of New Mexican History* (Cedar Rapids, IA: Torch Press, 1917), 356–58.

25. Cañon (from the Spanish *cañón*) means canyon.

desire to promote their welfare; that the principle is not to destroy, but to save them if they are disposed to be saved. . . .

## The U.S.-Mexican War and the U.S. Civil War[26]

*Many of the most notable military figures of the U.S. Civil War first experienced war during the U.S.-Mexican War. Among these were future presidents Franklin Pierce (1804–1869) and Ulysses S. Grant (1822–1885) and notable figures of the U.S. Civil War, such as Robert E. Lee (1807–1870), Jefferson Davis (1808–1889), Thomas "Stonewall" Jackson (1824–1863), George B. McClellan (1826–1885), David Twiggs (1790–1862), and Gideon Pillow (1806–1878). When Lee surrendered to Grant at Appomattox, Virginia, in April 1865, the two spoke about their memories of the war in Mexico.*

### Ulysses S. Grant Remembers the Lessons of the War (1885)

Generally the officers of the army were indifferent whether the annexation was consummated or not; but not so all of them. For myself, I was bitterly opposed to the measure, and to this day regard the war, which resulted, as one of the most unjust ever waged by a stronger against a weaker nation. It was an instance of a republic following the bad example of European monarchies, in not considering justice in their desire to acquire additional territory. . . . The occupation, separation and annexation were, from the inception of the movement to its final consummation, a conspiracy to acquire territory out of which slave states might be formed for the American Union.

. . .

My experience in the Mexican war was of great advantage to me afterwards. Besides the many practical lessons it taught, the war brought nearly all the officers of the regular army together so as to make them personally acquainted. It also brought them in contact with volunteers, many of whom served in the war of the rebellion afterwards. Then, in my particular case, I had been at West Point at about the right time to meet most of the graduates who were of a suitable age at the breaking out of the rebellion to be trusted with large commands. Graduating in 1843, I was at the military academy from one to four years with all cadets who graduated between 1840 and 1846—seven classes. These classes embraced more than fifty officers who afterwards became generals on one side or the other

26. Ulysses S. Grant, *The Personal Memoirs of Ulysses S. Grant* (New York: C. L. Webster and Co., 1885), 191–92, 490.

in the rebellion, many of them holding high commands. All the older officers, who became conspicuous in the rebellion, I had also served with and known in Mexico: Lee, J. E. Johnston, A. S. Johnston, Holmes, Hebert and a number of others on the Confederate side; McCall, Mansfield, Phil. Kearney and others on the National side. The acquaintance thus formed was of immense service to me in the war of the rebellion—I mean what I learned of the characters of those to whom I was afterwards opposed. I do not pretend to say that all movements, or even many of them, were made with special reference to the characteristics of the commander against whom they were directed. But my appreciation of my enemies was certainly affected by this knowledge. The natural disposition of most people is to clothe a commander of a large army whom they do not know with almost superhuman abilities. A large part of the National army, for instance, and most of the press of the country, clothed General Lee with just such qualities, but I had known him personally, and knew that he was mortal; and it was just as well that I felt this.

### Grant and Lee Reminisce about Mexico at Appomattox in 1865

We soon fell into a conversation about old army times. He remarked that he remembered me very well in the old army; and I told him that as a matter of course I remembered him perfectly, but from the difference in our rank and years (there being about sixteen years' difference in our ages), I had thought it very likely that I had not attracted his attention sufficiently to be remembered by him after such a long interval. Our conversation grew so pleasant that I almost forgot the object of our meeting. After the conversation had run on in this style for some time, General Lee called my attention to the object of our meeting, and said that he had asked for this interview for the purpose of getting from me the terms I proposed to give his army.

## The Plight of the Mission Indians (1883)

*Between 1769 and 1823, the Franciscan Order of the Catholic Church established twenty-one missions along the coast of California from San Diego in the south to Sonoma in the north. Although the missions sought to convert California's Indians to Christianity, they also functioned as vital centers of agriculture and industry during the Spanish colonial period. Large numbers of the so-called Mission Indians (they were originally from a variety of different backgrounds) were forcibly segregated within mission walls to provide the labor on which the economic success of the missions was predicated. Yet, American Indian peoples who became a part of mission culture both inside and outside the walls of the mission also suffered greatly after the Treaty of Guadalupe Hidalgo, when an influx of new settlers displaced them from their land. Moreover, the sparsely populated California underwent a dramatic demographic spike thanks to the California gold rush. In 1882, Helen Hunt Jackson, a writer-activist for Indian rights, investigated the living conditions of the Mission Indians in California as a special commissioner of the U.S. government. Helen Hunt Jackson published the following letters to alert the government and American public to the suffering of the Mission Indians and soon afterward published a bestselling novel titled* Ramona *(1884) on the same subject. The first two letters presented below relate to the Indian village of Saboba in San Diego County. The village was located on a Mexican land grant that was later sold to an American landowner who threatened to eject its inhabitants unless the U.S. government bought the land from him. The California Supreme Court ultimately sided with the inhabitants of Saboba and allowed them to stay on their land.*

## Letter to the President of the United States by Ramón Cavavi[27]

To the President of the United States:

Mr. PRESIDENT—DEAR SIR: I wish to write a letter for you, and I will try to tell you some things. The white people call San Jacinto rancho their land, and I don't want them to do it. We think it is ours, for God gave it to us first. Now I think you will tell me what is right for you have been so good to us, giving us a school and helping us. Will you not come to San Jacinto some time to see us, the school, and the people of Saboba village? Many of the people are sick, and some have died. We are so poor that we have not enough good food for the sick, and sometimes I am afraid that we are all going to die. Will you please tell what is good about our ranches, and come soon to see us.

Your friend,

RAMON CAVAVI

## Letter to Helen Hunt Jackson, Indian Agent, by Antonio León[28]

Mrs. JACKSON:

MY DEAR FRIEND: I wish to write you a letter about the American people that want to drive us away from own village of Saboba. I don't know what they can

27. Helen Hunt Jackson and Abbot Kinney, *Report on the Condition and Needs of the Mission Indians of California* (Washington, DC: Government Printing Office, 1883), 17.
28. Helen Hunt Jackson and Abbot Kinney, *Report on the Condition and Needs of the Mission Indians of California* (Washington, DC: Government Printing Office, 1883), 17.

be about. I don't know why they do so. My teacher told me she was very sorry about the town, and then my teacher said, I think they will find a good place for you if you have to go; but I do hope they will not drive you away. Then it will be very good for all the people of Saboba. It is a very good town for the people. They have all the work done on their gardens, and they are very sorry about the work that is done. My work is very nicely done also. The people are making one big fence to keep the cows and the horses off their garden.

Your true friend,

ANTONIO LEON

## Letter to the Secretary of the Interior of the United States by José Jesús Castillo[29]

San Jacinto, May 29, 1882

Mr. Teller.

Dear Sir,—At the request of my friends, I write you in regard to the land of my people.

More than one hundred years ago my great-grandfather, who was chief of his tribe, settled with his people in the San Jacinto valley. The people have always been peaceful, never caring for war, and have welcomed Americans into the valley.

Some years ago a grant of land was given to the Estudillos by the Mexican Government.[30] The first survey did not take in any of the land claimed by the Indians; but four years ago a new survey was made, taking in all the little farms, the stream of water, and the village. Upon this survey the United States Government gave a patent. It seems hard for us to be driven from our homes that we love as much as other people do theirs; and this danger is at our doors now, for the grant will be assigned to some of the present owners of the grant.

And now, dear sir, after this statement of facts, I, for my people (I ask nothing for myself), appeal to you for help.

Cannot you find some way to right this great wrong done to a quiet and industrious people?

---

29. Helen Hunt Jackson, "The Present Condition of the Mission Indians of Southern California," *The Century Magazine* 26, no. 4 (August 1883): 523.

30. José Antonio Estudillo (1805–1852) was one of the most affluent and respected landowners and political figures in Mexican California. Beginning in 1829, the Estudillo family began acquiring large stretches of mission land in Southern California, including the properties of Mission San Luis Rey in the San Jacinto Valley.

Hoping that we may have justice done us, I am
Respectfully yours,

José Jesús Castillo

## Affidavit of Patricio Soberano and Felipe Joqua of the Township of Pala[31]

Patricio Soberano and Felipe Joqua, being duly sworn by me through an interpreter, and the words hereof being interpreted to each and every one of them, each for himself deposes and says: I am an Indian belonging to that portion of the San Luisenos Indians[32] under the captainship of José Antonio Sal, and belonging in the rancheria[33] of Pala. I have occupied the land in question ever since my childhood, together with Geronimo Lugo and Luis Ardillo, our wives and families numbering in all twenty-nine persons. I have resided on the land in question continuously until December, 1882. About five years ago one Arthur Golsh rented of Luis Ardillo a portion of said land for three months at a rental of $5 per month. After this, said Golsh claimed the property of Ardillo and of the three other Indians; ordered them to leave; used threats; on one occasion aimed a pistol at Patricio Soberano. He then proceeded to file on the land, and obtained a patent for the land while these Indians were still residing upon it. The said Indians had upon the said land four houses, one of which is adobe, various enclosed fields, and a long ditch for bringing irrigation water to the said lands. In spite of the threats of Arthur Golsh and others, we continued to occupy the lands until December, 1882, when we were informed by Agent S. S. Lawson that if we did not leave voluntarily we would be put off by the sheriff.

Said affiants therefore pray that said land be returned to the said Indians by the United States Government.

Signed by Patricio Soberano and Felipe Joqua in presence of the justice of the peace, in Pala.

---

31. Helen Hunt Jackson and Abbot Kinney, *Report on the Condition and Needs of the Mission Indians of California* (Washington, DC: Government Printing Office, 1883), 30.

32. An Indian group named after the San Luis Rey Mission.

33. Village.

# VI

# Literature, Culture, and Memory

## *Heroes*

### Major Samuel Ringgold, Martyr of the Battle of Palo Alto (1849)[1]

*Tales of heroism and hero martyrs are central to all nationalist interpretations of war. The most important and celebrated hero martyr to emerge from the U.S.-Mexican War on the side of the United States was Samuel Ringgold (1800–1846), the son of Senator Samuel Ringgold (1770–1829) of Maryland and the grandson of a notable veteran of the American Revolution, General John Cadwalader (1742–1786). The document that follows is an 1849 article about Ringgold's death at the Battle of Palo Alto (May 8, 1846) and the reception of the news of his death in Baltimore and Philadelphia.*

He then received the wound which caused his death. It was occasioned by a six-pound cannon shot, which struck the middle of his right thigh, passed through it, and through the shoulders of his horse, and came out through the left thigh. Men and officers came to his assistance, but he waved them away, exclaiming, "Don't stay with me; you have work to do—go ahead."

He was immediately carried from the field under the direction of Dr. Byrne, who dressed his wounds. Although nearly all the anterior muscles were torn from each thigh, yet no bones were broken nor any important artery divided. His pain was trifling, and up to the time of his death, he conversed cheerfully with his attendants upon the incidents of the battle. He steadily grew worse, however, until one o'clock on the morning of the 10th, when he expired. His burial took place on the following day.

Major Ringgold was formed by nature to be popular. No man possessed more of the affection and obedience of the soldiers, and no one was ever more sincerely lamented. Even those who had known him only for a few months, partook of the

1. *The Mexican War and Its Heroes: Being a Complete History of the Mexican War, Embracing All the Operations under Taylor and Scott with a Biography of the Officers* (Philadelphia: Grigg, Elliot and Co, 1849), 175–78.

general sorrow; and when it was announced throughout the United States that Ringgold had fallen, the shout of victory was dashed with a wail of sympathy. At the Monument Square[2] a meeting convened to hear the details of the struggles of the 8th and 9th. Colonel Davis was one of the speakers; and when he announced that Ringgold had been killed, a deep silence settled over the dense mass, and every head was uncovered. The Baltimore county court adjourned on learning the melancholy event. On that occasion the honorable Judge Le Grande made the following remarks:

"In the motion of the attorney general the court recognizes a becoming appreciation of the sad feeling which the announcement of the death of our brave townsman has inspired in the bosoms of our entire community. It is fitting that the court and indeed every branch of the government should exhibit the sincerest evidences of the affliction which all have sustained in the death of one who has surrendered his life in the defense of his country. Custom has prescribed, amongst its usual cold ceremonials, the expression of grief at the final departure of any distinguished citizen; but when the resolute and noble defender of the honor of the country and the integrity of it soil is swallowed up in the jaws of death, whilst in the act of adding by his daring intrepidity another brilliant page to its history, the patriotic heart properly demands, and will have the tribute which the just and the grateful ever promptly pay to the gallant dead. To us all this is evident by the gloom which is everywhere in our city; and which the enunciation of a succession of the glorious victories of our arms cannot dispel. . . . Major Ringgold was a citizen of Baltimore, known to us all, to some of us intimately, and by whomsoever and wheresoever known, recognized as a gentleman of the highest sense of honor, and of the kindliest feelings of which humanity is susceptible. He is gone, but the fame his late brilliant conduct won will henceforth constitute a part of the pride and history of his country."

. . .

"The death of this accomplished officer," says the *Philadelphia North American*, "is a heavy loss to the country. . . . His death has stricken thousands of hearts that gush under the blow with feelings which no ordinary public calamity could have excited. He was generally known and appreciated in this city as the Bayard of the age[3]—the star of the war; and his career was watched with anxious eyes and hearts. That it would be glorious no one doubted; but who thought that an orb so bright would sink so early? The soul of chivalry and honor, accomplished as a soldier, lofty as a patriot, beloved as a man, it demands an agonizing struggle to reconcile us to such a sacrifice. And yet it is a noble one. In the flash of his fame he has died as he lived—for his country. The offering was doubtless a glad one. He desired no better fate than such a death; he could have no richer inheritance than

2. In Baltimore, Maryland.

3. A reference to the French knight Pierre du Terrail Bayard (1475–1524), who fought in many wars with valor and entered into myth for his sacrifice, courage, and virtue.

such an example. While we feel as if destiny had robbed the future of the fame which such a nature must have won, we dare not repine that his career has been closed in its morning with this sunburst of glory. His memory will be gratefully cherished so long as honor has victory, freedom a hero, or his country a name."

## The Child Heroes of Chapultepec (1901)[4]

*On the Mexican side, the most famous and enduring hero martyrs of the war with the United States are known as the "Child Heroes of Chapultepec" (In Spanish,* Los niños héroes de Chapultepec*). During the storming of Chapultepec Castle on September 13, 1847, cadets of the military school housed there aided in the defense of Mexican positions. History has singled out the cadets Juan de la Barrera, Juan Escutia, Francisco Márquez, Agustín Melgar, Fernando Montes de Oca, and Vicente Suárez as heroes for sacrificing their lives for their nation. According to legend, one of the cadets wrapped himself in a Mexican flag and hurled himself to his death from the castle defenses.[5] A U.S. officer who witnessed the battle wrote that the cadets were "pretty little fellows from ten to sixteen years of age" who died fighting "like demons, and indeed, they showed an example of courage worthy of imitation by some of their superiors in rank."[6] The document below is a 1901 account of the death of the children cadets of Chapultepec, typical of the cult of heroism that emerged around them in late nineteenth-century Mexico, which has endured until the present.*

Amid that horrible din and confusion, all enveloped in clouds of gunpowder, they fought, they struggled, they died between the American "hurrahs" and our soldiers' shouts of "Long live the motherland."

The columns rose beset by the volleys of fire, until with their ladders they reached the castle defended by the brave students of the military school.

The first attackers rolled down over the rocks.

The bulk of the columns attack converging on one point as if it were the endpoint of their victory.

The military school fans out making fire on the invader.

Those children had the inspiration of fighters, the ardent valor of heroes.

The volunteers fire a heavy volley and Lieutenant Barrera falls dying.

---

4. José Mateos, *Sangre de niños (Una página de Chapultepec)* (Mexico City: Lynotipia de "El Mundo" y "El Imparcial," 1901), 131–32. Translated by Gustavo Pellón.

5. It was a grown man named Margarito Suazo who, when mortally wounded, wrapped himself in the Mexican flag at the Battle of Molino del Rey on September 8, 1847.

6. Edward Mansfield, *The Mexican War* (New York: A. S. Barnes and Burr, 1860), 298.

"Now it's my turn!" shouts Melgar and falls with his breast torn.

"Now, me!" says Suárez, with rage and hurls himself on the enemy.

With a shout or rather with a roar, he dies pierced by bullets.

Then Márquez and Montes de Oca come in, embrace in the middle of that disaster, and die cheering the motherland.

The students continue to make fire until surrounded and taken prisoner by the enemy, having upheld the honor of the national flag.

As that din died out and the awful shouting made by that unchained army as they raised their victorious flag on the high tower of the castle ended, when the smoke of the gunpowder had dissipated, they turned to the field and saw that the corpses scattered there were "children," the Americans recoiled, ashamed of their victory.

The officers kissed the foreheads of the dead! . . . [7]

They picked up the children and rendered military honors to them.

A nation for which even the children die is invincible.

Over that field of blood, float the names of those heroes, whom history gathers in its most brilliant pages.

Sleep the slumber of glory, for the aura of immortality rests upon you!

Sleep in peace! . . . The murmuring of the old Montezuma cypresses repeats your last words and the wind that caresses your tombs gathers the last echoes of your glory.

Sleep in peace! . . . That mountain is your glorious sarcophagus; there is the proud epitaph that carries your names to history!

You have died for the motherland; may you be blessed!

The moans of yesterday become today's anthems of military honor over the torn up combat arena!

The national flag floats above your ashes.

The only tears that moisten your tombs are the tears of your motherland!

## *Caricature*

### Uncle Sam's Taylorifics (1846)

*The caricature Uncle Sam's Taylorifics (1846) was a popular, much reprinted lithograph by Edward Williams Clay (1799–1857). The image in this section contains two important stock characters, Brother Jonathan, representing the American people, and John Bull, standing in for the British. According to popular*

---

7. U.S. accounts of the children of Chapultepec are scarce and vague, and although praising their heroism, do not corroborate this act, rumored to have been carried out by General Worth.

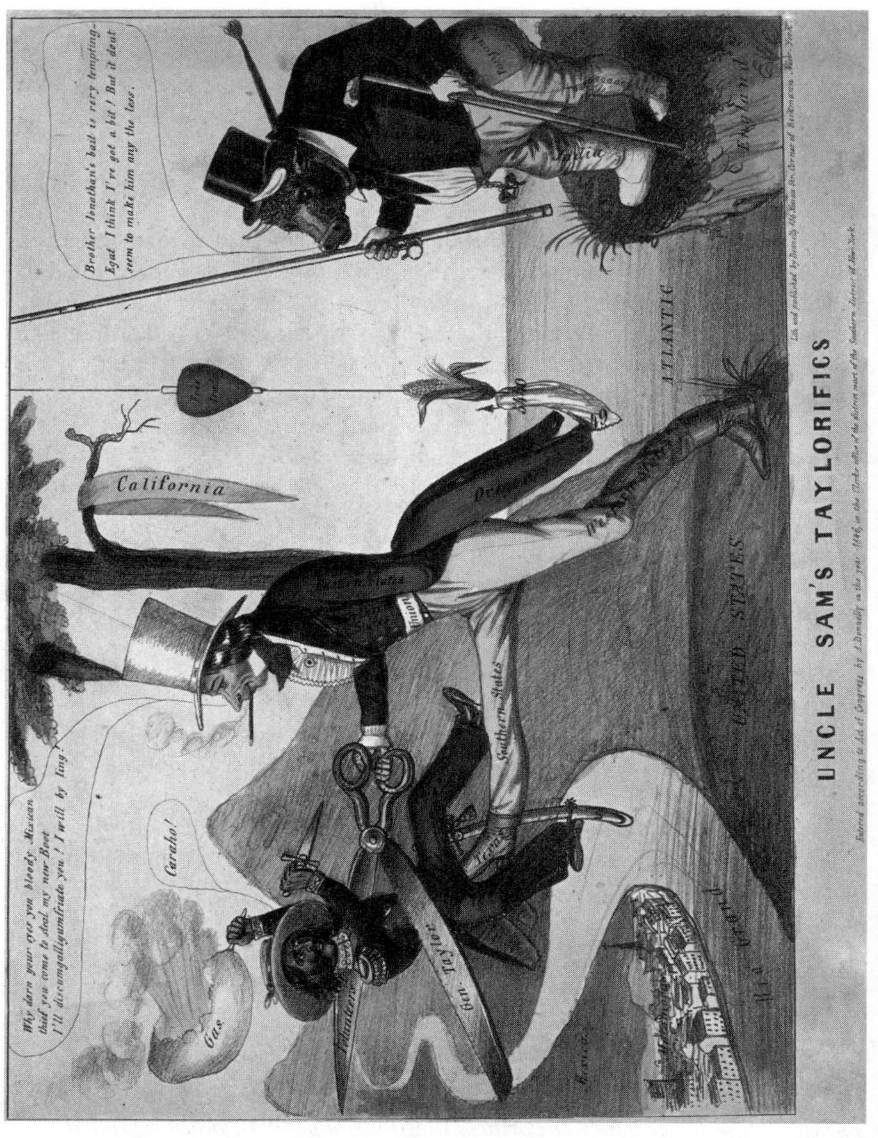


Uncle Sam's Taylorifics. 1846 lithograph by Henry R. Robinson, after a drawing by Edward W. Clay; negative no. 48482. Collection of The New-York Historical Society.

Brother Jonathan: "Why darn your eyes you bloody Mixican [sic] thief you come to steal my new Boot I'll discumgalligumfrigate you! I will by Jing!" His body is labeled "Union" (sash), "Texas" (right boot), "Southern States" (right leg), "Western States" (left leg), "Eastern States" (left arm), "Oregon" (coat tail). John Bull: "Brother Jonathan's bait is very tempting. Egat I think I've got a bit! But it don't seem to make him any the less." His fishing rod is labeled "Free Trade" and 54°40′. The Mexican exclaims "Caraho!" (damn it!) as he is cut by scissors labeled "Volunteers" (upper blade) and "Gen. Taylor" (lower).

*belief, the name Brother Jonathan came about as a result of a turn of phrase once used by George Washington during the Revolutionary War. At a difficult juncture in one of his campaigns, Washington is reported to have said, "We must consult Brother Jonathan," referring to his friend Jonathan Trumbull (1710–1785), the governor of Connecticut. In the first half of the century, the figure of the overly confident, young, and thin Brother Jonathan was the main pictorial symbol of the United States. He was overtaken by the bearded figure of Uncle Sam in the second half of the nineteenth century. (The phrase "Uncle Sam" had been in use since the War of 1812.) The earliest known example of the figure of John Bull as a symbol of Great Britain is a 1712 caricature by the Scottish mathematician John Arbuthnot (1667–1745). The word* caraho, *as uttered by the Mexican general in the caricature, is a rendering of the Spanish expletive* carajo, *meaning "penis," but is often used as an exhortation equivalent to "damn it" in English.*

## The Battle of Cerro Gordo (1847)

*The cartoon in this section shows President Polk asking his envoy Nicholas Trist (man with hose) to "cool down" General Winfield Scott, who is offering the retreating General Santa Anna a "hasty bowl of soup" at the Battle of Cerro Gordo. The dialogue in the caricature goes as follows: Scott: "General Santa Anna!! do stop and take 'a hasty plate of soup?'" Santa Anna: "I thank you, Sir, your soup's too hot—I must be off!" Polk: "Trist, take care & cool 'old Hasty's' soup, before our friend meets him again." Trist: "Your Excellency will pardon me, but I've tried in vain to cool 'Old Hasty's' soup." Polk: "Then put out 'Old Hasty's' fire, or that fatal soup will burn our fingers yet!" Trist: "Your Excellency would do well to send 'Old Hasty' home and give our friend 'a Pillow' for his Comfort." The reference to "hasty soup" originated in General Winfield Scott's tense relationship with President Polk, who at one point removed the general from command for what he perceived to be Scott's timid approach to war planning. Scott famously wrote that he was having a "hasty plate of soup" when news arrived that Polk was going to find a replacement for him in the field. Polk, who saw Scott as a political rival, ultimately reinstated the commander, and Scott went on to successfully lead the Veracruz and Mexico City campaigns. When Polk sent Nicholas Trist as his envoy to Mexico, Trist and Scott at first clashed but later developed a close relationship. The cartoon creates a contrast between the pairing of Polk and Trist, who seek a negotiated settlement with Santa Anna, and Scott, who chastens Santa Anna with overly hot soup. The cartoon also refers to General Gideon Pillow, a Polk loyalist who was Scott's second-in-command.*

Battle of Cerro Gordo. 1847 lithograph. Library of Congress.

# *Wartime Songs (1846–1848)*

## "Uncle Sam and Mexico"[8]

*The song "Uncle Sam and Mexico" is drawn from the* Rough and Ready Songster *(c. 1848), a pamphlet of song lyrics that U.S. soldiers carried with them in Mexico during the war. The tune of "Uncle Sam and Mexico" is "Old Dan Tucker," a minstrel song published in 1843 by Daniel Decatur Emmett (1815–1904), whose song "Dixie" became the fighting song of the Confederacy. Emmett was a member of the Original Virginia Minstrel company, and the lyrics of his smash hit "Old Dan Tucker" depicted and exaggerated black vernacular speech: "I came to town de udder night, / I hear de noise, / den saw de sight, / De watchman dey (was) runnin' roun', / Cryin' 'Ole Dan Tucker's come to town.' / Git outen de way / Git outen de way / Git outen de way, Ole Dan Tucker, / You's too late to come to your supper."[9] The tune of "Old Dan Tucker" was so popular and ubiquitous that in the next twenty years it was parodied in Gold Rush and abolitionist songs as well as in a song about Abraham Lincoln. In more than one memoir of the war, U.S. soldiers recalled the "negro" songs that were sung during the war, and during the occupation of Mexico City an anonymous Mexican observer published an article in a Mexican newspaper describing the strange gatherings of U.S. soldiers performing in blackface.*

Throughout de land dar is a cry,
And folks all know de reason why,
Shy Mexico's two legged b'ars,[10]
Am 'tacking Uncle Sammy's stars.

*Chorus wid drum.—*
Den march away,
Den march away—
Den march away, bold sons of freedom,
You're de boys can skin and bleed 'em.

---

8. An American Officer, *The Rough and Ready Songster: Embellished with Twenty-Five Splendid Engravings Illustrative of the American Victories in Mexico* (New York: Nafis and Cornish Publishers, 1848), 91–92.

9. Charles Burleigh Galbreath, *Daniel Decatur Emmett: Author of Dixie* (Columbus, OH: Press of Fred J. Heer, 1904), 49.

10. Bears.

Dey're kicken up gunpowderation,
About de Texas annexation,
Since Mexico makes sich ado,
We'll flog her and annex her too.
        Den march away, &c.

Young Texas came ob age quite jam,[11]
And den she married Uncle Sam,
She sewed her stars fast to his flag,
An it shall shine dar[12] while dar's a rag.
        Den march away, &c.

Dey met us on de Rio Grandy,
We showed 'em Yankee Doodle Dandy,[13]
But when brave Taylor cross de line,
He'll make 'em snort like steam bullgine.[14]
        Den march away, &c.

Little Texas when quite in her teens,
Did give 'em a dos of leading [sic] *beans,*[15]
An' now old Sammy is called out,
Dey'll catch salt-petre sour crout.[16]
        Den march away, &c.

Since Texas cut off Sant Anna's peg,
We'll *Amputate* Ampudia's leg,
An' so his carcass de air shan't spoil,
We'll boil it in his own hot oil.

---

11. Young.

12. There.

13. Soldiers sang variants of "Yankee Doodle Dandy" in battle during the Texas Revolution and the U.S.-Mexican War.

14. Slang for a steam locomotive.

15. In U.S. slang, to give someone beans was to punish or give them a beating.

16. Sauerkraut sprinkled with saltpeter (potassium nitrate), an ingredient in gunpowder.

# "La Pasadita"[17]

*The* corrido *is a uniquely Mexican folk song with roots in medieval Spanish poetry that traveled to the New World with conquistadors and early colonists. The meter and strophe structure of Mexican* corridos *vary widely, from octosyllabic to decasyllabic meter, and to stanzas structured as quartets, quintets, or sextets. Commonly sung with guitar accompaniment,* corridos *constitute an oral tradition that documents Mexican life and history as seen from a popular point of view and in the speech of rural and working-class people. "La Pasadita" is an early Mexican* corrido *that dates to late 1847 or early 1848 and documents the U.S. occupation of Mexico City. "La Pasadita" was popular and enduring enough to be rewritten years later to refer to a different historical event, in this case the French occupation of Mexico of 1861–1867. The excerpt that follows is from the memoir of Antonio García Cubas (1832–1912), nineteenth-century Mexico's most important geographer, who was living in Mexico City with his family during the U.S. occupation of 1847–1848. In his memoir, García Cubas describes the circumstances that gave rise to the song "La Pasadita" and inserts a transcription of one of many extant versions of this anonymous but enduring song. Below we excerpt García Cubas' memories as well as his transcription of "La Pasadita."*

## Antonio García Cubas Introduces "La Pasadita"

Of a different order, but equally prejudicial to the soldiers, was their friendship with harlots of the lowest class and to whom the soldiers themselves gave the inappropriate name of *margaritas.*[18] Their meetings with them gave rise to coarse and immoral scenes that sometimes were enacted on the balconies of the Bella Unión Hotel,[19] and their audience was the rabble of the city, who mockingly applauded them and sang the popular song "La Pasadita:"

---

17. Antonio García Cubas, *El libro de mis recuerdos* (Mexico City: Imprenta de Arturo García Cubas, 1904), 439–40. Translated by Gustavo Pellón.

18. The name Margarite, from a Greek word meaning "pearl," has connotations of both purity and sexuality in Western culture. Among the poets who wrote about Margarite were Geoffrey Chaucer (c. 1343–1400), Guillaume de Machaut (c. 1300–1377), and Matthew Arnold (1822–1888). In the latter half of the nineteenth century, Margarite was a name often associated with courtesans and sexuality because of the popularity of the novel *The Lady of the Camellias* (1848) by Alexander Dumas fils (1824–1895).

19. According to *The Other Side* (1850), an important Mexican history of the war, the four-story Hotel Bella Unión housed the most popular ballroom of Mexico City during the U.S. occupation. The first floor was used for gambling, the second for saloons and dancing, and the third for accommodating prostitutes and their Johns (416). In his memoirs of the war, Col. L. A. Norton remembered that "over a million dollars changes hands in a single night" at the Bella Unión.

### *La Pasadita*

Oh! My friends,
I'm going to tell you
what happened to me
in this city:
in came the Yankees,
and I threw some stones,[20]
and on to La Pasadita,
tra-la-la-la.

All the Margaritas
speak English now,
you say: do you love me
and they answer: *jes,*
*I onderstan de money*
*ees very good,*[21]
and on to La Pasadita,
tra-la-la-la.

Only the women
Are so kind
As to traffic
with that nation,
and they say: Let's go,
but it isn't true,
and on to La Pasadita,
tra-la-la-la.

All those girls
at the Bella Unión
gaily dance
the *danza* and *rigodón:*
looking like ladies
really high class,
and on to La Pasadita,
tra-la-la-la.

¡Ay! Amigos míos,
les voy a contar
lo que me ha pasado
en esta ciudad:
entraron los yankees,
me arriesgué apedrear,
y á la pasadita,
*tan-darín-da-rán.*

Ya las Margaritas
hablan el inglés,
les dicen: me quieres
y responden: *yes,*
*mi entende de monis*
*mucho gueno está*
y á la pasadita
*tan-darín-da-rán.*

Sólo las mujeres
tienen corazón
para hacer alianza
con esa nación,
y ellas dicen: vamos,
pero no es verdad,
y á la pasadita
*tan-darín-da-rán.*

Todas esas niñas
en la "Bella Unión"
bailan muy alegres
danza y rigodón:
parecen señoras
de gran calidad,
y á la pasadita
*tan-darín-da-rán.*

---

20. In some versions of the song, *a pelear* (to fight). Here *apedrear* refers to popular resistance to the U.S. occupation of Mexico City, which took the form of throwing rocks from rooftops and balconies.

21. Here the lyric refers to the pidgin Spanish learned by the Margaritas to speak to their American clients and suitors.

When it comes to the men,
there's no need for mistrust,
because what they do
has no ill intent:
just like cats,
they know when to fawn,[22]
and on to La Pasadita,
tra-la-la-la.

Solo de los hombres
no hay que desconfiar,
pues lo que ellos hacen
no lo hacen por mal:
suelen como el gato
también halagar,
y á la pasadita
tan-darín-da-rán.

### Antonio García Cubas Describes the Balls in which Margaritas Danced with U.S. Soldiers

At the balls, the volunteers were living caricatures, trying to imitate the folk dances. Each had a margarita for a partner and following her example executed the *jarabe.*[23] With their bodies loose, they bent their legs a lot, and because of the movement produced by the stamping of their feet, the brims of their hats waved up and down, as did their bags of provisions that hung from straps over one of their shoulders. And it happened often that they tripped themselves as their legs attempted the footwork, imprisoned as they were in heavy boots. While some of them danced, others carried on a conversation with their sweethearts. I won't say an animated conversation because that would have been impossible with those harlots, whom the common people called by the name of an eight-legged insect. Nor could a conversation be considered animated when it took place by means of gestures, contortions, monosyllables, or a few phrases or sentences in which some version of the personal pronoun "I" appeared as subject followed by an infinitive and then, as direct object, some mangled word, for example: *mi querer osté.*[24]

22. A reference to proverbs (in the English and Spanish language) that describe cats fawning with their tails and scratching with their claws or biting with their mouths. The stanza implies that Mexican compliance is temporary and tactical.

23. The *jarabe* is a variable Latin American dance descended from the Spanish *jota* and characterized by the choreographed stamping of feet and heels.

24. *Mi querer osté* is a garbled version of the Spanish, *Yo la quiero a Usted,* or "I love you." An equivalent in English would be something like: "Me loving ya."

# *Wartime Poetry (1846–1851)*

## Two Poems by Guadalupe Calderón, Josefa Terán, and *Una Zacatecana* (1846)[25]

*The following selections are among the earliest known poems by Mexican women to be published in Mexico.*[26] *The collaborative aspect of these poems adds to their historical importance. Little is known about these pioneering women poets.* Una Zacatecana *(A Woman From Zacatecas) was the pseudonym of Mrs. Josefa Letechipía de González. The first poem, "To the Motherland," is typical of the kind of transparently patriotic Mexican poetry published in the Mexican press during the war. The second poem, "The Storm," represents the upheaval, menace, and ultimate transcendence of the nation's call to arms through the romantic commonplace of a storm.*

**To the Motherland**

Your glorious brow ringed with laurel
Oh dear motherland! My eyes beheld;
Cowardly trembled those oppressors,
Who so many sorrows heaped on you.

The spilt blood of loyal patriots,
Gives you new life, full of triumphs;
Breaking the chain that oppressed your neck,
Erasing the abominable mark, liberty is yours!

But, alas, discord tarnishes with its breath

**A la Patria**

Tu frente gloriosa de lauro ceñida,
¡Oh patria querida! mis ojos miraron;
Cobardes temblaron esos opresores,
Que tantos dolores causaron en ti.

De fieles patriotas la sangre vertida,
Te da nueva vida, de triunfos te llena;
Rompe la cadena que agovió tu cuello,
Borra infando sello, ¡tienes libertad!

Mas ¡ay! la discordia con su hálito empaña

---

25. Both poems were published in *El Republicano,* Friday, November 27, 1846, page 3.

26. Translated by Gustavo Pellón. For more on women's writing in Mexico, see "María de la Salud García, Mexican Patriot" in Part IV of this collection.

The glory that wrests a world from Spain:
Fearsome, it waves the torch of death,
And turns happiness to grief.

The fratricidal hand takes up the steel;
In deranged delirium, tearing your bosom:
Those who swore to avenge your injuries,
Oh, motherland! bring poison to your lips.

Indelible insult, the ravenous rapine
Of the fierce savage on you stamps its shame;
Your virgin countryside the Yankee profanes:
Mexican blood tinted the grass.

Defenseless motherland, what lies in store for you? . . .
Oh, destroyed Poland![27] Your image haunts me . . .
Anáhuac![28] Raise your clamor to Heaven,
Ask ardently for "peace and liberty."

La gloria que a España un mundo le quita:
Tremebunda agita su antorcha de muerte,
Y en duelo convierte la felicidad.

Empuña el acero fratricida mano;
En delirio insano desgarra tu seno:
¡Oh patria! veneno llevan a tus labios,
Los que tus agravios juraron vengar.

Oprobio te imprime, indeleble ultraje
Del feroz salvage la voraz rapiña;
Tu virgen campiña el yankee profana:
Sangre mexicana la yerba tiñó.

¿Qué es lo que te espera, patria desvalida? . . .
¡Polonia destruida! tu imagen me espanta . . .
¡Anáhuac! levanta tu clamor al cielo,
Pide con anhelo "paz y libertad."

**The Storm**

Already the black storm clouds darken
The horizon, and the terrible echoes
Of the deafening thunderbolt, that intimidate
Criminal and cowardly breasts,
Inspire awe in the silent woods,

**La Tempestad**

Ya negros nubarrones oscurecen
El horizonte, y los terribles ecos
Del rayo estrepitoso, que intimidan
A criminales y cobardes pechos,
Imponen en los bosques silenciosos,

---

27. In the late eighteenth-century, Poland was partitioned by Russia, Austria, and Prussia.

28. Mexico's central valley during the Aztec Empire.

Resounding in the vast hollows
Of the deep ravines, and seem to
Move the earth to its foundations.
Bright thunderbolts light
With the speed of thought,
The snows that crown the mountain,
The lake where they see their reflection.
On the neighboring rocks are drawn
The shadows of gigantic pines;
And their branches find themselves attacked
By the clashing gusts of the winds.
From the hill, the torrent already falls,
Improvised by strong cloudbursts,
And its insignificant white foam,
Disappears like the lightest vapor.
The gentle river now strains its bed;
Its waters overflow, and arrogantly
Dragging boulders in its flow,
Bending the grass on the ground,
Floods the cultivated fields;
The meadows where the lambs graze;
The leafy jungle, the fertile valleys
That other times it sweetly watered.
Startled, the bull seeks refuge
In the hollows of the hills;
Nor can the poor farmer find it
In the thatched-roofed cabin.
The innocent birds in their flight,
Cut the air, describing circles,
And return flustered to the nests
That once saw their fond wooing.
Oh, grandiose spectacle! Sublime!
Worthy of the great author of the universe!

Resuenan en los cóncavos estensos
De las hondas cañadas, y parecen
Conmover de la tierra los cimientos.
Relámpagos vivísimos alumbran
Con la velocidad del pensamiento,
Las nieves que coronan la montaña,
El lago do se miran sus reflejos.
En las rocas vecinas se dibujan
Las sombras de los pinos gigantescos;
Y sus ramas se miran combatidas
Por el soplo encontrado de los vientos.
De la colina, baja ya el torrente
Que improvisaron fuertes aguaceros,
Y sus blancas espumas deleznables,
Desaparecen cual vapor ligero.
Estrecho va en su cauce el manso río;
Desbórdanse sus aguas, y soberbio
Arrastrando en su curso los peñascos,
Doblegando la yerba de su suelo,
Inunda la llanura cultivada;
Los prados en que agostan los corderos;
La selva hojosa, los fecundos valles
Que otras veces regaba placentero.
Amedrentado el toro, busca asilo
En las concavidades de los cerros;
Y el pobre labrador no puede hallarlo
En la cabaña de pajizo techo.
Hendiendo el aire, círculos describen
Las inocentes aves con su vuelo,
Y azoradas se vuelven a los nidos
Que vieron sus amores lisongeros.
¡Oh grandioso espectáculo! ¡sublime!
¡Digno del grande autor del universo!

That overwhelms man, and elevates him,
Turning his affection away from the earth!

¡Que anonadas al hombre, que lo elevas,
Desviando de la tierra sus afectos!

Hacienda del Pabellón, September 1846
Guadalupe Calderón
Josefa Terán
Una Zacatecana

## "The Angels of Buena Vista" by John Greenleaf Whittier (1847)[29]

*The following poem about the Battle of Buena Vista by the U.S. poet John Greenleaf Whittier (1807–1892) was inspired by a widely disseminated eyewitness account of the Battle of Monterrey originally published in the* Louisville Courier *in late 1846. In the letter, a U.S. soldier reported seeing a Mexican woman tend to the wounded of both sides before being shot in crossfire: "While I was stationed with our left wing in one of our forts, I saw a Mexican woman busily engaged in carrying bread and water to the wounded men of both armies. I saw the ministering angel raise the head of a wounded man, give him water and food, and then bind up his ghastly wound with a handkerchief she took from her own head. After having exhausted her supplies, she went back to her house, to get more bread and water for others. As she was returning on her mission of mercy, to comfort other wounded persons, I heard the report of a gun, and saw the poor innocent creature fall dead. I think it was an accidental shot that struck her. I would not be willing to believe otherwise. It made me sick at heart; and, turning from the scene, I involuntarily raised my eyes toward heaven, and thought, Great God! and is this war? Passing the spot the next day, I saw her body still lying there, with the bread by her side, and the broken gourd, with a few drops of water in it,—emblems of her errand. We buried her; and while we were digging her grave, cannon-balls flew around like hail."[30] The anecdote was further popularized by songs and poems published during and immediately following the war, including the much reproduced poem "The Heroine Martyr of Monterey" by the Reverend J. G. Lyons,*

29. John Greenleaf Whittier, *The Writings of John Greenleaf Whittier,* vol. 1 (Boston and New York: Houghton Mifflin, 1892), 112–16.

30. The letter is reproduced in George Winston Smith and Charles Judah's *Chronicles of the Gringos: The U.S. Army in the Mexican War, 1846–1848* (Albuquerque: University of New Mexico Press, 1968), 90. In addition to the *Louisville Journal,* the letter appeared in numerous other newspapers across the country.

*published in February 1847.*[31] *Whittier's poem about the incident, though not the first, is the most famous retelling of this emblematic tale of the horrors of the U.S.-Mexican War. In his poem, presented in its entirety below with a prefatory note by the poet, Whittier changes the setting of the poem from Monterrey to the subsequent Battle of Buena Vista.*

> A letter-writer from Mexico during the Mexican war, when detailing some of the incidents at the terrible fight of Buena Vista, mentioned that Mexican women were seen hovering near the field of death, for the purpose of giving aid and succor to the wounded. One poor woman was found surrounded by the maimed and suffering of both armies, ministering to the wants of Americans as well as Mexicans, with impartial tenderness.
>
> John Greenleaf Whittier

Speak and tell us, our Ximena, looking northward far away,
O'er the camp of the invaders, o'er the Mexican array,
Who is losing? who is winning? are they far or come they near?
Look abroad, and tell us, sister, whither rolls the storm we hear.

"Down the hills of Angostura[32] still the storm of battle rolls;
Blood is flowing, men are dying; God have mercy on their souls!"
Who is losing? who is winning? "Over hill and over plain,
I see but smoke of cannon clouding through the mountain rain."

Holy Mother! keep our brothers! Look, Ximena, look once more.
"Still I see the fearful whirlwind rolling darkly as before,
Bearing on, in strange confusion, friend and foeman, foot and horse,
Like some wild and troubled torrent sweeping down its mountain course."

Look forth once more, Ximena! "Ah! the smoke has rolled away;
And I see the Northern rifles gleaming down the ranks of gray.[33]
Hark! that sudden blast of bugles! there the troop of Minon wheels;
There the Northern horses thunder, with the cannon at their heels.

"Jesu, pity I how it thickens! now retreat and now advance!
Right against the blazing cannon shivers Puebla's charging lance!
Down they go, the brave young riders; horse and foot together fall;
Like a ploughshare in the fallow, through them ploughs the Northern ball."

---

31. This poem may be found on this volume's title support page.

32. The hills of Angostura was the site of the Battle of Buena Vista, known in Spanish as the Battle of Angostura.

33. See note 35 to "The Horrors of War at Buena Vista" in Part III.

Nearer came the storm and nearer, rolling fast and frightful on!
Speak, Ximena, speak and tell us, who has lost, and who has won?
"Alas! alas! I know not; friend and foe together fall,
O'er the dying rush the living: pray, my sisters, for them all!

"Lo! the wind the smoke is lifting. Blessed Mother, save my brain!
I can see the wounded crawling slowly out from heaps of slain.
Now they stagger, blind and bleeding; now they fall, and strive to rise;
Hasten, sisters, haste and save them, lest they die before our eyes!

"O my heart's love! O my dear one! lay thy poor head on my knee;
Dost thou know the lips that kiss thee? Canst thou hear me? canst thou see?
O my husband, brave and gentle! O my Bernal, look once more
On the blessed cross before thee! Mercy! all is o'er!"

Dry thy tears, my poor Ximena; lay thy dear one down to rest;
Let his hands be meekly folded, lay the cross upon his breast;
Let his dirge be sung hereafter, and his funeral masses said;
To-day, thou poor bereaved one, the living ask thy aid.

Close beside her, faintly moaning, fair and young, a soldier lay,
Torn with shot and pierced with lances, bleeding slow his life away;
But, as tenderly before him the lorn Ximena knelt,
She saw the Northern eagle shining on his pistol-belt.

With a stifled cry of horror straight she turned away her head;
With a sad and bitter feeling looked she back upon her dead;
But she heard the youth's low moaning, and his struggling breath of pain,
And she raised the cooling water to his parching lips again.

Whispered low the dying soldier, pressed her hand and faintly smiled;
Was that pitying face his mother's? did she watch beside her child?
All his stranger words with meaning her woman's heart supplied;
With her kiss upon his forehead, "Mother!" murmured he, and died!

"A bitter curse upon them, poor boy, who led thee forth,
From some gentle, sad-eyed mother, weeping, lonely, in the North!"
Spake the mournful Mexic woman, as she laid him with her dead,
And turned to soothe the living, and bind the wounds which bled.

"Look forth once more, Ximena!" Like a cloud before the wind
Rolls the battle down the mountains, leaving blood and death behind;
Ah! they plead in vain for mercy; in the dust the wounded strive;
"Hide your faces, holy angels! O thou Christ of God, forgive!"

Sink, O Night, among thy mountains! let the cool, gray shadows fall;
Dying brothers, fighting demons, drop thy curtain over all!
Through the thickening winter twilight, wide apart the battle rolled,
In its sheath the sabre rested, and the cannon's lips grew cold.

But the noble Mexic women still their holy task pursued,
Through that long, dark night of sorrow, worn and faint and lacking food.
Over weak and suffering brothers, with a tender care they hung,
And the dying foeman blessed them in a strange and Northern tongue.

Not wholly lost, O Father! is this evil world of ours;
Upward, through its blood and ashes, spring afresh the Eden flowers;
From its smoking hell of battle, Love and Pity send their prayer,
And still thy white-winged angels hover dimly in our air!

## "A Solemn Moment. To My Motherland" by Guillermo Prieto (1847)[34]

*Guillermo Prieto (1818–1897) was nineteenth-century Mexico's most celebrated and popular poet and a widely read journalist. He was one of the founders of the Mexican Republic's first nationalist literary association, the Academia Letrán (1836), and a well-known journalist in the turbulent years of the U.S.-Mexican War and its aftermath. During the* Reforma *Movement, he was a close associate of Benito Juárez and later served in the Mexican congress for thirty years (1867–1897). Prieto's memoirs are rich with reminiscences of the U.S.-Mexican War, and he was one of the contributors to* The other side, or, Notes for the history of the war between Mexico and the United States *(1848), an early and influential history of the war.*

**A Solemn Moment. To My Motherland**

God of my fathers! God of nations!
Almighty God! Look on the sorrow

**Un momento de formalidad. A mi Patria.**

¡Dios de mis padres! ¡Dios de las naciones!
¡Omnipotente Dios! Mira el quebranto

34. Guillermo Prieto, *Colección de poesías escogidas, publicadas e inéditas* (Mexico City: Tipografía de la Oficina Impresora de Escampillas, 1895), 46–48. Translated by Gustavo Pellón.

of the adored motherland that to my eyes
first gave the light of day.
Why do you take the strength from her children?
Why when they see that vile men oppress them,
do their withered lips moan in torment,
instead of shouting, Oh God! War! Vengeance?
Veracruz, a corpse next to her seas,
queen without scepter, bloody victim
heard as she died the "hurrahs" of victory
from those who drenched her homes in blood! . . .
Won't you wake? Do the shouts of joy
that the triumphant invader hurls arrogantly
lull you in the lethargy of infamy? . . .
Oh torment! Oh outrage! Oh my motherland!
See! The families flee in terror
by the glare of the burning towns,
while the thousand mouths of the bronzes
of the foreigner, acclaim their dominion,
amid terror and extermination!
And where is the people whose wrathful
thunderbolt once struck in Dolores,[35]
and made embers out of the tyrant's throne?
And where are the people who like the lava

de la patria adorada que a mis ojos
dio por primera vez la luz del día.
¿Por qué a sus hijos quitas la pujanza?
¿Por qué al sentir que viles les oprimen,
sus labios mustios de tormento gimen,
y no claman, ¡oh Dios!, ¡guerra!, venganza?
¡Cadáver Veracruz junto a los mares,
reina sin cetro, víctima sangrienta
oyó al morir los ¡hurras! de victoria
del que empapó con sangre sus hogares! . . .
¿No despertais? ¿Los gritos de alegría
que ufano lanza el invasor triunfante
te arrullan de la infamia en el letargo? . . .
¡Oh tormento!, ¡oh baldón!, ¡oh patria mía!
¡Ved!, las familias huyen con espanto
a la luz del incendio de los pueblos,
mientras que las mil bocas de los bronces
del extranjero, aclaman el dominio,
¡en medio del terror y el exterminio!
¿Y dónde el pueblo está que en otro tiempo
de su ira el rayo fulminó en Dolores,
e hizo pavesa el trono del tirano?
¿Y dónde el pueblo está que cual la lava

35. Dolores was where the Mexican independence movement was born under the leadership of Miguel Hidalgo y Costilla. See note 60 in Part II of this volume.

of the colossal volcano, broke their fetters,
became great, and took heart in glory,
and announced a land of heroes to the world,
sublime with the sun of victory?

Beautiful land of Hidalgo! My land!
Like outcasts in your lovely soil,
we shall eat the bread of agony;
like beggars, to the masters of our land,
we shall go on our knees to plead
for soil on which to sleep the final sleep! . . .
Our anguish shall be their pleasure;
the children of our love, their slaves;
and our women will give them comfort
alas, amid the remains of our brave men.
No, let our anger dry our tears;
No, let us die a thousand times, for sorrow
in the face such affronts is sterile shame,
when the heart bursts with rage.
No, because our lips thirst for fury;
such thirst is only sated by blood;
we must purify them, to raise
hymns of praise to you, oh my motherland!

The invader with reckless tread,
scattered the limbs of those they found in the streets
begging for mercy and dragging their wounded bodies.

del tremendo volcán, rompió sus hierros,
se tornó grande, se alentó en la gloria,
y de héroes una patria anunció al mundo
sublime con el sol de la victoria?

¡Patria hermosa de Hidalgo! ¡Patria mía!
¡Como proscriptos en tu hermoso suelo,
comeremos el pan de la agonía;
como mendigos, de la patria al dueño,
iremos a pedir arrodillados
tierra para dormir el postrer sueño! . . .
¡Serán nuestras angustias sus placeres;
de nuestro amor los hijos, sus esclavos;
y les darán solaz nuestras mujeres
entre los restos, ¡ay!, de nuestros bravos.
No, que el enojo seque nuestro llanto;
No, mil veces morir, que a tanta afrenta
es un oprobio estéril el quebranto,
cuando de rabia el corazón revienta.
No que está el labio de furor sediento;
la sed, sólo con sangre se sacia;
fuerza es purificarlo, para alzarte
cánticos de alabanza, ¡oh patria mía!

El invasor con planta temeraria,
los miembros dispersó del que en las calles
reclamando piedad, se arrastró herido.

Virgins, children, to place themselves at their feet,
ran in droves to their trenches,
and those cowards gorged on their lives
with the cruelty and avidness of panthers . . .

Clamor for peace . . . ask them for peace, villains,
while the waves on the beach kiss
the bones of unburied Mexicans!
Ask for peace, the insolent will sign,
dipping his enormous quill,
in the throbbing wound of him
who is expiring because he tried to safeguard our country.
Ask for peace beside the violated bed
of the wife and the ravished virgin;
ask for peace, you slave, pleased
to receive it from the invader's sword;
renounce all claim to your people's memory
to become scum of the scum
that envelops, and humiliates, and degrades you!

God who hung a sapphire sky
as a canopy, over my beloved country,
fair jewel of America the fertile,
beautiful and gracious, and rich, and admired;
land of the fountains with crystalline waters;
land of the rich and varied flowers;
land full of fecund, virgin treasures;
enchanting pearl of the two worlds;
cradle of beauties, opulent land;
august mother of illustrious warriors . . .
To die? To die! Amid disgrace?

Las vírgenes, los niños a sus plantas
corrieron en tropel a sus trincheras,
y en sus vidas cobardes se cebaron
con crueldad y ansia de panteras . . .

¡Clamad por paz . . . pedídsela, villanos,
mientras besan las olas en la playa
los huesos de insepultos mexicanos!
Pedid la paz, la firmará insolente,
humedeciendo su tremenda pluma,
del que por darnos patria está expirando
en la herida latente.
Pedid la paz junto al violado lecho
de la esposa y la virgen ultrajada;
pedid la paz esclavo satisfecho
que el invasor te otorgue con la espada;
renuncia de tu pueblo a la memoria
para quedar escoria de la escoria
¡que te envuelve, y te humilla, y te degrada!

Dios que tendiste un cielo de zafiro
Como dosel, sobre mi patria amada,
Joya hermosa de América la fértil,
Bella y gentil, y rica, y admirada;
¡la de las fuentes de aguas cristalinas;
la de las ricas y variadas flores;
la de tesoros vírgenes, fecundos;
la perla encantadora de dos mundos;
la de beldades cuna, la opulenta;
la madre augusta de ínclitos guerreros . . .
¿Morir, ¡morir!, en medio de la afrenta?

To be the booty of foreign bandits?
Aren't you our God? Most Holy God!
At whose sign of mercy the thunderbolt
gathers his wing under your high mantle?
Aren't you our God, He who erased
from the terrified face of the earth
with the intelligent wave of the Red Sea
the furious host of Pharaoh?[36]
Are you no longer our God? Why don't you breathe
strength into the brave, valor into our souls
so that we can sink the vile forehead of the impious invader
into the mud made with our blood and our own soil? . . .
WAR! WAR without end! May a hundred towns
rise up roaring like wounded lions,
let us lift our avenging foreheads . . .
already I hear the din of combat,
already the steed neighs, the trumpet blasts,
Already the dawn of hope shines,
already the whole nation has one voice
that clamors ceaselessly: war and vengeance!
War! War! Descendants of Hidalgo,
War! War! Land of Morelos,[37]

¿Ser botín de bandidos extranjeros?
¿No eres tú nuestro Dios?, ¿Dios sacrosanto!
A cuyo signo de piedad el rayo
recoge el ala bajo tu alto manto?
¿No eres tú nuestro dios, el que borraste
de la faz espantada de la tierra
con la ola inteligente del Mar Rojo
de Faraón las huestes furibundas?
¿No eres ya nuestro Dios? ¿Por qué no infundes
fuerza a los bravos, a las almas brío
para hundir en el fango que ha formado
con nuestra sangre en nuestro propio suelo
la frente vil del invasor impío? . . .
¡GUERRA! ¡GUERRA sin fin! Alcense aullando
como el león herido, pueblos ciento,
levantemos las frentes vengadoras . . .
ya escucho el estridor de los combates,
ya relincha el bridón, suena la trompa,
ya reluce una aurora de esperanza,
ya toda la nación tiene un acento
que clama sin cesar: ¡guerra y venganza!
¡Guerra! ¡Guerra!, de Hidalgo descendientes,
¡guerra! ¡guerra!, la patria de Morelos,

36. A reference to the parting of the Red Sea by Moses and the subsequent destruction of Pharaoh's army (Exodus 14:28).

37. See introduction to "Oath of Allegiance of the *La Insurgente Guadalupana Guerrilla* Fighters (April 23, 1847)" in Part III of this volume.

everything draws strength, our
 foreheads undaunted
drink the light of glory from the skies!

Good, thus let us die, simply as
 brothers
fighting against infamous invaders,
and the flag waves, guiding Mexicans,
to where this new happy light glides
illuminating the children of Dolores
the adored banner of Iguala!

Motherland, motherland, my love, if
 this is a dream
it is the dream of a son who adores
 you
and sheds tears for your adverse lot;
but if it is a dream and no more,
 implore God
that the fatal dawn may hide from
 me
the deathly shadow of your disgrace!

todo se alienta, ¡ímpavidas las
 frentes
beben la luz de gloria de los cielos!

Bien a morir así, tan sólo
 hermanos
luchando contra infames invasores,
y flota, dirigiendo mexicanos,
donde esa nueva luz feliz resbala
alumbrando los hijos de Dolores
¡el adorado pabellón de Iguala!

Patria, patria, mi amor, si éste es un
 sueño
es el sueño de un hijo que te
 adora
y vierte llanto por tu adversa suerte;
mas si es sueño y no más, ¡de Dios
 implora
que le oculte la sombra de la
 muerte
de tu ignominia la funesta aurora!

## "Illuminations for Victories in Mexico" by Grace Greenwood (1851)[38]

*Sara Jane Clark Lippincott (1823–1904) was a suffragist and abolitionist who wrote under the pseudonym of Grace Greenwood. Greenwood was one of the most prolific and well-known women journalists of her time. Her articles appeared in numerous newspapers and magazines, including* Godey's Lady's Book, The New York Times, The National Era, Saturday Evening Post, *and* The Little Pilgrim, *a children's magazine. Greenwood published more than twenty books in her lifetime, including several children's books, such as* Stories and Legends of Travel and History for Children *(1857) and* Nelly, the Gipsy Girl *(1863). Greenwood is primarily known for her prose writings, but the following poem, which was probably composed and first published during the war, is a dramatic counterpoint to nationalist and martial poems and writings about the war. The poem unflinchingly condemns the loss of civilian life and explores the relationship between gender and perceptions of the war.*

38. Grace Greenwood, *Poems* (Boston: Ticknor, Reed and Fields, 1851), 102–3.

Light up thy homes, Columbia,[39]
For those chivalric men
Who bear to scenes of warlike strife
Thy conquering arms again,
Where glorious victories, flash on flash,
Reveal their stormy way,—
Resaca's, Palo Alto's fields,
The heights of Monterey!

They pile with thousands of thy foes
Buena Vista's plain;
With maids and wives, at Vera Cruz,
Swell high the list of slain!
They paint upon the Southern skies
The blaze of burning domes,—
Their laurels dew with blood of babes!
Light up, light up thy homes!

Light up your homes, O fathers!
For those young hero bands,
Whose march is still through vanquished towns,
And over conquered lands!
Whose valor, wild, impetuous,
In all its fiery glow,
Pours onward like a lava tide,
And sweeps away the foe!

For those whose dead brows glory crowns,
On crimson couches sleeping,
And for home faces wan with grief,
And fond eyes dim with weeping,
And for the soldier, poor, unknown,
Who battled, madly brave,
Beneath a stranger soil to share
A shallow, crowded grave.

Light up thy home, young mother!
Then gaze in pride and joy
Upon those fair and gentle girls,
That eagle-eyed young boy;
And clasp thy darling little one
Yet closer to thy breast,

39. Columbia denotes the United States of America.

And be thy kisses on its lips
In yearning love impressed.

In yon beleaguered city
Were homes as sweet as thine;
Where trembling mothers felt loved arms
In fear around them twine,—
The lad with brow of olive hue,
The babe like lily fair,
The maiden with her midnight eyes,
And wealth of raven hair.

The booming shot, the murderous shell,
Crashed through the crumbling walls,
And filled with agony and death
Those sacred household halls!
Then, bleeding, crushed, and blackened, lay
The sister by the brother,
And the torn infant gasped and writhed
On the bosom of the mother!

O sisters, if ye have no tears
For fearful tales like these,
If the banners of the victors veil
The victim's agonies,
If ye lose the babe's and mother's cry
In the noisy roll of drums,
If your hearts with martial pride throb high,
Light up, light up your homes!

# *The War and Its Legacy in Fiction*

## *Legends of Mexico* by George Lippard (1847)[40]

Legends of Mexico *(1847) by George Lippard (1822–1854) is a collection of fictionalized historical episodes written in a melodramatic, violent, and lurid style designed to provoke strong sensations in the reader. Along with Ned Buntline (1821–1886), the author of* Magdalena, The Beautiful Mexican Maid *(1847),*

40. George Lippard, *Legends of Mexico* (Philadelphia: TB Peterson, 1847), 15–16, 37–39.

*Lippard is considered to be one of the most important practitioners of popular "sensationalist" fiction at mid-century. Lippard was a strong critic of the corruption of modern city life and made a name for himself writing urban gothic novels such as* The Quaker City; Or, The Monks of Monk Hall *(1845). Below we present two selections from* Legends of Mexico. *The first is drawn from the opening section of the book titled "The Crusade of the Nineteenth Century." It is emblematic of the lengthy digressions about race, identity, and history that Lippard intersperses throughout his narrative, as well as the ideology of Manifest Destiny in this period of time. The second is an excerpt from the melodramatic tale "The Dead Woman of Palo Alto," in which a handsome U.S. soldier marries the daughter of a Mexican general who imprisons the American and later fights him on the fields of Palo Alto. The lengthy story also contains surprising twists and turns, including an astonishing family revelation, rape, and murder.*

## From "The Crusade of the Nineteenth Century"

There is a deeper reason, in all this, than meets the superficial eye. Beneath the bloody foam of battle, flows on, forever, the serene and awful current of divine truth.

Do you ask the explanation of this mystery? Search the history of the North American People, behold them forsake the shores of Europe, and dare the unknown dangers of the distant wilderness, not for the lust of gold or power, but for the sake of a religion, a Home.

An Exodus like this—the going forth of the oppressed of all nations to a new world—the angels never saw before. All parts of Europe, sent their heart-wounded, their down-trodden thousands to the wilds of North America.

The German and the Frenchman, the Swede and the Irishman, the Scot and the Englishman, met in the wild, and grouped around one altar—Sacred to the majesty of God and the rights of man. From this strangely mingled band of wanderers, a new People sprung into birth.[41]

A vigorous People, rugged as the rocks of the wilderness which sheltered them, free as the forest which gave them shade, bold as the red Indian who forced them to purchase every inch of ground, with the blood of human hearts. To this hardy People—this people created from the pilgrims and wanderers of all nations—this People nursed into full vigor, by long and bloody Indian war and hardened into iron, by the longest and bloodiest war of all, the Revolution, to this People of Northern America, God Almighty has given the destiny of the entire American continent.

---

41. Here, Lippard anticipates Frederick Jackson Turner's "The Significance of the Frontier in American History" (known as the "Frontier Thesis"), which argued that the struggle between the emigrant and the American frontier was central to the forging of the American character.

The handwriting of blood and fire, is upon British America and Southern America.

As the Aztec people, crumbled before the Spaniard, so will the mongrel race, moulded of Indian and Spanish blood, melt into, and be ruled by, the Iron Race of the North.

You cannot deny it. You cannot avoid the solemn truth, which glares you in the face.

God speaks it, from history, from the events now passing around us, from every line of the career of the People, who followed his smile into the desert.

As the People of the Old Thirteen states, rose like one man, against the juggernaut of government, the British Monarchy, so the serfs of Canada will rise, trample the thing of blood into dust, and in the gore of the battlefield plant the olive tree of peace and freedom.[42]

Thanks be to God, the time comes, when Niagara, will no longer extend from a free land to a British despotism. Before many years that awful cataract will sing the anthem of a free Continent.

God Almighty has given the destiny of the Continent, into the hands of the free People of the American Union.

Not the Anglo-Saxon race,[43] for such a race has no existence, save in the brains of certain people, who talk frothily about immense nothings. You might as well call the American People, the Scandinavian race, the Celtic race, the Norman race, as to apply to them, the empty phrase, Anglo-Saxon. This ridiculous word, has been in the mouths of grave men, who should know better, for years; it is high time, that we should discard it for some word, with a slight pretense of meaning.

. . .

We are the American people. Our lineage is from that God, who bade us go forth, from the old world, and smiled us into an Empire of Men. Our destiny to possess this Continent, drive from it all shreds of Monarchy, whether British or Spanish or Portuguese, and on the wrecks of shattered empires, build the Altar, second to the Brotherhood of Man.

Then come with me, and look upon our Banner of the Stars, as it goes in glory and gloom over the Continent, freedom's pillar of cloud by day, her pillar of fire by night. Our fathers loved that Banner in the days of old. Its stripes were painted with the blood of martyrs. Its stars flashed through the clouds of Bunker Hill and Brandywine, and Saratoga, and came shining out in the cloudless sky of Yorktown. Let us follow it then, and bid God's blessing on it, as its stars gleam awfully through the bloody mists of Mexico.

---

42. Lippard here links the war against Mexico with the prospect of a Canadian rebellion against the British Crown. At the start of the U.S.-Mexican War, relations between the United States and Great Britain continued to be strained over the nonrenewal of the Treaty of Joint Occupation of Oregon. See Introduction.

43. See note 2 in Part II of this volume.

Let us not heed the miserable cant of the traitors among us, who advise the Mexicans to give the American soldier a bloody and hospitable grave. Though these traitors increase like vipers under a hot sun, though they poison our air, in the Senate and the Press, let us pass them by, with a simple prayer, that God will be merciful to the pitiful dastard, who—under the cloak of British or Mexican Sympathy—would turn traitor to a land like ours.

WASHINGTON, you all remember, sat in his Camp at Cambridge, in September, 1775, his eyes fixed upon the map of the Continent, his finger laid upon Canada, while his unsheathed sword, reached from Labrador to Patagonia. In the silence of the night, even as he planned the conquest of Canada, he recognized this great truth—God has given the American Continent to the free.

Let us follow then, the American Banner, and while our souls are awed by the thunder flash of battle; while the horrible world of carnage with its shrieks and groans, its dead armies and butchered legions widens and crimsons around us, let us never for one moment forget, that mysterious Symbol of our destiny—THE UNSHEATHED SWORD OF WASHINGTON RESTING UPON THE MAP OF THE NEW WORLD.

### From "The Dead Woman of Palo Alto"

It was in the last hour of that fight—when the battle, which we will shortly look upon in all its details, was about to close—that a solitary Mexican officer, flying from the field, spurred his bay horse through the devious path of the chaparral.

Look yonder, and by the light of the solitary sun, you may behold his pursuer, a young American, mounted on a dark steed. With the uniform torn in ribands from his right arm, he brandishes his sword—it drops blood upon his broad chest—and dashes on.

He nears the Mexican, he is within twenty paces, when the flying soldier is about to leave the path, and seek the shadows of the chaparral. The American raises his pistol—fires! The bay-horse totters to and fro, and falls on his forefeet, precipitating his rider on the sod.

Beside his dying horse—whose life-blood wells from the fatal wound—that rider stands and confronts the enemy. The American starts in his saddle, and pulls his bridle-rein, throwing his dark horse, back on his haunches, as he beholds him.

For in that American officer stained from head to foot with blood, you recognize the pale face and full deep eyes of the Virginian, husband of the Lady Inez. Look upon that Mexican, his green uniform rent with sword thrusts, his white moustache, dyed with crimson drops, his bronzed face traversed by a fearful wound, and you behold *her father*.

Words of deep meaning were spoken there in that lonely chaparral.

"Yield, General!" cried the Virginian in Spanish. "You are faint with wounds. I will not fight with the father of my wife."

There was something terrible in the silent malignity which shone from the old man's eyes.

"You are mounted," he quietly said—"My horse is dying—" and then wiping the blood from his sword blade with his left hand, grasped the hilt with his right, and stood prepared for a deadly fight—"Come!" he cried in the settled tone of a mortal hatred—"You escaped from the prison of Mexico, but cannot escape *me*!"

It was interesting to notice the conduct of that young Virginian, whose blue uniform was in many places turned to red, by the blood of his foes. He quietly dismounted, flung the rein on the neck of his dark steed, wiped the battle sweat from his face, and then struck the point of his sword into the sod.

He then calmly advanced along the path, with the wall of the chaparral on either side. Stern and unrelenting, the old General awaited him.

"General you see me, unarmed, defenseless before you!" said the Virginian advancing—"Let me ask you once for all—why do you pursue me with this unrelenting hatred? I came to your Mexican home, a stranger from the far north, and was grateful for your generous hospitality. I met your daughter—we loved—were joined in marriage before the altar of your solemn cathedral. Why hurl me from your daughter's arms, into a prison, only reserved for the vilest outcast? Why, even as I rotted in the dungeon, did you drag my wife from the city, force her to accompany you in your march, and last night bid her prepare, for the miserable nuptials which were to take place to day? Come—be friends with me—in this hour, when you are forced to leave the field, a fugitive, I will aid your flight!"

There was an earnestness in the young man's tone, that would have touched the hardest heart. Frankness was written on his pale face, and honor spoke in the gleam of his large hazel eye.

"Where is my daughter?" said the Mexican General, in a low voice, but still keeping his hand on the hilt of his sword.

"Last night, when I bore the message of Fort Brown, to our General—that message which called for help, in direst extremity—I left Inez in a *ranche*[44] (farm house) some few hundred yards to the west of this place. When the battle is over,—I will join her again."

"Coward! You will never join her again! After I have laid you dead upon the sod, I myself will go and bear your message to my daughter."

With a ferocious look in his eye, the General dashed upon the unarmed man, making a thrust, with all the vigor of his right arm. To say the least, there was something cowardly in this movement, indeed, it looked very much like Assassination.

The VIRGINIAN darted aside, but the sword passed between his side and his left arm, transfixing a piece of his coat. As quick as thought he turned, darted on the Mexican who had been almost thrown on his face by the impetus of his ineffectual thrust and clutched his throat with a grasp of iron.

"This your Mexican chivalry! To stab an unarmed man!"

---

44. A misspelling of the Spanish word *rancho*.

He shook him fiercely in that tightening grasp—the General made an effort to shorten his grasp of the sword, and use it as a dagger, but the blade fell from his hand—he sank backward on the sod, with the knee of the Virginian on his breast.

He uttered an incoherent groan—his eyes began to start from their sockets.

The Virginian, touched with pity released his grasp, but seized the fallen sword.

"I hate you"—slowly said the Mexican General, raising himself on one hand, while his face grew deathly pale—"Not so much because you stole my daughter, as that you are one of the accursed race, whose destiny it is, to despoil our land, extinguish our name, annihilate our flag!"

He tore open the breast of his coat, and disclosed a mortal wound, which had been killing him, slowly, for hours.—

"If there is one word, that may express the hatred of a dying man, better than another, I fling it in your face and curse you with that breath, whose passing, leaves my lips cold forever!"

There was something so terrible in these last words of a dying man, uttered with rattling breath and a pale face, deformed by hideous contortions, that the American soldier shrunk from his touch, and gazed upon him in silent horror.

He never spoke again, save to murmur, in his Spanish tongue—"Water! Water!"

Reaching forth his arms, he grasped the blade of his sword which the Virginian held—kissed the hilt, and fell back, with a torrent of blood, streaming from his mouth.

## "Don Luis Martínez de Castro or The National Guard" by Niceto de Zamacois (1847)[45]

*In the years leading up to the war, Luis Martínez de Castro (1819–1847) was one of the most educated and talented members of Mexico City's intelligentsia. He was a graduate of the city's finest school, the Colegio de Minería, where he mastered several languages, and he was a respected member of the Academia Letrán (1836), the country's first nationalist literary* salón. *During the war, Martínez de Castro assisted in the publication of pamphlets calling for U.S. soldiers to desert and join the Mexican army, and he distinguished himself at the Battle of Churubusco (August 20, 1847), where he was mortally wounded. Two months after his death from gangrene in Mexico City, while the U.S. occupied the capital, a Spanish-born writer named Niceto de Zamacois (1820–1885) published a short story about Martínez de Castro's heroic death in the newspaper* El Monitor Republicano.

---

45. Niceto de Zamacois, "Don Luis Martínez de Castro o El guardia nacional," *El Monitor Republicano,* October 24, 1847, 1–2. Translated by Gustavo Pellón.

*Zamacois' fanciful representation of Martínez de Castro's heroics and his relationship with a fictional woman named Matilde led several of Martínez de Castro's friends to lodge a written complaint with the newspaper against Zamacois for distorting and diminishing the man's true character and actions. Zamacois' short story treats the theme of love and sacrifice and features a cross-dressing woman warrior, in this case possibly inspired by the actions of Doña María de Jesús Dosamantes of Monterrey (see Part III of this volume). Below are three excerpts from this controversial story.*

"Matilde, listen: listen one moment, and I swear I'll obey you if after you hear me you command me to stay by your side, indifferent to the cause of our independence."

"Speak, speak, I'm listening, I'm listening impatiently."

"Someday—if by some fate the enemy triumphs—do you want my compatriots to say, pointing at me: 'That one who goes there, is one of the many who because they didn't run to join the fight contributed to the ruin of our country.' Or do you want them to exclaim as they see me beside you: 'He is one of the brave who with his blood saved the republic from shameful slavery?'

"You win, you win. Leave, my love, leave, yes; and forgive me if for one moment I tried to lead you away from the most sacred of duties; but before leaving I beg you don't deny me a favor."

"What can I deny you? . . . What favor do you wish?"

"Embrace me . . ."

"Ah! . . . Yes . . . and a kiss as pure as our souls."

. . .

Death decimates the ranks of the Mexicans, while their cannon sow the battlefield with the corpses of North Americans. In the end, the Guardia Nacional finds itself flanked, and begins to retreat in some disorder. In such critical circumstances a young Mexican appears with the flag of the Independencia regiment in his hand, seeking out the place of the greatest danger. He exhorts his comrades to defend him until not one of them is alive. This conduct gives courage to the Mexicans, who begin to attack with greater fury, managing to repel the enemy three times, inflicting a horrible slaughter. But just when they begin to believe that victory is theirs, an enemy bullet pierced the chest of a gallant officer, who with his valor and example was sustaining the indecisive victory, and he fell to the ground with a terrible "Oh!" When they see him down, the few soldiers who are still alive lose heart and retreat to take the heights of the Churubusco convent, to renew the resistance, abandoning that valiant officer in the field, wallowing in his blood and that of the comrades who had preceded him in death.

Only the young man with the flag won't abandon him. On the contrary, he gives the flag to an officer so that it will not fall into enemy hands and hurls himself with the speed of an eagle on the brave wounded man, trying to stanch with his lips the blood that spurts from the wound. The invaders then advance with celerity, and when they break into the fort, an American soldier raises his saber to take the life of the young man who was holding the dying officer in his arms. The flag bearer, however, with undaunted serenity, takes off his cap, letting two beautiful braids fall on her back, saying: "Wound, wound this unhappy woman from whom you have taken the only treasure she had in the world!" The soldier, seeing the attitude and the beauty of that angel, held back his arm, and the hapless wounded man, who had heard clearly the last words, opened his dying eyes and recognized . . . his adored Matilde! . . .

. . .

When she saw him expire, Matilde went out to the street screaming horribly, and when she reached her home, flung herself into the arms of her unhappy mother, who was looking at her in surprise.

"Matilde! . . . My daughter! . . . What does this garb mean and this despair? . . ."

"He is dead! . . . He is dead! . . . Now there is no happiness for me! . . . Everything has ended! . . ." And she told the poor old woman everything that had happened. . . .

Eight days after this fatal adventure, a great number of private carriages with their blinds up were in ______ Street. A hearse with mules caparisoned in black with plumes of the same color was before them, and a moment later, they placed in it the coffin that held the body of a sixteen-year-old girl. It was Matilde, because a spotted fever, that came from her constant weeping and suffering took her soul to the region where the Eternal has his radiant throne, to reunite her with that of the hero Luis Martínez de Castro, whose blood, spilled in Churubusco, marks the way to true glory.

## "A Faithful Negro" by Thomas Bang Thorpe (1848)[46]

*In an 1861 debate on the floor of the U.S. House of Representatives on African Americans in the U.S. Army, Samuel R. Curtis of Iowa—who supported their employ in the military—asked an opponent, Henry C. Burnett of Kentucky, whether or not he knew if African Americans had carried arms in the Mexican War. When Burnett replied that he did not, Curtis said: "I know they did." The historian Robert E. May has shown that large numbers of African Americans participated in the U.S.-Mexican War as servants to white soldiers and some*

---

46. Thomas Thorpe, *The Taylor Anecdote Book. Anecdotes and Letters of Zachary Taylor* (New York: D. Appleton and Company, 1848), 127–28.

*fought in battle.*[47] *Below appears an anecdote from Thomas Bang Thorpe's* The Taylor Anecdote Book *(1848), a collection of brief accounts of interesting, humorous, and inspiring incidents of the war. Thorpe, who was one of the most popular humorists of his time, followed Taylor for part of his Mexican campaign as a correspondent for the* New Orleans Tropic *and wrote two books about the war. Because Thorpe's writing career before and after his stint as a war correspondent was marked by fabulation and humor, the authenticity of the tales contained in* The Taylor Anecdote Book *cannot be taken at face value. Be that as it may, his anecdotes are revealing of the mind-set of the time and were read as fact by many of his readers. Thorpe's "The Faithful Negro" is a representative example of the stereotype of the obedient and submissive slave who honors his master. In fact, the very phrase "faithful negro" is a commonplace of late eighteenth- and nineteenth-century representations of black masculinity.*[48]

During the battle of Cerro Gordo, Aaron King, a faithful dark-skinned, but true-hearted servant, was left in the camp at Plan del Río, where during the fight, news was received that the 2d. Tennessee and our (his) Pennsylvania regiment had both been cut to pieces and driven out of the field. Further, that Captain Blinder's German company, and that with which his master was connected, were utterly routed, and their captains killed or wounded.

When King heard the report he burst into tears, and uttering one or two sobs, he suddenly sprang from the spot on which he was sitting, and exclaimed: "Poor captain! he may want water, aid, assistance, and I here idle!"

Quick as thought, he seized two very large canteens, ran to the creek, filled them, snatched up a musket belonging to one of the sick men, which he loaded, crying the whole time, and thus rendering the scene at once ludicrous and affecting, and exclaiming, as he returned the ramrod,— "Gosh, if I find the captain killed, I'll do something, I know."

He then ran to the road, seized the first horse he found there, rode him at the top of his speed to the battle-field, where, dismounting, he hurried through all points, inquiring for the Pennsylvania regiment. Great was his master's surprise to see him with his musket and two canteens of water, but far greater was his on discovering him. His joy was exhibited in the most striking manner. At first he did not speak, but his big eyes sparkled in a truly extraordinary way, and giving

47. Robert E. May, "Invisible Men: Blacks and the U.S. Army in the Mexican War," in *A Question of Manhood: A Reader in U.S. Black Men's History and Masculinity,* ed. Darlene Clark Hine and Earnestine Jenkins, 473–88 (Bloomington, IN: Indiana University Press, 1999).

48. For more on this stereotype, see George Boulukus, *The Grateful Slave: The Emergence of Race in Eighteenth-Century British and American Culture* (Cambridge, UK: Cambridge University Press, 2008).

his large body, for he is over six feet high, two or three singular twists, he burst into tears.

## *The Life and Adventures of Bandit Joaquín Murieta, the Celebrated California Bandit* by John Rollin Ridge (1854)[49]

*The realities of life in Gold Rush era California are depicted in* The Life and Adventures of Joaquín Murieta, the Celebrated California Bandit *(1854) by John Rollin Ridge, the first California novel and the first novel ever written by an American Indian (Ridge's Cherokee name was Yellow Bird). Ridge's father, Major Ridge, was a Cherokee notable who supported U.S. proposals to relocate the Cherokee to Oklahoma and was murdered before his son's eyes by political rivals. Ridge mined for gold in California and became a well-known journalist and editor. Inspired by more than one Mexican bandit, including one called Joaquín Murieta, Ridge fashioned an early story of frontier crime and punishment. The excerpt below explains how his protagonist, the peaceful young Murieta, is transformed into a bloodthirsty bandit.*

The first that we hear of him in the Golden State is that, in the spring of 1850, he is engaged in the honest occupation of a miner in the Stanislaus placers, then reckoned among the richest portions of the mines. He was then eighteen years of age, a little over the medium height, slenderly but gracefully built, and active as a young tiger. His complexion was neither very dark nor very light, but clear and brilliant, and his countenance was pronounced to have been—at that time—exceedingly handsome and attractive. His large black eyes, kindling with the enthusiasm of his earnest nature, his firm and well-formed mouth, his well-shaped head from which the long, glossy, black hair hung down over his shoulders, his silvery voice full of generous utterance, and the frank and cordial bearing which distinguished him made him beloved by all with whom he came in contact. He had the confidence and respect of the whole community around him, and was fast amassing a fortune from his rich mining claim. He had built him a comfortable mining residence in which he had domiciled his heart's treasure, a beautiful Sonoran girl, who had followed the young adventurer in all his wanderings with that devotedness of passion that belongs to the dark-eyed damsels of Mexico.

It was at this moment of peace and felicity that a blight came over the young man's prospects. The country was then full of lawless and desperate men, who bore the name of Americans but failed to support the honor and dignity of

49. John Rollin Ridge (Yellow Bird), *The Life and Adventures of Joaquín Murieta, the Celebrated California Bandit* (San Francisco: W.B. Cooke, 1854), 8–12.

that title. A feeling was prevalent among this class of contempt for any and all Mexicans, whom they looked upon as no better than conquered subjects of the United States and having no rights that could stand before a haughtier and superior race. They made no exceptions. If the proud blood of the Castilians mounted to the cheek of a partial descendant of the Mexiques, showing that he had inherited the old chivalrous spirit of his Spanish ancestry, they looked upon it as a saucy presumption in one so inferior to them. The prejudice of color, the antipathy of races, which are always stronger and bitterer with the ignorant and unlettered, they could not overcome; or if they could, would not, because it afforded them a convenient excuse for their unmanly cruelty and oppression.

A band of these lawless men, having the brute power to do as they pleased, visited Joaquín's house and peremptorily bade him leave his claim, as they would allow no Mexicans to work in that region. Upon his remonstrating against such outrageous conduct, they struck him violently over the face, and being physically superior, compelled him to swallow his wrath. Not content with this, they tied him hand and foot and ravished his mistress before his eyes. They left him, but the soul of the young man was from that moment darkened. It was the first injury he had ever received at the hands of the Americans, whom he had always hitherto respected, and it wrung him to the soul as a deeper and deadlier wrong from that very circumstance.

. . .

He had gone a short distance from Murphy's Diggings to see a half brother, who had been located in that vicinity for several months, and returned to Murphy's Diggings upon a horse that his brother had lent him. The animal proved to have been stolen, and being recognized by a number of individuals in town, an excitement was raised on the subject. Joaquín suddenly found himself surrounded by a furious mob and charged with the crime of theft. He told them how it happened that he was riding the horse and in what manner his half brother had come in possession of it. They listened to no explanation, but bound him to a tree, and publicly disgraced him with the lash. They then proceeded to the house of his half brother and hung him without judge or jury.

It was then that the character of Joaquín changed, suddenly and irrevocably. Wanton cruelty and the tyranny of prejudice had reached their climax. His soul swelled beyond its former boundaries, and the barriers of honor—rocked into atoms by the strong passion that shook his heart like an earthquake—crumbled around him. Then it was that he declared to a friend that he would live henceforth for revenge and that his path should be marked with blood. Fearfully did he keep his promise, as the following pages will show.

## *The Coiner* by Nicolás Pizarro Suárez (1861)[50]

*The Mexican novel* The Coiner (El Monedero) *by Nicolás Pizarro Suárez (1830–1895) was published in 1861. The novel explores Mexico's defeat at the hands of the United States in relation to the corruption of Mexico's ecclesiastical, military, and economic elites. In opposition to these essentially corrupt forces, Pizarro presents his readers with a utopian community inspired by the ideals of the French socialist Charles Fourier (1772–1837). The extract below describes the fall of Mexico City to U.S. forces and is rich with symbolic and allegorical connotations. The headings in brackets are presented to assist the reader and are not in the original novel.*

### [Don Domingo Dávila]

The clock of the Cathedral of Mexico City had just finished slowly tolling midnight, announcing that the fatal day, September 14, 1847, had run its course. The moon, veiled almost completely by thick clouds, feebly lit the buildings of the city that was submerged in a deep silence interrupted at times by rifle shots that the echo repeated distinctly, as the city returned to apparent calm. At the conclusion of the twelve strokes of the bell, a thousand voices broke forth in a prolonged shout, saying: "Sentinel! A—lert!" that other more distant voices repeated, adding, "Death to the Yankees!" at which shout the first voices replied, "Death!"

In the streets at the center of the city, already occupied by the Americans, marauders passed each other loaded with spoils, while others endeavored to force the doors of the houses, shooting the locks with their guns. Among those that were looted that horrible night was the house of Don Domingo Dávila, whom our readers already know. The gentleman had been hopelessly ill for a few months. His illness had been brought on by the moral heartache caused by the loss of almost his entire fortune in a deal that promised huge profits and had appeared to be safe owing to the respectability of the persons involved. He had been obliged to lend large sums, and he had not been able to recover them. His major misfortune was that there was no court where he could humanly appeal, because the persons who had served as surety signing the documents he had in his keeping were powerful and had great influence in the privileged court. The transaction from which those now worthless liabilities derived was not of the kind that can be published in search of the support of public opinion. In such a desperate situation, Señor Dávila still had to maintain the appearance of wealth in his home and thus had come to two wrecks at once, that of the fortune he had amassed through continual toil for the space of many years and that of his health.

50. Nicolás Pizarro Suárez, *El Monedero* (Mexico City: Imprenta Nicolás Pizarro, 1861), 244–50. Translated by Gustavo Pellón.

His daughter Rosita, who was totally unaware of the state of her household, continued to display her beauty and her finery until the seriousness of her father's condition had made her give up all diversions, becoming the most careful nurse at the bedside of the patient, at whose side she was at the moment we have spoken about at the beginning of this chapter.

. . .

The bedside lamp, which shed a bluish light at the moment we are speaking of, gave a sepulchral aspect to the room in which Rosita and Clara were taking care of the sick man. The former, dressed in black, was sitting on her father's bed, on whom she fixed a disconsolate gaze, and the latter was dozing in an armchair. The patient's symptoms were terrible: he had not spoken for the last twenty-four hours, a deathly pallor extended over his whole face, his eyes were closed and sunken, his lips almost white, bordered by a dark, circular stain that reached the end of his chin. Suddenly he sighed deeply, half-opened his eyes, and cast his vague, languid gaze over the objects before him and closed them again as he said with a lifeless voice:

"Rosa, Rosita!"

"I'm here Papa; don't you recognize me?" The young woman started to cry.

"What will become of you, my daughter?"

Rosita was unable to answer, choked by the sobs that she vainly tried to repress. Surely it took a great effort on the part of the patient to utter those words, because he was immediately attacked by a cavernous, dry cough that left him in a state of total prostration. Clara, who had allowed herself to be won over by sleep, awoke then. She suggested to Rosita that they give the sick man a drink they had prepared, but his teeth were clenched tightly and he was not able to drink it, which made Rosa burst into tears.

Later the patient's cough came back with greater force. Hearing his daughter cry, his pale face became colorless, his eyes became fixed and lusterless, and one would have thought him dead if one had not heard him pronounce with great difficulty these incoherent words:

"Rosita . . . the Feb . . . ruary . . . de . . . cree! They repu . . . diate the debt, my . . . daughter!"

Just then they heard a horrible noise, as if the vestibule door were being torn down, after a few shots, and the young women looked at each other filled with terror. Meanwhile, all the servants of the house came into Don Domingo's room in a mad rush, almost out of breath, saying with the greatest anguish: "They're here! They're coming!"

## [The Invaders and Their Allies Discover Dávila's Nurse and Her Daughter in the House]

When the Americans and the antiguerrilla force penetrated to the upper rooms of the house, "El Chato," who was guiding them, asked the nurse, who awoke in the greatest terror, where the money and the family were. The old lady did not answer, and angered by her silence that he interpreted as resistance, he gave her a kick in the chest. Then the daughter started to scream, and in order to silence them, an American alternately hit the mother and daughter with his rifle butt, leaving the former without life and the latter unconscious. When the long-haired Yankee returned to that room, the daughter of the nurse was beginning to recover. Not remembering what had happened to them, she was trying to wake her mother, thinking she was asleep, and making laborious efforts at getting up, since the pain she then felt impeded her.

"Mother! Mother dear! What happened?"

Attracted by that plaintive voice, the Yankee came near the girl, who had managed to sit, as she was pressing her forehead as if to free herself from the vision that seemed like a dream. The Yankee spoke to her in English, mixing in some Spanish words, of which the girl understood only "mucho bueno"[51] repeated by him with tenacity. Overcome with terror, she screamed again and tried to hide under the dead woman.

In such a state, the American conqueror found the daughter of the poor nurse beautiful . . . and the same bed witnessed the death of the mother and the rape of the daughter.

## *"Captain Ray, the Young Leader of the Forlorn Hope" (A True Story of the Mexican War)* by General James A. Gordon (1920)[52]

*Dime novels were inexpensive, melodramatic paperbacks that were immensely popular in the second half of the nineteenth century and the start of the twentieth. Beginning in the 1870s, these publications sported black-and-white illustrated covers and, later, color covers. Some of the more popular protagonists of these adventure stories were frontier heroes such as Buffalo Bill and Kit Carson, the outlaw Deadwood Dick, the detective Nick Carter, and Fred Fearnot, an enterprising and brave college student. The excerpts presented below are from a well-known dime series called* Pluck and Luck, *which ran from 1898 to 1929. The story of Captain Ray is not "true" as the title indicates, and General James A. Gordon was a pseudonym.*

51. *Mucho bueno* is this American soldier's attempt to say *muy bueno* or "very good."

52. James A. Gordon, "*Captain Ray: the young leader of the forlorn hope*" *(a true story of the Mexican War), Pluck and luck. No. 1160* (New York: Harry E. Wolff, Publisher, Aug. 25, 1920), 2–4, 11–12.

"Captain Ray," the general asked, "how old are you?"

"I am just twenty-one, general."

"Ah, you are young, and life is no doubt sweet to you."

"Yes, general," he replied, "life is sweet to me, but mine belongs to my country."

The general looked him in the face in silence for a minute or two, and said: "Yes, a soldier's life belongs to his country. Some of us must die tomorrow. The enemy is in our front, strongly entrenched and outnumbering us nearly three to one."

"But we can whip him out of his boots, general," remarked the young officer.

"So we can, and we must do it; but it will be at a terrible cost. I want a brave, determined officer to lead a forlorn hope of one hundred men, every man of whom will probably fall, and. . . ."

"Let me lead them, general," exclaimed the young officer, with sudden eagerness.

"It will cost you your life, captain."

"No matter, general, only let me lead them."

The general extended his hand to the young officer and silently pressed that of the young captain.

"Captain Ray," he said, in a husky tone of voice, "you will go to your death, but your fall will save the lives of hundreds of your comrades and give us that stronghold of the enemy in front of us."

. . .

At last Captain Ray turned to his men, and said: "Men, we are to go right over those breastworks.

When you rise and charge, give a yell, and when the startled enemy shows himself over the top of the works, give him your bullets full in the face. Then you can go over ere the others rally. Up and at them, now."

The one hundred brave fellows sprang to their feet and uttered a defiant yell that startled the whole Mexican camp. Then they rushed forward with fixed bayonets, on a fast run. When they were about halfway the Mexican sentinel fired his gun and uttered a cry of alarm. A few moments later the startled Mexicans had sprung to arms and rushed to the defense of the breastworks. As they showed themselves, the Forlorn Hope poured a volley into their ranks and sent many a one to his long account. Then they rushed furiously up the steep breastworks. Young Captain Ray was the first to scale them. With sword in hand he cheered on his men and a moment later was engaged in a hand-to-hand conflict with three stalwart Mexicans. The wild cry of the combatants, and the fierce oaths of desperate men, coupled with the sickening thrusts of bayonets through quivering flesh, combined to make a scene that utterly beggars description. The loss of life was terrible. The one hundred brave men melted away like snow under the heat of a summer's sun, but the survivors struck right and left, not a man flinching or dropping a weapon till his life dropped with it. The Mexican officers ran hither and thither, swearing in copious Spanish, waving their swords above their heads, and trying to rally their panic-stricken men. But all their efforts were in vain. The resistless sweep of the Americans, with the brave Smith at their head, carried the day, and in fifteen or twenty minutes from the time the first shot was fired Contreras was captured, together with nearly a thousand prisoners.

. . .

Colonel Cardenas, accompanied by his officers, repaired to the spot where Anita was seated with young Ray and Lieutenant Graham.

"Señorita," he said, without noticing Ray, "I have come for you."

"You can go without me," she replied; "I will not go."

"Then I will be compelled to use force."

"Force!" exclaimed Ray, springing to his feet and facing the burly Mexican. "This lady has appealed to me for protection, and any attempt at force will be met with force."

"Indeed!" sneered Cardenas. "What have Americanos to do with Mexico, now that the war has ended?"

"Nothing—but to get out of it as soon as we can," said Ray. "But, while we are here, whoever seeks protection under the American flag will find it," and seizing the Stars and Stripes, where they were lying near, he threw them over the beautiful girl, completely enveloping her. "Now touch her if you dare!" he exclaimed.

Anita gathered the folds of the flag about her person with a gracefulness that served to heighten her beauty.

"Señor Capitan Ray," said Cardenas, "this is a usurpation I will not submit to. I have 300 men, and all will give you battle. The consequences be upon your head."

"I will take the consequences," said Ray.

"Do you know you are violating the terms of the treaty?" Cardenas asked.

"No, I do not know, nor do I care. The lady has appealed to the protection of the American flag, and she shall receive it."

"The lady belongs to Mexico," said Cardenas; "you have no right to interfere."

"She can belong to the United States if she wishes to," replied Ray, and then turning to Anita he said: "Señorita, I have learned to love you, and if you can reciprocate my love I will make you my wife within an hour. Then the American army will protect you, even if it has to reconquer all Mexico."

Anita uttered a glad cry and sprang into the arms of the young officer.

"Oh, Señor Capitan," she cried, "I love you, I love you, and that is why I could not marry him."

And she threw her arms around his neck and kissed him repeatedly.

# Suggestions for Further Reading

The U.S.-Mexican War has produced a vast and ever-growing bibliography. The following list does not pretend to be exhaustive and favors more recent works of scholarship.

**General Histories, Reference, Biography**

Alcaraz, Ramón, ed. *The Other Side; or Notes for the History of the War between Mexico and the United States.* Translated by Albert C. Ramsay. New York: Burt Franklin, 1970.

Bauer, Jack. *The Mexican War, 1846–1848.* Lincoln: University of Nebraska Press, 1992.

Chávez, Ernesto. *The U.S. War with Mexico: A Brief History with Documents.* New York: Bedford/St. Martin's, 2007.

Crawford, Mark, David Stephen Heidler, and Jeanne T. Heidler. *Encyclopedia of the Mexican-American War.* Santa Barbara, CA: ABC-CLIO, 1999.

Fowler, Will. *Santa Anna of Mexico.* Lincoln: University of Nebraska Press, 2007.

Frazier, Donald, ed. *The United States and Mexico at War: Nineteenth-Century Expansionism and Conflict.* New York: Simon Schuster/Macmillan, 1998.

Griswold del Castillo, Richard. *The Treaty of Guadalupe Hidalgo: A Legacy of Conflict.* Norman: University of Oklahoma Press, 1990.

Haynes, Sam W. *James K. Polk and the Expansionist Impulse.* New York: Pearson Longman, 1997.

Henderson, Timothy. *A Glorious Defeat: Mexico and Its War with the United States.* New York: Hill and Wang, 2007.

Libura, Krystyna, Luis Gerardo Morales Moreno, and Jesús Velásco Márquez, eds. *Echoes of the Mexican-American War.* Translated by Mark Fried. Toronto, Canada: Groundwood Books, 2004.

Robinson, Charles M. *Texas and the Mexican War: A History and a Guide.* Austin: Texas State Historical Association, 2004.

University of Texas at Arlington Library, Jenkins Garrett, and Katherine Goodwin. *The Mexican-American War of 1846–1848: A Bibliography of the Holdings of the Libraries, the University of Texas at Arlington.* College Station: Texas A&M University Press, 1995.

**Mexican Politics and Perspectives**

Alamán, Lucas. Selection from "The History of Mexico (1849)." In *Nineteenth-Century Nation-Building and the Latin American Intellectual Tradition: A Reader,* translated and edited by Janet Burke and Ted Humphrey. Indianapolis: Hackett Publishing Company, 2007. 173–198.

Bazant, Jan. "From Independence to the Liberal Republic, 1821–1867." In *Mexico since Independence,* edited by Leslie Bethell. Cambridge, UK: Cambridge University Press, 1991. 1–48.

Brack, Gene. *Mexico Views Manifest Destiny, 1821–1846: An Essay on the Origins of the Mexican War.* Albuquerque: University of New Mexico Press, 1975.

Colcleugh, M. Bruce. "War-Time Portraits of the Gringo: American Invaders and the Manufacture of Mexican Nationalism." *Journal of the Canadian Historical Association* 6 (1995): 81–101.

Colcleugh, M. Bruce. "'La Invasión Yanqui': The Crucible of Elite Nationalism in Mexico." *Canadian Review of Studies in Nationalism* 24, no. 1–2 (1997): 1–11.

Costeloe, Michael. *The Central Republic in Mexico, 1835–1846: 'Hombres de Bien' in the Age of Santa Anna.* Cambridge, UK: Cambridge University Press, 2002.

DePalo, William A., Jr. *The Mexican National Army, 1822–1852.* College Station: Texas A&M University Press, 1997.

Goffin, Aivin M. "Nationalism and Mexican Interpretations of the War of the North American Invasion, 1846–1848." *Canadian Review of Studies in Nationalism* 19, no. 1–2 (1992): 129–138.

Hale, Charles A. *Mexican Liberalism in the Age of Mora, 1821–1853.* New Haven, CT: Yale University Press, 1968.

Levinson, Irving W. *Wars within Wars: Mexican Guerrillas, Domestic Elites, and the United States of America, 1846–1848.* Fort Worth: Texas Christian University Press, 2005.

Mora, José María Luis. "On Ecclesiastical Wealth." Selection from "The History of Mexico (1849)." In *Nineteenth-Century Nation-Building and the Latin American Intellectual Tradition: A Reader,* translated and edited by Janet Burke and Ted Humphrey. Indianapolis: Hackett Publishing Company, 2007. 37–50.

Robinson, Cecil, ed. *The View from Chapultepec: Mexican Writers on the Mexican-American War.* Translated by Cecil Robinson. Tucson: University of Arizona Press, 1989.

Rodríguez Díaz, María del Rosario. "Mexico's Vision of Manifest Destiny during the 1847 War." *Journal of Popular Culture* 35, no. 2 (2001): 41–50.

Santoni, Pedro. *Mexicans at Arms: Puro Federalists and the Politics of War, 1845–1848.* Fort Worth: Texas Christian University Press, 1996.

Weber, David J. *Foreigners in Their Native Land: Historical Roots of the Mexican Americans.* Albuquerque: University of New Mexico Press, 1973.

Weber, David J. *The Mexican Frontier, 1821–1846: The American Southwest under Mexico.* Albuquerque: University of New Mexico Press, 1982.

Zoraida Vázquez, Josefina, and Lorenzo Meyer. *The United States and Mexico.* Chicago: University of Chicago Press, 1985.

**The War in U.S. Culture and Literature**

Alemán, Jesse, and Shelley Streeby. *Empire and the Literature of Sensation: An Anthology of Nineteenth-Century Popular Fiction.* New Brunswick, NJ: Rutgers University Press, 2007.

Flores, Richard R. *Remembering the Alamo: Memory, Modernity, and the Master Symbol.* Austin: University of Texas Press, 2002.

Greenberg, Amy S. *Manifest Manhood and the Antebellum American Empire.* Cambridge, UK: Cambridge University Press, 2005.

Gruesz, Kirsten Silva. *Ambassadors of Culture: The Transamerican Origins of Latino Writing.* Princeton, NJ: Princeton University Press, 2001.

Johannsen, Robert Walker. *To the Halls of the Montezumas: The Mexican War in the American Imagination.* New York: Oxford University Press, 1985.

Kazanjian, David. *The Colonizing Trick: National Culture and Imperial Citizenship in Early America.* Minneapolis: University of Minnesota Press, 2003.

Streeby, Shelley. *American Sensations: Class, Empire, and the Production of Popular Culture.* Berkeley: University of California Press, 2002.

Sundquist, Eric J. *Empire and Slavery in American Literature, 1820–1865.* Jackson: University Press of Mississippi, 2006.

**Miscellaneous**

Amon Carter Museum of Western Art, Martha A. Sandweiss, Rick Stewart, and Ben Huseman. *Eyewitness to War: Prints and Daguerreotypes of the Mexican War, 1846–1848.* Washington, DC: Smithsonian Institution Press, 1989.

Dugard, Martin. *The Training Ground: Grant, Lee, Sherman, and Davis in the Mexican War, 1846–1848.* New York: Little, Brown, 2008.

Foos, Paul. *A Short, Offhand, Killing Affair: Soldiers and Social Conflict during the Mexican-American War.* Chapel Hill: University of North Carolina Press, 2002.

Francaviglia, Richard, and Douglas W. Richmond, eds. *Dueling Eagles: Reinterpreting the U.S.-Mexican War, 1846–1848.* Fort Worth: Texas Christian University Press, 2000.

Gómez, Laura. *Manifest Destinies: The Making of the Mexican American Race.* New York: New York University Press, 2007.

May, Robert E. "Invisible Men: Blacks and the U.S. Army in the Mexican War," In *A Question of Manhood: A Reader in U.S. Black Men's History and Masculinity*, edited by Darlene Clark Hine and Earnestine Jenkins. Bloomington: Indiana University Press, 1999. 473–484.

Miller, Robert Ryal. *Shamrock and Sword: The Saint Patrick's Battalion in the U.S.-Mexico War*. Norman: University of Oklahoma Press, 1989.

Reilly, Tom. "Jane McManus Storms: Letters from the Mexican War, 1846–1848." *Southwestern Historical Quarterly* 85 (July, 1981): 21–44.

Smith, George W., and Charles Judah. *Chronicles of the Gringos: The U.S. Army in the Mexican War, 1846–1848*. Albuquerque: University of New Mexico Press, 1968.

Stevens, Peter F. *The Rogue's March: John Riley and the St. Patrick's Battalion, 1846–48*. Washington, DC: Brassey's, 1999.

Tijerina, Reies. *They Called Me "King Tiger": My Struggle for the Land and Our Rights*. Translated and edited by José Angel Gutiérrez. Houston, TX: Arte Público Press, 2000.

**Selected Works in Spanish**

García Cantú, Gastón. *Las invasiones norteamericanas en México*. Mexico City: Fondo de Cultura Económica, 1996.

Herrera Serna, Laura. *México en guerra, 1846–1848: Perspectivas regionales*. Mexico City: Consejo Nacional para la Cultura y las Artes, Museo Nacional de las Intervenciones, 1997.

Martín Moreno, Francisco. *México mutilado: La raza maldita*. Col. del Valle, Mexico: Alfaguara, 2004. [novel]

Solares, Ignacio. *La Invasión*. Mexico City: Alfaguara, 2005. [novel]

Vázquez, Josefina Zoraida. *México al tiempo de su guerra con Estados Unidos, 1846–1848*. Mexico City: Fondo de Cultura Económica, 1997.

Velasco Márquez, Jesús. *La guerra del 47 y la opinión pública (1845–1848)*. Mexico City: Secretaría de Educación Pública, 1975.

# Index